LIBRARY OF RELIGIOUS BIOGRAPHY

Edited by Mark A. Noll, Nathan O. Hatch,
and Allen C. Guelzo

The LIBRARY OF RELIGIOUS BIOGRAPHY is a series of original biographies on important religious figures throughout American and British history.

The authors are well-known historians, each a recognized authority in the period of religious history in which his or her subject lived and worked. Grounded in solid research of both published and archival sources, these volumes link the lives of their subjects — not always thought of as "religious" persons — to the broader cultural contexts and religious issues that surrounded them. Each volume includes a bibliographical essay and an index to serve the needs of students, teachers, and researchers.

Marked by careful scholarship yet free of footnotes and academic jargon, the books in this series are well-written narratives meant to be *read* and *enjoyed* as well as studied.

LIBRARY OF RELIGIOUS BIOGRAPHY

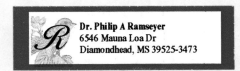
BLAISE PASCAL

Reasons of the Heart

Marvin R. O'Connell

WILLIAM B. EERDMANS PUBLISHING COMPANY
GRAND RAPIDS, MICHIGAN / CAMBRIDGE, U.K.

© 1997 Wm. B. Eerdmans Publishing Co.
255 Jefferson Ave. S.E., Grand Rapids, Michigan 49503 /
P.O. Box 163, Cambridge CB3 9PU U.K.

Printed in the United States of America

02 01 00   7 6 5 4 3 2

Library of Congress Cataloging-in-Publication Data

O'Connell, Marvin Richard.
    Blaise Pascal : reasons of the heart / Marvin R. O'Connell.
       p.   cm. — (Library of religious biography)
    Includes index.
    ISBN 0-8028-0158-7 (pbk. : alk. paper)
    1. Pascal, Blaise, 1623-1662. 2. Jansenists — France — Biography.
3. Apologetics — History — 17th century. 4. France — Intellectual
life — 17th century. I. Title. II. Series.
BX4735.P26026 1997
282'.092 — dc21
[B]   97-10578
                                          CIP

FOR MKT

"Nulle n'est heureuse, comme une vrai chrétienne,
ni raisonnable, ni vertueuse, ni amiable."

Contents

CONTENTS

Foreword

IF WE are to abide by the conventional descriptions of the Enlightenment in Europe, then we will probably think of it as the age of Voltaire, or at least as the age in which the intellectual and scientific revolutions of the seventeenth century that we associate with Newton, Galileo, and Descartes were brought to an elegant and rational fizz by those great popularizers of the new learning, the *philosophes*. But this conventional view ignores how, alongside the new learning and the *philosophes*, Europe was convulsed in the seventeenth and eighteenth centuries by an equally powerful reawakening of the most intense and aggressive forms of devotional Christianity. It came in a bewildering variety of shapes: in Protestant Germany, it appeared in the form of what became known as Pietism; in France, it took the form of Jansenism; in England, it appeared in both the writings and the lives of the Non-Jurors and, later on, the Methodist revivals of John Wesley. But its appeal was powerful. At the same time as Voltaire was busy discrediting Christianity as a facade of impostures, the demand for Christian devotional literature achieved new heights in both volume and readership. As late as 1740, the writings of the *philosophes* may have comprised up to 5 percent of the German book trade; that was dwarfed by the 20 percent of German book production that was still given over to Christian devotional literature.

First on the stage in this renewal of spirituality were the Jansenists, a movement for spiritual renewal in Roman Catholic France in the seventeenth century, and first among the Jansenists was their most famous convert, the scientific prodigy Blaise Pascal. Born in 1623 and raised in Paris, he was already experimenting in physics by the time he was ten, and by age twelve, he had written a treatise on sound and on his experiments with vibrations, and worked out the thirty-second proposition of Euclid on his own hook. But in 1646, Pascal also met two doctors, who began to speak to him of religion, of grace, of predestination, and of the bankruptcy of human reason. They were Jansenists, and they marked the starting point of the conversion of Blaise Pascal. Over time, Pascal moved from being merely a well-wisher to the Jansenists to being an active ally, until finally, on the night of November 23, 1654, while reading the biblical account of the crucifixion of Christ, Pascal was shaken by a vision of the crucifixion that confirmed him as both a Jansenist and a Christian. From that time onward, Pascal began assembling notes that he planned to publish as a defense of Christianity, and, indeed, as an argument against the whole notion that reason and science could lead people to God. However, the book he had planned was never finished. In 1670, a selection was published under the bland title of *Pensées* ("Thoughts"); successive editions reprinted still more of the notes, but the whole body of Pascal's sketches had to wait until 1844 before it received a thorough editing and publishing.

Pascal himself left only the vaguest hints at the order and arrangement of his *Pensées;* nevertheless, they have a certain order of their own, and running through them all is Pascal's basic conviction of the weakness and inadequacy of human reason to discover truth. It was not that Pascal had no use for reason at all: "If we submit everything to reason, our religion will be left with nothing mysterious or supernatural," Pascal claimed, but "if we offend the principles of reason our religion will be absurd and ridiculous." The point is that human reason cannot function effectively in the search for truth when left *alone:* "Submission and the use of reason: that is what makes true Christianity." If reason operated rightly, it would not deceive us with delusions about reason's greatness. Instead, it would remind us how little reason can discover:

"Reason's last step is the recognition that there are an infinite number of things which are beyond it."

Far better than relying solely on reason is to admit that "man's condition is dual." No one can function without the use of reason, but "without the aid of faith he would remain inconceivable to himself." And faith is as dependent on the operation of what Pascal called "the heart" as reason is upon the operation of the mind. In Pascal's vocabulary, "the heart" is a term that means, not simply feelings or emotions, but intuition — the immediate comprehension and understanding of certain things that we have without having to reason our way to them. Through "the heart," we immediately apprehend basic principles that reason cannot discover on its own, and that reason requires as givens for its own operation. Through the "heart," in fact, we apprehend truths that reason, if left to its own devices, would never touch. In one of the most famous portions of the *Pensées*, Pascal warns the lovers of reason that "the heart has its reasons of which reason knows nothing. . . . It is the heart which perceives God and not the reason. That is what faith is: God perceived by the heart, not by the reason."

The problem of Pascal's own time was that the new learning, fully as much as the old learning based on Aristotle and the study of logic, had deceived the "philosophers and scholars" into thinking that they knew more about the world than they actually did know or could know, or that reason could lead them to the discovery of a God of natural religion to replace the God of traditional Chrisitianity. But no one was in a better position as a mathematician and physicist to understand the folly of that proposition than Pascal.

> The Christian's God does not consist merely of a God who is the author of mathematical truths . . . but the God of Abraham, the God of Isaac, the God of Jacob. The God of the Christians is a God of love and consolation: he is a God who fills the soul and heart of those whom he possesses: he is a God who makes them inwardly aware of their wretchedness and his infinite mercy: who united himself with them in the depths of their soul: who fills it with humility, joy, confidence and love: who makes them incapable of having any other end but him.

The "philosophers and scholars" placed their confidence in nature

xi

and reason. But what was nature, after all? "I look around in every direction and all I see is darkness," Pascal wrote. "Nature has nothing to offer me that does not give rise to doubt and anxiety." What is human reason, after all? The discoverer and master of a world that it has found tick-tocks along through the ages in sweetly mechanical and predictable fashion? To the contrary, says Pascal, the human mind is a monkey in the middle of the yawning abyss of a mysterious universe, too small to comprehend the vastness of the universe and too clumsy to pierce its tiny secrets. When Pascal beheld the universe, he did not see in it a routine mechanism: he beheld something so awesome that he felt wretched by comparison. Galileo, Descartes, Newton, and all the others may have felt certain that they had found a universe that was discoverable, rational, and ready to be made useful for any human endeavor. Not so Pascal. No single sentence in the *Pensées* tells us more about Pascal's religious consciousness or the distance he felt between himself and his fellow scientists of the 1600s than this: "The eternal silence of these infinite spaces fills me with dread."

On those terms, "what amazes me most," Pascal added, "is to see that everyone is not amazed at his weakness." But the seventeenth century was not prepared for the wretchedness that Pascal was preaching to them. It was a century of genius, and genius does not like to acknowledge its limitations. Voltaire, in his *Philosophical Letters,* dismissed Pascal as a gloomy, cheerless fanatic:

> As for me, when I look at Paris or London I see no reason whatever for falling into this despair that M. Pascal is talking about; I see a town that in no way resembles a desert island, but is peopled, opulent, civilized, a place where men are as happy as human nature allows. Who is the wise man who will be ready to hang himself because he does not know how to see God face to face. . . ? Why make us hate our nature? Our existence is not so unhappy as they try to make us think.

But in truth, there were more heads in the Enlightenment who were inclined to agree with Pascal than Voltaire liked to admit, and within that company were Wesley, Francke, Zinzendorf, and Jonathan Edwards.

Marvin O'Connell, in this graceful and eloquent journey into the world of Blaise Pascal, makes us understand the passion that drove the man, and the radical spirituality he sought in his own heart. There are surely few biographies more difficult to write than Pascal's, not only because the man was a mathematical and scientific genius of Mozartean scale, but because the pieces of his life are imbedded in such a dense context of political intrigue, of winner-take-all struggle between Jansenist and Jesuit, and of the sheer geographical complexity of Paris and Port-Royal. No other Pascal biographer, however, steers us through these complexities as well as O'Connell. He provides us not only a life well told, but a spirit, a bold spirit, to admire.

ALLEN C. GUELZO

Preface

ONE DAY in July, 1945, a young American wandered into the church of Saint-Germain-des-Prés in Paris and saw inscribed upon the wall lines describing "a night of vision": "From about half-past ten in the evening until about half-past twelve — FIRE. God of Abraham, God of Isaac, God of Jacob, not of the philosophers and scholars. God of Jesus Christ." These were the first words of the *mémorial* Blaise Pascal wrote down as a record of the ecstatic moment of his conversion to a living religion. The American remembered a half-century later that just before his visit to the church he had come into possession of a copy of Pascal's *Oeuvres*. "I was uplifted by it. This was truly a gift for life. Pascal combined the greatest possible intelligence with the most acute need of God. In a style that already astonished me by its perfect transparency, he brought me to my knees."

Alfred Kazin was not yet the world-renowned literary critic he was to become, but as a Jewish intellectual in a Paris so recently liberated from the Nazis, and in a world just becoming aware of the horrors of Auschwitz and Buchenwald, he was intensely conscious of "the universe of death that was the war world of the Jews." And what had Pascal to say about all this? Nothing directly, of course, but the calm and reverential strains of the *Pensées* intimated a civilized voice too often stilled in his century and in our own: "This family, or people, is the most ancient within human knowledge, a fact that seems to me to inspire a peculiar veneration for it. If God had from all time revealed himself to men, it is to these we must turn for knowledge of the tradition."

Other contemporary Jews with Western roots, like Simone Weil and Hannah Arendt, have also admired Pascal. But they were not alone. Only weeks after Kazin's poignant pilgrimage to Saint-Germain-des-Prés, half a world and a whole culture away, an atomic bomb was dropped on Nagasaki, Japan. A "universe of death" indeed. Takashi Nagai, already by that time a celebrated radiologist and university professor, dedicated himself for the rest of his life to the care of the survivors of the blast in which his wife had been killed. Eventually he became a victim himself; in 1951 he, like so many others, died of radiation exposure. He had joined the Catholic Church twenty years earlier, first attracted to it by reading Pascal's *Pensées*. Like Pascal he matured into a poet-scientist, and one of his twenty books — *The Bells of Nagasaki* is its title in English — will stand always as a monument to courage, endurance, and faith. Dr. Nagai was, like Pascal, a devotee of the Latin liturgy, which, he maintained, harmonized perfectly with the Japanese ethos.

With such testimonials as these, it should matter little that Voltaire and Condorcet and other luminaries of the Enlightenment were aghast at Pascal's religiosity and went to considerable lengths to besmirch his reputation. This should come as no surprise. Perhaps, with the wisdom of hindsight, one might even argue that Pascal had been attempting to stave off the development of the kind of intellectual milieu in which the likes of Voltaire and Condorcet could flourish. However that may be, one remains startled to hear that fiercest of atheists, Friedrich Nietzsche, proclaim, "Pascal's blood flows in my veins!" The metaphor notwithstanding, what, one wonders, had they in common, save a weakness for introspection?

Still, the judgment of T. S. Eliot appears to have much justice on its side, echoing as it does the sentiments of Pascal's own hero, St. Augustine of Hippo: "I can think of no Christian writer, not Newman even, more to be commended than Pascal to those who doubt, but who have the mind to conceive, and the sensibility to feel, the disorder, the futility, the meaninglessness, the mystery of life and suffering, and who can only find peace through a satisfaction of the whole being."

"There will always be room for more books about Pascal," Ronald Knox wrote nearly fifty years ago. Certainly his observation has been borne out by the steady stream of publications that has appeared since he made it, and, needless to say, I hope there is indeed room for one more. I claim no particular originality for this book; I claim only to have tried to illumine to a modest degree Pascal and his times with a chronological narrative based upon the published sources. One reward in any case I have already received, a three-year intimacy with this remarkable human being and luminous Christian believer.

My best thanks must go to my friend and colleague, Professor Mary Katherine Tillman, who read the entire typescript and not only turned upon it her sharp editorial eye but also, and more importantly, gave it the benefit of her sensitivity to the personal and experiential nature of Pascal's faith. Without her counsel I would have missed many "reasons of the heart."

MARVIN R. O'CONNELL
London, England, and
Notre Dame, Indiana
1993-1996

A Chronology

1635   Saint-Cyran becomes spiritual director of Port-Royal de Paris

1636   Jansenius appointed bishop of Ypres

1637   Étienne Pascal, to avoid arrest by Richelieu, retires to Clermont

1638   Arrest and imprisonment of Saint-Cyran
Death of Jansenius
"The Solitaries," male Jansenist sympathizers, settle into a monastic routine at the old Port-Royal, now called Port-Royal des Champs
Birth of Louis XIV

1639   Étienne Pascal, restored to Richelieu's favor, appointed by the cardinal as tax-assessor in Normandy

1640   After repression of local disorder, the Pascal family settles in Rouen
Posthumous publication of Jansenius's *Augustinus*

1641   Publication of Blaise Pascal's first work, *Essai pour les coniques*
Marriage of Gilberte Pascal and Florin Périer

1642   Death of Richelieu; Cardinal Mazarin becomes First Minister

1643   Blaise Pascal begins work on his calculating machine
Death of Saint-Cyran
Death of Louis XIII; regency headed by Anne of Austria, the queen mother, and Mazarin
Publication of Antoine Arnauld's *De la fréquente communion*
Jean Guillebert, disciple of Saint-Cyran, becomes *curé* of Rouville, near Rouen

1646   Winter and spring. "First conversion" to Jansenist principles of Blaise, then Jacqueline, and finally Étienne Pascal
Summer and autumn. Blaise Pascal begins a series of experiments on the vacuum

1647   February. Blaise Pascal's controversy with the free-thinker Saint-Ange
September. An ailing Blaise Pascal returns to Paris, accompanied by Jacqueline; both begin to frequent services at Port-Royal de Paris
October. Publication of Blaise Pascal's preliminary researches on the vacuum

1648   A contingent of nuns from Paris, headed by Mère Angélique Arnauld, take up residence again at Port-Royal des Champs; the Solitaries resettle nearby

Publication of Blaise Pascal's extended treatise on conics (now lost) and of his treatise on the equilibrium of liquids

Celebrated experiment related to the vacuum performed at the instance of Blaise Pascal by Florin Périer at the Puy-de-Dome, near Clermont

Étienne Pascal, now retired, returns to Paris

1649 May. In response to the civil disturbances collectively known as the Fronde (1648-1652), Étienne, Blaise, and Jacqueline Pascal leave Paris for Clermont and reside with Gilberte and Florin Périer

1650 November. The three Pascals return to Paris

1651 Blaise Pascal engages in published controversy over his theories related to the vacuum

Death of Étienne Pascal

1652 January 4. Jacqueline Pascal becomes a nun at Port-Royal de Paris over her brother's strong objections; estrangement follows

April. Pascal presents his calculating machine to the public

October. Pascal travels to Clermont and resides with the Périers

1653 May. Pascal returns to Paris, quarrels with Jacqueline over her inheritance, and works on three treatises in physics and mathematics (all published posthumously)

May. *Cum occasione* of Pope Innocent X condemns five propositions allegedly found in the *Augustinus* of Jansenius

September. Pascal accompanies the duc de Roannez to Poitu; reflections on probability and games of chance

1654 January. Pascal returns to Paris; begins process of reconciliation with Jacqueline

November 23-24. "The night of fire," Pascal's second and definitive conversion

1655 January. Pascal's first retreat at Port-Royal des Champs; critique of Epictetus and Montaigne

1656 January. Antoine Arnauld condemned by the Sorbonne

January 23. Pascal publishes the first of the eighteen *Provincial Letters* defending Arnauld and attacking the Jesuits

March 24. Cure of Marguerite Périer, the "miracle of the Holy Thorn"

September. Pascal begins to gather materials for his *apologie* for the Christian religion (the *Pensées*)

1657   Pascal composes a treatise on divine grace and another on the elements of geometry (both published posthumously)
        March 24. Pascal publishes the eighteenth and last of the *Provincial Letters*
        December. Pascal begins his collaboration with the anti-Jesuit polemic sponsored by the *curés* of Paris
1658   Summer. Pascal publishes his treatise on the cycloid and invites European mathematicians to offer alternative theories; composes short works on geometry and rhetoric (both published posthumously)
1659   Widespread rumors that Pascal's health is deteriorating
1660   May-December. The ailing Pascal resides first with the Périers in Clermont and then with Roannez in Poitu
1661   February 1. Assembly of the Clergy imposes anti-Jansenist oath but allows reservations
        March. Death of Mazarin; Louis XIV begins his personal rule determined to destroy Jansenism; oath reimposed but this time without reservations
        August. Death of Mère Angélique Arnauld
        October 4. Death of Jacqueline Pascal
1662   January. Pascal launches a plan to provide public transport in Paris
        June 29. Gilberte Périer moves her desperately ill brother to her Parisian home
        August 19. Death of Blaise Pascal
1670   First edition of Pascal's *Pensées*

Prologue

THE BOULEVARD Saint-Michel and the rue Saint-Jacques, on the left bank of the Seine, run parallel to each other, up the gentle slope toward what Parisians from time immemorial have called the Mont Sainte-Geneviève. Both these thoroughfares begin at the foot of bridges that link them to the Ile de la Cité, the island in the middle of the river, the ancient heart of Paris, where Roman legionaires once fixed their eagles and where Capetian kings presided over courtly tournaments. Defying the tumults of centuries, great monuments to the ages of faith still stand there: the Hotel Dieu, the oldest hospital in Europe; the incomparable Sainte Chapelle, built by King St. Louis IX to house the Crown of Thorns he had brought back from the crusades; and the majestic cathedral of Notre-Dame de Paris.

To walk up either street is to feel the strong pulse of intellectual life, to be reminded that here, in the Latin Quarter, throngs of friars gowned in white and brown once loudly disputed with one another in the language reserved for scholars — Thomists against Scotists, realists against nominalists, and, later, Jansenists against black-robed Jesuits. Latin, to be sure, is heard no more, and the tonsured masters and students who framed their arguments in it have disappeared as surely as have the questions they argued about. But the scholars remain.

1

Where the Saint-Jacques intersects with the rue des Écoles stands the Collège de France, whose lecture halls still echo to the voices of Renan and Bergson. Round about are the great preparatory academies, the *lycées* named for Louis le Grand and Henri IV, for Montaigne and Lavoisier, and the specialty schools in chemistry and music and geology.

Almost at the top of the hill, between the Saint-Michel and the Saint-Jacques, lies a massive pile, crammed with laboratories, libraries, and classrooms, and named for Robert de Sorbon, who, at the time when young Thomas Aquinas was acquiring a Parisian reputation as a lecturer, founded on this site and endowed a *collège* to support sixteen students of theology. Over succeeding centuries the Sorbonne evolved into a theological faculty so prestigious that its authority in Catholic France ranked scarcely less than that of the pope himself. The Revolution of 1789 ended its ecclesiastical status, and under Napoleon's educational reforms the Sorbonne became the showpiece of the national *université* and then merely a constituent part of the ever-sprawling University of Paris. The building whose somber stone façade now fronts the Saint-Jacques is of relatively recent construction, but not so the church attached to it off the courtyard that leads to the Saint-Michel. This sumptuous classical structure was commissioned in 1635 by the then rector of the Sorbonne, Armand-Jean du Plessis, Duc and Cardinal de Richelieu. His remains lie entombed just inside, which gives one the ghostly feeling that the cardinal, who during his lifetime made it his business to know everything about everybody, now listens attentively to the chatter of the students as they lounge round the Corinthian pillars guarding the entrance.

From there the boulevard Saint-Michel, descending gradually, crosses the Place Edmond Rostand and skirts the lush greenery and dazzling flower beds of the Luxembourg Gardens, until it reaches the boulevard de Port-Royal. The flourishing convent of nuns for which this busy street was named was closed down three centuries ago. Now in its stead stretches out an imposing medical complex that features a large maternity hospital. Here, just off a small, hedged cloister — a quiet retreat from the urban hubbub swelling up all round — is a modest chapel where the bones of the foundress of the convent, Angélique Arnauld, were interred. With none of the pomp of heraldry and epitaph that marks the cardinal's grave, this place breathes a serene austerity;

2

it suggests rather than asserts high idealism and a lost cause. Mère Angélique, who brought her sisters in religion here in 1625 — just as Richelieu was beginning his tenure as King Louis XIII's first minister — spoke of it in terms that expressed, perhaps better than she knew, the ethos of a movement at once noble and foredoomed to failure by the weight of its own gloomy tenets; our chapel, she said confidently, will be the most beautiful and the most reverent in Paris, because it will be the most simple.

One who chooses to return from the Port-Royal to the Mont Sainte-Geneviève by way of the rue Saint-Jacques will find the street here narrower and less bustling. At the bottom of it stands the baroque splendor of the Val-de-Grace, the church built in imitation of St. Peter's in Rome by Louis XIII's queen, Anne of Austria, in thanksgiving for the birth of a son after twenty-three years of wedded childlessness. And at the top, a few hundred yards to the west of the Saint-Jacques, the Panthéon rises like a Greek temple. An abbey dedicated to Sainte-Geneviève, the patron saint of Paris, occupied this lofty space in Mère Angélique's days, but now the site accommodates the enormous monument to the triumph of nationalism and of humanistic values unfettered by religion, the secular shrine in memory of "great men from their grateful country," as the inscription that runs across its external pillars proclaims. The "great men" commemorated in the Panthéon include not only the likes of Voltaire and Mirabeau, of Napoleon and his generals, but also of Victor Hugo and Émile Zola and Jean Moulin, who are buried there. Nothing testifies so eloquently as the contrast between the Val-de-Grace and the Panthéon to the uneasy ambivalence in the French heritage, at once deeply Catholic and deeply pagan.

Underscoring that ambivalence is the church of Saint-Étienne-du-Mont, standing as it does, quite literally, in the shadow of the Panthéon. This small jewel of Renaissance architecture was built to serve as the parish church for the servants of the nearby abbey. It bears the name of St. Stephen, but the cultus of St. Genevieve — the shepherdess who in the fifth century, legend has it, saved Paris from the ravages of the Huns — has always thrived here, and one of its side chapels boasts a sarcophagus that supposedly contains a stone from her original grave site. The church glows brightly within, especially the white marble rood screen with the two decorative staircases flanking it, and yet the building remains cool and restful, even at midday in summer. On the wall of the ambulatory, just off the choir, is a fulsome epitaph, written in over-ripe Latin, extolling the virtues of a man interred nearby. More moving, however, is a simple notice of that same man inscribed on one of the pillars at the entrance to the Lady Chapel, behind the main altar. "Pray for the soul," it says, "of Blaise Pascal, a member of this parish, who died on August 19, 1662, and whose ashes are lodged here."

Richelieu, Arnauld, Pascal: three names that evoke even now, after so long a time and after so many momentous changes, a spirit that can still be detected even amid the smells and noises of a great modern city. Other names, to be sure, might serve a similar purpose, might bring to mind the immense vitality of France in the seventeenth century, *le grand siècle*. Louis XIV, whose birth was commemorated by the construction of the Val-de-Grace, towered like a colossus over Europe for sixty years; if he left behind a dubious testament — a mixture of grandeur and tyranny, of bounty and bloodshed — by the time he died French culture had become the norm against which civilized societies everywhere measured themselves. Personages of lesser rank also crowd their way into the consciousness of their posterity: statesmen like Mazarin and Colbert, soldiers like Turenne, Villars, and the Great Condé, spell-binding churchmen like Bossuet and Fénélon all have left their mark upon the generations that followed them. Even more so have the thinkers and the artists; it is not too much to say that Western philosophy owes its present orientation to the speculations of René Descartes and that modern drama still finds inspiration in the work of Racine, Molière, and Corneille. The paintings of Champaigne and Poussin, the literary fancies of La Fontaine, the classical architecture of François Mansard — these, too, testify to a society brimming over with creative impulse.

Yet Richelieu, Arnauld, and Pascal will serve well enough. The cardinal, with his single-minded consistency, with his rare ability to meld the theoretical with the practical, was the creator of the modern French state. Certainly circumstances played into his hands: years, indeed scores of years, of disorder that characterized the decay of the medieval world helped to engender an almost universal yearning for the kind of stability only a strong centralized regime could provide. Then, too, as the old idea of Christendom fell to pieces under the blows of religious war, the sense of French nationhood, a nascent patriotism, was nurtured by Richelieu's aggressive policies and by his glamoriza-

4

tion of the monarchy. Not that he acted without allies and surrogates and, above all, successors — most notably Mazarin and Louis XIV himself. Nor did the cardinal fancy himself an agent of dramatic change; the political materials he found at hand he put to use to aggrandize the power of his anointed royal master, which power, he firmly believed, was of natural and divine necessity. Nevertheless, it was Richelieu more than any other person who set the public agenda in France during his own time and over the three hundred fifty years since.

The family Arnauld ultimately fell victim to the repressive machine Cardinal Richelieu devised, but not before leaving upon posterity an imprint of its own. Mère Angélique and her nine siblings, along with her nieces and nephews, formed the heart of the Jansenist movement in its early, palmy days, and afterward, after king and pope had combined to suppress it, they remained its abiding symbols. The denizens of the convent of Port-Royal, however, did not advance their stern creed out of a moral vacuum. Rather, the Jansenism they propagated was a constituent part of the religious revival that had begun the previous century with the preaching of the great Protestant Reformers and that since then had swept across Europe. The Catholic variety of that revival — misleadingly called the Counter-Reformation — came late to France, but when it did it coincided with the burst of dynamic energy that was to make French culture dominant in the West for centuries to come. The impact of this circumstance upon the development of modern Catholicism is incalculable. And the Jansenism of Mère Angélique Arnauld, even after as formal doctrine it had been driven underground, continued to play its part in the process, almost to the present day. Recall the restrictive eucharistic piety of generations of Catholics of all nationalities. Witness the severity of the sexual code routinely preached by Irish pastors, who for so long were trained in French seminaries because Ireland was allowed no seminaries of its own. Read the novels of François Mauriac.

And what of Blaise Pascal, one of the greatest luminaries of France's *grand siècle*, the scientist and poet and religious zealot, whose random thoughts — his *pensées* — have intrigued thoughtful people ever since? Genius of course imposes its own criteria for judgment, but even the genius lives in a shared milieu that affects his values and goals. Even the genius must come to terms with whatever physical and spiritual limitations are peculiarly his. These always include time and space; and, in Pascal's case, they included also family ties of unusual strength and a physique of unusual frailty. He never really departed from his father's house, never really gave up his two sisters, though one left him for a husband and the other for a nunnery. That fragile vessel, his body, was always ill, or almost so, and he died before he was forty. Often he was moved to ruminate about what seemed to him the accidental character of his being. "When I consider the short duration of my life, swallowed up in the eternity before and after, the little space that I fill, and even can see, engulfed in the infinite immensity of spaces of which I am ignorant, and which know me not, I am frightened and astonished at being here rather than there; for there is no reason why here rather than there, why now rather than then."

He met Richelieu only once, on a ceremonial occasion when he was an adolescent, but the political and social order the cardinal was imposing became Pascal's own; he can scarcely be understood outside it. Yet, even so, he could not but kick against the goad. "Tyranny," he wrote, "is wanting to have by one means what can only be had by another. It consists in the desire to dominate everything regardless of order." And of whom but Richelieu and his heirs could he have been thinking when he added: "When it comes to deciding whether we should make war, kill so many men, condemn so many Spaniards to death, it is a single man who decides, and an interested party at that; it ought to be an impartial third party." The genius defies ordinary categorization.

Pascal was a mature man, already with a considerable reputation as an intellectual, when he fell under the influence of Angélique Arnauld and her party. The conversion he experienced on "the night of fire" led him to accept the saving formulae they recommended. The starting point was, for them and for him, a recognition of human wretchedness. "Man is vile enough to bow down to beasts and even worship them." "Man is nothing but a subject full of natural error that cannot be eradicated except through grace. Nothing shows him the truth, everything deceives him." Yet, despite these convictions, his restless mind never ceased probing and inventing, his restless heart never quite purged itself of a lust for fame and worldly success. More than once, both in word and deed, he uttered his *cri de coeur:* "For a religion to be true it must have known our nature; it must have known its greatness and smallness, and the reason for both. True religion teaches us our duties, our weaknesses, pride and concupiscence, for Jesus is a God whom we can approach without pride and before whom we can humble ourselves without despair."

One might well walk out of the stillness of Saint-Étienne-du-Mont and across the Place de Panthéon toward the Sorbonne reflecting upon many things. Not least appropriately perhaps upon the last words Blaise Pascal ever spoke, words not inscribed on his splendid epitaph: "May God never abandon me."

1 Prodigy from the Auvergne

CLERMONT-FERRAND, capital of the Auvergne, lies some two hundred miles south of Paris, midway between Limoges to the west and Lyons to the east. The hyphenated name dates from the eighteenth century when, by royal decree, the medieval village of Mont-ferrand was incorporated into the much older community of Clermont. The city is built on both banks of the Tretaine, a small tributary of the Allier River, and squats in a kind of geological bowl, a bowl broken on one side, with hills rising steeply all round, except eastward where the suburbs merge gently into the the Limagne plain, fertile for maize and grain and in pasturage for fat white cows. Conical hills, called *puys*, dominate the landscape, for this is the northern edge of the *massif central*, a mild misnomer for the hilly region that stretches southeast toward Rodez and Nîmes. Close to Clermont-Ferrand itself are more than a hundred *puys*, each with its distinctive shape and size, most scooped out at the center by dry and empty craters, whose volcanic eruptions 50,000 years ago left behind a testament of grey rock and of sweet, allegedly curative waters gathered into sparkling little lakes or into springs guarded jealously by the nearby settlements at Vichy, Volvic, and Perrier. Towering above the others to almost 5,000 feet, and darkly green with its covering of pine, oak, and scrub, stands the craterless Puy-de-Dôme, atop which the Romans once built a temple to Mercury and, long before that, the Celtic Auverni had worshiped gods of their own.

The Roman legions, under the command of Julius Caesar, first appeared in the vicinity in the spring of 52 B.C. and were promptly driven off by local tribesmen, led by their formidable chieftain, Vercingetorix. But Caesar, not to be deterred by a single setback from his intention to conquer *Galliam omnem,* returned later that year, and this time the Gallic army was routed. Vercingetorix was taken alive and transported in triumph back to Rome, where eventually, at Caesar's order, he was strangled to death in the dungeons of the Mamertine prison. The Romans called the town they founded near the site of their victory Augustonemetum, and, like so many other places from Bath to Cologne to Arles, it flourished modestly under an enlightened if rigorous administration and enjoyed the fruits of the *pax Romana.* Even before the collapse of the Empire at the end of the fourth century, and the consequent disintegration of the rich Gallo-Roman culture, had come the Christian missionaries, most notably St. Austremoins, remembered, mostly in legend and in faded frescoes, as the first bishop of the town now renamed Clermont. During the feudal centuries that followed Austremoins's successors held political as well as religious sway, sharing the former, however, with the neighboring barons, while a wholly new culture emerged under the inspiration of the Benedictine monks, whose foundations, with their splendid Romanesque churches, spread out from the great abbey of La Chaise-Dieu, thirty miles or so away.

A defining moment in the medieval life of the Auvergne came in 1095, when Pope Urban II traveled from Rome to attend the Council of Clermont and urged the participants to mount a crusade to liberate the Holy Land from the domination of Islam. "God wills it!" cried the pontiff to the cheering assembly. A hundred years later, about the time the crusading spirit had reached its highest pitch, construction began on a new cathedral for Clermont, dedicated to Our Lady of the Assumption. Its spaciousness and soaring lines were evidence that the Romanesque style had given way to the Gothic. But even this mammoth undertaking did nothing to alter the slow rural rhythms of medieval life and indeed, absorbing as it did the creative energies of several generations, became a familiar part of that life. Clermont remained a marketing center of a few thousand inhabitants, sweltering in the hazy heat of August and shivering from the sharp north winds of December. Down a gentle hill from the cathedral lay the heart of the town, the *port* or commercial quarter, where vendors' kiosks stood in the shadow of the old church of Notre-Dame du Port, a Romanesque gem of yellow stone, its interior brightened by stripes of paint on its walls and by the light filtered through its little stained-glass windows. Here an unlettered populace could study, if so inclined, the rudiments of their biblical faith from the cunningly carved capitals set atop the church's pillars.

One Bible lesson in which they hardly needed instruction was that lean years alternated with fat, famine with feast, that all human endeavor was dependent finally upon sun and rain and harvest. The local cheeses, *bleu* and *gaperon,* were hearty, and the *pralines* — sweets concocted from almonds and caramel — succulent. But good wines had to be brought in cross-country, beaujolais from Roanne and burgundies from Dijon. Except for that circumstance, the world outside hardly mattered at all. From the thirteenth century the Auvergnats were technically subjects of the Capetian kings, but Paris was a long way off, and France continued to be what it had been for nearly a thousand years, a huge patchwork of petty jurisdictions. The Black Death came and went, and the Black Prince with his English freebooters marched to the borders of the Auvergne, but then he too went away. And if for a while there was a French pope at Avignon and an Italian one at Rome, each fiercely claiming the mantle of St. Peter, it made small difference to the routine pieties of the people, who looked for relief from the anxieties of a chancy life almost as much to the intercession of the Virgin and the saints as to the mercy of God himself.

Change came slowly and almost imperceptibly to this static society, but change came relentlessly nonetheless. Gunpowder revolutionized the arts of warfare, just as the printing press revolutionized the techniques of scholarship. Tales penetrated even into the Auvergne about the discovery by Spanish and Portuguese sailors of exotic new lands and peoples. An explicitly capitalist and entrepreneurial bourgeoisie had gradually evolved from the guild masters of an earlier time — an urban middle class, that is, with none of the inhibitions about profit-making or usury that had formerly been basic assumptions within an essentially subsistence economy. A new dynasty, the Valois, had ascended the throne of St. Louis, intent upon forging out of the disparate provinces and independent communes like Clermont a unitary regime similar to those taking shape in England and Spain. Not that these kings, like François I or Henri II, worked in accord with some abstract plan of campaign; rather, by purchase, by marriage contract, when necessary and feasible by force, they proceeded out of a scarcely articulated sense of the potentialities of feudal expansion to extend the effectiveness of the royal writ and the reach of the royal tax collector. The birth pangs of the centralized French state had begun.

Out of Italy, meanwhile, had emerged, little by little, a whole set of novel ideas, rooted in the rediscovery of the ancient Latin and Greek classics. Art and poetry, politics and science and moral discourse — hardly any area of inquiry was left untouched by the rush of this new learning. The academic establishment, so long dominated by a Christianized version of an Aristotelian *Weltanschauung,* was shaken to its foundations. The scholastic masters in the old universities like Paris, Oxford, and Bologna found their carefully crafted commentaries and the subtle syllogisms not only dismissed but laughed at. And no longer was the intellectual élite of Europe restricted to the clerical caste. It may have been a respectable priest in faraway Prussia who put forward the most revolutionary notion of all, that the very earth, far from being the center of the universe as had always been supposed, could be shown by mathematical demonstration to be no more than a planet revolving around the sun, which itself was merely a bright speck among an infinite multiplicity of suns. But by and large the priests most avidly read and listened to were not reputable canons like Copernicus but rather those who refused to abide by traditional clerical standards, like Rabelais, the profligate Franciscan friar, or the monk Erasmus of Rotterdam, who spent a lifetime avoiding the cloister. Pico della Mirandola and Galileo in Italy, Thomas More in England, Miguel de Cervantes in Spain — among many others — all testified, in quite different ways, to the ripening of a lay culture that, though by no means indifferent to religious concerns, enjoyed a status free from the ordinary requirements of the Church's canon law. Not least among such scholars and literati was a French nobleman of lesser rank, Michel de Montaigne, who lived in the environs of Bordeaux, just over the range of *puys* from Clermont; his elegant *essais* presented a view of the human condition that appeared little in tune with what had prevailed among the learned classes since the time of Thomas Aquinas.

11

Yet all these savants lived and died as Catholics, and one of them was a martyr. Neither their collective rebuke of what they considered shopworn ideas nor their anticlerical mockery ever went so far as to reject the basic tenets of the old religion or its claim to their formal adherence. Much more severe, therefore, was the contemporaneous challenge to Catholicism that arose first in Germany and Switzerland and then appeared in France — more severe because the Protestant Reformers were intent not upon recasting traditional teaching in terms consistent with humanistic insights but upon asserting an interpretation of scriptural revelation that did in fact reform, and radically so, the understanding of the relationship between God and the believer. In France this movement was led by a native of Picardy, Jean Cauvin — John Calvin — who combined industry, eloquence, rigid selfdiscipline, and remarkable organizational talents with utter devotion to and confidence in the rightness of his cause. The converts to that cause, called by the mysterious name Huguenots, were statistically few — perhaps ten percent of the population of the country by the time Montaigne died, in 1592 — but they represented out of all proportion the productive middle class and the skilled artisans in the towns.

They also counted among their adherents some of the eminent noble families of the realm, including the Bourbons, cousins of the Valois and so princes of the blood royal. Eventually the Valois, grown effete and ineffective, died out, leaving as heir to the throne the Calvinist head of the house of Bourbon, Henri of Navarre. But before that France had been plunged into a series of grim civil wars, usually and appropriately called the Wars of Religion, because they pitted Catholic against Huguenot. Yet these struggles could also be seen as part of a continuing duel between a centralizing monarchy and the powerful barons anxious to maintain the control they had exercised over their enclaves from time immemorial. That is not to say that religious fervor did not play a predominant role in the bloody mayhem that gripped France for three decades. Though the twentieth century has witnessed the slaughter of scores of millions for the sake of an ideological slogan here or a bit of colored bunting there, it remains an enigma difficult to understand in the post-Christian era that civilized people were once prepared to die — and, even more significantly, to kill — over seemingly abstruse theological dogmas and practices, over a preference for Catholic sacramental good works (*la messe*) or for the defining Protestant appeal to justifying faith *(le prêche)*. Navarre, however, very much a man of his times, recognized that political status could not be separated from confessional commitment; and, having brought the Wars of Religion to an end by converting to Catholicism, he was joyfully welcomed into Paris as King Henri IV. A few years later, in 1598, while the royal court was in residence at Nantes, the king issued an edict granting the Huguenots, not religious toleration in the Anglo-American sense of that word, but rather the limited rights of peaceful coexistence. With that the conflict, for the time being, rested.

Two years before the famous edict was promulgated at Nantes, René Descartes was born not far away, up the Loire valley in Touraine. And twenty-five years afterward, in a house on the rue de Gras that stood within the shadow of the Clermont cathedral's tall façade of grey volcanic stone, Blaise Pascal was born, on June 19, 1623.

Pascals had figured prominently in the affairs of the Auvergne for at least two centuries. One branch of the family indeed had been ennobled as early as 1480, while another had produced several generations of wealthy merchants representative of the increasingly affluent and powerful bourgeoisie. About 1580 these two clans merged when Marguerite Pascal, a daughter of the noble house, married Martin Pascal. Martin at the time of his marriage was already a royal functionary, a tax collector for the commune of Clermont, and in 1586 he was promoted by Henri III, the last of the Valois kings, to the important post of treasurer or chief fiscal officer in the *generalité* of Riom, one of the sixteen *generalités* that served as the basic bureaucratic units of the expanding monarchy. This prestigious position, for which Martin made a cash payment to the royal exchequer, brought with it the equivalent of noble rank, not, to be sure, of the traditional aristocracy to which his wife's forebears had belonged — the nobility of the sword, the *noblesse d'épée* — but rather of a distinct group of royal administrators who came to be designated the *noblesse de robe.* For such ambitious men of the middle class, service of the crown not only satisfied social aspirations but also promised significant financial rewards, because incumbents were exempted from direct taxation and could expect ample income through the administrative fees they charged. It was an investment well worth paying for. And it was worthwhile, too, from the point of view of the crown, which, besides the revenues received from the sale of the offices themselves, had provided for itself an unsalaried civil service and a class to counterbalance the old warrior aristocracy. Tax farmers like Martin Pascal — tough businessmen who knew where the money was in their localities and how best to secure it — were the ideal allies of kings anxious for the resources that would enable them to extend and consolidate their sway.

Of the seven children born to Marguerite and Martin Pascal, Étienne was the oldest son, born in 1588. In his late teens he went to study law in Paris; while there, he made the acquaintance of a fellow-Auvergnat and one of his father's former colleagues, the distinguished advocate Antoine Arnauld — a small harbinger of the intertwined destinies of Étienne's children and Arnauld's. When he came back to Clermont in 1610, Étienne Pascal purchased an office in one of the lesser tax boards of the *gereralité*, and fourteen years later he assumed the vice presidency of the provincial *Cour des aides*, the court that exercised jurisdiction, civil and criminal, over all matters related to indirect taxation. From then on, as one of the leading personages in the Auvergne, he could rightly claim the title *chevalier*. The *Cour des aides* had its headquarters in Montferrand, but Étienne followed the example of his father, who had kept separate his offices in Riom from his home in nearby Clermont. Here Étienne took his place in an upper-class élite composed largely of congenial associates who shared his own wide-ranging intellectual interests. Like most of them he regularly performed his religious duties at the cathedral or at Notre-Dame du Port, but with no remarkable fervor.

There may also have been romantic reasons to explain his choice of residence. In 1616, Étienne Pascal married twenty-year-old Antoinette Begon, daughter of a prominent Clermont merchant. The couple had four children, three of whom survived: Gilberte, born in 1620, Blaise in 1623, Jacqueline in 1625. The next year their mother died, leaving behind only the shadowy memory, testified to by her granddaughter, of a pious young woman devoted to charitable work among the poor. No doubt the bereaved husband's friends and peers expected him, after a decent interval of mourning, to remarry and so provide maternal care for his three small children. This, however, Étienne did not do, nor is there evidence that he ever considered doing so. Instead, he assumed for the rest of his life the full parental role and forged between himself and his son and two daughters extraordinarily close bonds.

Information about Blaise Pascal's childhood in Clermont can be gleaned only from snippets of family remembrance. His sister Gilberte, writing after his death, recalled how precocious the little boy was, how strikingly appropriate was his conversation, and how the questions he asked surprised everybody by their acuity. It was because of these early marks of unusual promise that their father, she said, determined to educate his son himself, and in fact Blaise never attended any school or university. He was in good hands; Étienne Pascal not only was a genuinely cultivated man but also possessed the gifts of a born teacher and of a shrewd educational theorist. "The principal maxim of his methodology," remembered Gilberte, who benefited from it no less than did her brother, "was to keep the pupil always at a level above the work he was doing," that is, to instill in the child confidence in the learning process by matching his studies to his level of maturity. Thus Étienne, much at odds with the pedagogical establishment of the time, decided that Blaise should not begin the study of classical languages until he was twelve years old and mathematics until he was sixteen — far different from the regime experienced a generation earlier by Descartes at the much-heralded Jesuit college of La Flèche. Instead, the father explored with his son the general rules of grammar common to all languages so that when he came to read Greek and Latin he would understand that the art of communication has its regularity no less than its specific exceptions. Or else Étienne concentrated his instruction on attracting a childish imagination or on answering a young boy's questions. How does gunpowder work? Why does a knife striking a porcelain plate make a certain sound that stops when one puts one's hand on the plate?

But this sweet reasonableness, with its comfortingly modern ring, does not by itself characterize the annals of the Pascal family. Witness the curious tale recounted by Gilberte's daughter, Marguerite Périer. When Blaise was about a year old, she said, he began to manifest a strange languor accompanied by strong, almost violent, reaction to the sight of water and, "even more astonishing, to the sight of his parents in physical proximity to one another. He enjoyed the caresses of each of them individually, but when they approached him together he would cry out and twist and turn violently." As this peculiar behavior appeared to grow more pronounced and even life-threatening, an explanation presented itself. Among the poor women who came monthly

15

to the house on the rue de Gras to receive the benefactions of Madame Pascal was one widely reputed to be a witch. At first Étienne and Antoinette scoffed at the notion that their son might be the victim of this woman's spell, but, when all forms of treatment appeared to fail, they finally confronted her; she blandly told them that the Devil had a grip on the infant and that a cure could be effected only by transferring his malady to a scapegoat and then killing it. When Étienne Pascal, a humanist who abhorred such superstitious practices, mockingly offered one of his horses for the required sacrifice, the woman replied that a cat would do. Priests were consulted, but they offered no solution. At one point in the negotiations a furious Étienne knocked the alleged witch down the stairs of his house. But ultimately a desperate Antoinette had two cats tossed out a high window to their deaths, and, in accord with the witch's directions, she applied a herbal poultice to little Blaise's stomach. Three tense weeks followed, at the end of which "the baby was entirely cured, began to put on flesh, and was never again troubled by this evil condition."

Whatever one makes of this story now, one can hardly doubt that Blaise Pascal's niece believed it to be true. She may have learned it from her mother — who did not record it — or possibly, when she was a little girl, from her grandfather, or even from her uncle himself. The state of apathy or languor she described as an infantile affliction may in fact have been related to the ill health from which Blaise Pascal suffered all through his short life. Her calm acceptance in any case of a magical cure may be difficult for later generations to countenance, but not so for Marguerite, who herself, when a child, was healed of a hideous disease by what was universally agreed to have been a miraculous intervention. That event, when it occurred, profoundly affected her uncle, who perhaps compared it to what had happened to him when he was a baby.

In 1631 Étienne Pascal moved his household to Paris. It would seem that his primary purpose in doing so was to expand his own intellectual horizons as well as those of his children. Separation from the Auvergne, however, was by no means complete: at first the family continued to spend two or three months a year there, and later on, especially when Gilberte settled in Clermont after her marriage in 1641, it became a place for lengthy holidays and, sometimes, for refuge. For reasons not altogether clear, the Pascals had some difficulty in establishing a permanent home in the rapidly expanding capital, though they always resided in or near its more fashionable districts. Étienne first leased a house on the rue de la Tissanderie, on the edge of a former marshland, the *Marais*, lying between the Hotel de Ville and the Bastille, where noblemen and wealthy financiers had begun to build their elaborate *hôtels* and where Henri IV had located two new palaces along with symmetrical rows of interconnected service buildings around the sparkling greenery of the Place des Vosges. A few years afterward the family was living across the Seine in the aristocratic Faubourg Saint-Germain, and so found itself in the most elegant of neighborhoods. Blaise and his sisters could look out their front windows at the *hôtel* of the Prince of Condé, the king's cousin and the most influential nobleman in France; and virtually next door to them stood the magnificent Luxembourg, recently completed for the queen mother, Marie de' Medici, in a style calculated to remind her of the Pitti Palace in her native Florence. By 1636, however, Étienne and the children had returned to the right bank and the *Marais* and had taken a house on the rue Brise-miche, a quiet street abutting the cloisters of the church of Saint-Merri. Here they went to Mass and observed the various feasts and fasts of the liturgical year as dutiful if quite conventional Catholics, accompanied regularly by Mademoiselle Louise Default, whom Étienne had engaged as governess and *maitresse de maison*. She remained with them for twenty years.

They had come to the Paris of Cardinal Richelieu. Three centuries of analysis and learned commentary about the career of this diminutive churchman — the wily politician who midwifed the modern French state — have made it difficult to address an admittedly prosaic question: What impact might the cardinal and his regime have had upon a legal gentleman of scholarly habits just arrived in Paris from the provinces or, even more difficult, upon that gentleman's impressionable young son? Blaise Pascal in his maturity took little direct interest in political affairs, except insofar as they affected the religious causes he came to espouse. Yet he grew up in the household of a servant of the crown and therefore could never be indifferent to the policies or indeed to the whims of the all-powerful first minister of the king. It was no laughing matter when, as in fact happened, Étienne Pascal fell under the cardinal's displeasure. But that event proved to be a passing crisis, while Richelieu's overall agenda was one that, for the privileged bourgeoisie minority to which the Pascals belonged, possessed a permanent coherence and value.

One sign of the cardinal's eminent position was the huge palace he had constructed for himself — now the *palais royal* — beginning in 1632. The site was only a few hundred yards from his royal master's residence in the Louvre and not far from the rue de la Tissanderie. It seems not unlikely that nine-year-old Blaise Pascal may have been brought here on occasion to watch the builders at work, placing stone upon splendid stone. Their task, and the thought and patience required to bring it to fulfillment, provide an analogy to the cardinal's conduct during the years of his supremacy. Like an architect who has drawn up his blueprints, like an on-site foreman who oversees the specific implementation of such plans, Richelieu forged both the strategy and the tactics required to construct out of the materials at hand a new French polity. The foundations had been laid, in a haphazard fashion, by the able but unsystematic Henri IV. During the regency following that king's assassination the state-building process had collapsed into a confusion of conflicting interests. That Richelieu was able to take it up again, and pursue it with characteristic ruthlessness and rationality, was due to the trust placed in him by the new king. For all his personal limitations — he was a man of only modest intelligence, highly strung, scrupulous to a fault, physically brave but almost constantly ill — Louis XIII had a lofty sense of his royal prerogatives and responsibilities, and, once convinced of the merits of the cardinal's program, he never swerved in his support of it. Nor did either man have any doubt as to the gist of that program. "I promised your Majesty," Richelieu wrote in his celebrated *Testament politique*, "to employ all my industry and all the authority which it pleased you to grant me to ruin the Huguenot party, to abase the pride of the great nobles, to reduce all your subjects to the obedience that they owe you, and to restore your name among foreign nations to the position which it should rightly hold." In order to keep these promises, the cardinal held tight the reins of foreign and domestic policy for eighteen years, and, at the cost of battlefields drenched in blood and of a populace left for the most part inarticulate and often impoverished, he succeeded in his campaign to identify the monarchy with the nation, so that Louis XIII's son was able to boast a generation later, and without undue exaggeration, *"L'état, c'est moi."*

In 1634 Étienne Pascal signaled his intention to remain permanently in Paris by selling his office in the *Cour des aides* of Montferrand. By that time he had become a familiar in the lively intellectual circles of the capital. Richelieu himself took public notice of Étienne's scientific reputation by appointing him to a commission charged with inquiring into the proper method of determining lines of longitude. But Monsieur Pascal indulged himself in rather more frivolous activities as well, by appearing, for example, at the salon of Madame Sainctot, an aging court beauty with a notorious past, around whom had gathered a coterie of poets and pundits. Her three children were often the playmates of the young Pascals. Though Étienne was more amused than shocked by the often ribald and sometimes imprudently radical conversation he heard at Madame Sainctot's *soirées,* his own more scholarly interests gradually drew him away from such occasions and often into the company of Marin Mersenne, a Franciscan friar who had recently founded an *académie* devoted to the study of science. Indeed, it may have been his desire to locate himself closer to Mersenne's research center that prompted Étienne to leave the Faubourg Saint-Germain for the rue Brise-miche. He found here in any event regular fellowship with the physicists and mathematicians whose studies were most congenial to him. One fruit of this association was the publication, in 1637, of a tract written by Étienne Pascal and one of his new colleagues, which voiced serious reservations about René Descartes's *Discours de la Méthode.*

His father's erudite pursuits, as well as the frequent visits to the house on the rue Brise-miche paid by his father's learned friends, no doubt exerted weighty influence upon young Blaise. It may well be that he overheard conversations there critical of the speculations of Descartes, criticisms that may have colored his own judgments later on. But one subject was never discussed in the boy's presence. "My father," Gilberte Périer remembered, "was a very accomplished mathematician, and he cultivated those of similar bent." Yet because Étienne wanted Blaise to learn the classical languages before turning his attention to mathematics, "and because he knew mathematics is something so fulfilling and satisfying to the mind, he did not want my brother to be distracted by an acquaintance with it, for fear that it would make him negligent in studying Latin and other languages which he, my father, wanted him to perfect." And so Étienne "locked away all the books in the house that treated of mathematics and, when my brother was in the room, even refrained from discussing the subject with his friends."

Blaise, however, his precocious curiosity piqued by "this resistance," pestered his father until the latter relented enough to explain that, "in general, mathematical science provided the means to make accurate figures and to determine the proportions that prevailed among them." Étienne would say no more, but what he had said was sufficient to set his son's mind whirling. Off by himself during recreation time, he took a piece of charcoal and began drawing figures on the flagstone floor — "attempting, for example," said Gilberte, "to make a perfectly round circle, a triangle whose sides and angles were equal, and other similar forms." The boy did not know any mathematical terminology, so he invented names for his own use: a circle was a *"rond,"* a line was a *"barre."* He worked steadily, ever more fascinated by the discoveries he made. After definitions came demonstrations and then axioms and corollaries until, Gilberte maintained, "he had pressed his researches so far forward that he could propound, without knowing it was so, the thirty-second proposition of the first book of Euclid."

One day, and quite by chance, Étienne Pascal entered the room where Blaise was at work on his explorations into geometry. "It is difficult to say who was more surprised: the son chagrined at having been discovered in an activity explicitly forbidden him, or the father in seeing his son standing amidst these sophisticated drawings." A tense exchange followed, and, when Blaise shyly showed an astonished Étienne the papers on which he had scrawled the results of his investigations, the father realized that his son, scarcely twelve years old, had indeed arrived, by his own unaided efforts, at Euclid's conclusion that the sum of the angles of a triangle is equal to two right angles. Overcome with emotion, Étienne left the room and repaired to the nearby house of a friend who was also a learned mathematician. The friend inquired anxiously why Étienne was so disturbed, why he appeared to be close to tears. " 'I do not weep from affliction but from joy,' " was the reply. " 'You know the pains I have gone to to keep my son from the knowledge of geometry, because I did not want him distracted from his other studies. However, look what he has done.' " It took the friend but a moment's perusal of the papers spread out before him to insist that Étienne, whatever his pedagogical principles, could no longer deprive his son of formal instruction in mathematics. So it was that Blaise was given a copy of the *Elements* of Euclid to read, a task the lad took on with predictable enthusiasm. And from that time Étienne no longer hesitated to discuss mathematical matters in his son's presence; on occasion, he even had Blaise accompany him to the conferences of savants held regularly at Father Mersenne's academy.

The reliability of this reminiscence of Gilberte, with all its romantic overtones, has understandably been questioned ever since she published it some years after her brother's death. Many have assumed that young Blaise, in defiance of his father's directive, had somehow got hold of a copy of the *Elements* and studied the book secretly. This is not an unreasonable hypothesis, but even if such were the case, the accomplishment would still rank as remarkable for a boy of twelve. Other commentators, however, have noticed one point insisted upon by Gilberte that lends some credibility to her account. She claimed that her brother, by himself, had demonstrated Euclid's thirty-second proposition, not that he had worked his way through the whole classical treatise — which would have been far more difficult to achieve. There is at any rate plenty of evidence in Blaise Pascal's career to suggest that his mathematical acumen might have manifested itself at a very early age.

Gilberte, the faithful family chronicler, also wrote a memoir of her sister, Jacqueline, in which she narrated the double crisis the Pascals had to endure at the end of the 1630s. Jacqueline, a beautiful child with a sweet and sunny disposition, was the darling of her father and of her siblings. When she was seven years old Étienne assigned Gilberte, five years her senior, to teach her to read. This task proved unexpectedly troublesome, indeed impossible, until "one day, by chance, I recited aloud some poetry to Jacqueline, the rhythms of which delighted her so much that she said to me: 'When you want to make me read, have me read from a book of verse, and then I will say my lesson just as you please.'" Her devotion to poetry, and all that that implied about her imagination and intuition, appeared to pervade little Jacqueline's life. She was only eleven when, with her two close friends, the daughters of Madame Sainctot, she composed, produced, and performed in a verse-play of five acts and multiple scenes, much to the delight of the fashionable matrons of the Parisian *haut monde* who witnessed it.

Early in 1638 it was confirmed that Louis XIII's wife, Anne of

Austria, was pregnant. This was momentous news, for after more than twenty years of marriage the royal couple was childless — a dangerous circumstance in a dynastic state — and it had been widely assumed in court circles that a permanent sexual incompatibility existed between the scrupulous, insecure king and the fun-loving queen. Amid the universal rejoicing, there was much cosseting of Queen Anne, much effort to distract her as her delicate condition progressed toward term. Among those brought forward to amuse her at the palace of Saint-Germain was Étienne Pascal's clever daughter, who had written pretty verses in honor of the blessed event to come. The queen made a great fuss over the child, as did the king himself. But not long afterward Jacqueline was struck down by small pox, and for a time her life hung in the balance. Her inconsolable father was beside himself with worry, and he kept constant watch by her bedside. The fever subsided at last, but Jacqueline, her once beautiful face scarred and pitted, bore for the rest of her short life the mark of that cruel disease. Gilberte — who never missed an opportunity to make a pious point — recalled that her sister accepted her lot with cheerfulness, that "she even wrote some verses in thanks to God, in which she said she regarded her scars as guardians of her innocence and as proof that God wished to preserve her in it."

In the midst of these trying days, Étienne Pascal suddenly found himself in serious trouble of another kind. He had invested most of his money in government bonds, the income from which supported him and his family in considerable style. In 1638 a directive came down from the highest authority that the interest paid on these securities should be drastically reduced. When Étienne and two or three others protested, an irritated Cardinal Richelieu issued terse orders that they should be sent to the Bastille. Pascal, to avoid detention, prudently withdrew to Clermont, leaving his children in the care of the formidable Madame Defaut. Meanwhile, the cardinal, who was, after all, chief courtier as well as chief minister, expressed a wish to be entertained by the children who had so charmed the king and queen. Accordingly, and in collusion with Madame Sainctot and other friends of the elder Pascal, it was arranged in February 1639 that Jacqueline, now recovered from her illness, should perform at a special fête in honor of the cardinal, with the hope that she might get a chance to intercede for her father. So indeed it turned out. Richelieu, delighted by the girl and taking her

22

on his lap, promised that Étienne Pascal would be restored to favor. Then Jacqueline said, " 'Monseigneur, I have one more favor to ask of your Eminence.' The cardinal was so entranced by this sweet and childish boldness that he replied: 'Ask what you want, and it will be granted to you.' " She begged that her father, upon return from his temporary exile in the Auvergne, "might have the honor of making in person his reverence to the cardinal, in order to thank him for his forebearance." Shrewd little Jacqueline understood full well that admittance to the presence of the mighty was itself an assurance of rehabilitation. "M. le Cardinal said to her: 'Not only do I grant your request, but I heartily desire its fulfillment. Tell your father to come to see me in all confidence, and when he comes he should bring his whole family with him.' " Six months later Étienne Pascal was appointed the king's commissioner of taxation for the province of Normandy, in the *generalité* of Rouen.

Rehabilitated though he now was, Étienne may yet have reflected that Richelieu had handed him a poisoned chalice. For years Normandy had been on the verge of full-scale rebellion. The chief cause of unrest was the crushing burden of taxation that had impoverished bourgeois, peasant, and gentleman alike. But the government now demanded from this western province even more money to support the seemingly endless war against Austria and Spain. In the summer of 1639, looting erupted in Rouen and disorder spread across the countryside, testimony to the wretchedness of a population made immeasurably worse by outbreaks of the plague. Troops had to be sent from Paris to quell the disturbances, and it took an army commanded by a field marshal to force its way into Rouen on the second day of the new year, the intendant and the new tax assessor in its train. Only then, and under these inauspicious circumstances, did Étienne Pascal assume the unpopular duties that were to be his for the next decade.

Blaise and his sisters joined their father only after Normandy had been officially declared pacified, though in fact Rouen and its environs witnessed sporadic outbursts of violence for some time yet. In later life Blaise Pascal gave few signs of an interest in politics as such, but he did take for granted that any decent society had need of a strong central authority. Exposure at an impressionable age to the Norman *jacquerie* and, later, to the depredations associated with the Fronde went a long way to confirm attitudes that were his anyway by reason of class and religious conviction. He labored under no democratic or populist illusions. In the *Pensées* he would quote approvingly the Gospel of Luke: "When a strong man armed keepeth his palace, his goods are in peace."

When they settled in Rouen, Gilberte was twenty years old, Blaise nearly seventeen, Jacqueline fifteen. They lived in a comfortable house located in the tangle of narrow streets behind the monastery of Saint-Ouen, a district on the northwest edge of the city reserved mostly for government functionaries. Their mode of life was pretty much what it had been in Paris, though on a more restricted scale. As the popular unrest gradually subsided, they could drink in the charms of the gently hilly medieval town, with its sycamores and early morning mist off the Seine, its timber-framed houses whose upper storeys jutted out over the street, its collection of little churches and shrines stuck off in odd corners — like the squat Saint-Maclou, the ultimate in flamboyant architecture, and the somber plague cemetery nearby. They could walk up the bustling rue du Gros Horloge, from the spot where Jeanne d'Arc had been burned by the English and Burgundians two centuries before, pass beneath the arch upon which rested the great clock with its single hand, embellished by simple bas-reliefs depicting the Good Shepherd, and arrive finally at the cathedral, its spire rising like a needle into the sky and, inside, its stained glass shimmering in reds and startlingly deep blues. But the gaunt cathedral was almost dowdy compared to the abbey church of Saint-Ouen, a vast Gothic cavern of flying buttresses and pinnacles, flooded with light and poignant shadow, whose magnificent carved stone portal the Pascals strolled by most days. Even deep into the autumn they could gather the flowers that grew helter-skelter among the sloping lawns around the monastery, and in the cool of the evening they could watch the great orange ball of the sun, streamers of cloud across its face, descend behind the hills to the west.

In the summer of 1641, Gilberte Pascal — by now a handsome young woman with large dark eyes, a cupid's bow mouth, and black hair falling softly to her shoulders — married her cousin from Clermont, Florin Périer, for whom her father had obtained a government post. Jacqueline, the budding poet, continued to pursue her muse and indeed won a measure of local fame for her verses. "She was awarded a prize for them," her sister primly reported, "at a grand ceremony heralded by trumpets and drums, all of which she looked upon with admirable indifference." If Jacqueline matured in her art during these adolescent years, one cause may have been the encouragement of Pierre Corneille; the Norman tragedian, just then reaching the height of his powers, became a family friend of the Pascals at this time. At any rate the severely classical sentiments expressed in Corneille's plays, like *Cinna* and *Le Cid*, found an echo in the young girl's *Stances contre l'amour*, in which she celebrated the triumph of reason over the tyranny of erotic passion. Perhaps, given her convictions on this tender subject, it is not surprising that — in Gilberte's words — "Jacqueline, while living at Rouen, had many opportunities to marry, but God always permitted some obstacle to arise that prevented her."

Blaise, as befitted the son and heir, spent much time with his father, often traveled with him on Étienne's official trips round the *generalité* and occasionally to Paris or Clermont, and continued to receive, whether at home or abroad, his father's rigorous tutoring. The first fruit of that instruction to gain public notice — and the first taste of the celebrity Blaise Pascal was to hanker after all his life — came early in the family's residence in Rouen. The *Essai pour les coniques*, composed during the winter of troubles in Normandy and published in 1640 — no doubt at Étienne's expense — was a leaflet of several closely reasoned pages of text and appropriate geometric drawings, which purported to explain the properties of conic sections as they relate to the circle. Though it could not claim any particular originality, the *Essai* nevertheless demonstrated a remarkable aptitude in a lad of sixteen, who appeared to have read and absorbed all the pertinent literature on his subject and who clearly had begun to frame in his mind a projective geometry more sophisticated than its Euclidian roots. As a progression in mathematical knowledge, the *Essai* proposed a theorem later known as the "mystic hexagram": when a figure of six sides is drawn within a circle, the meeting points of the opposite sides are in a straight line. Eight years later Blaise would elaborate his ideas on conics with a full-blown Latin treatise (now lost save for a few excerpts preserved by Leibniz), but for the moment he basked in the praises of his proud father and of his father's learned associates. Into this laudatory chorus, however, a sour note was introduced by one prominent member of the intellectual community. René Descartes, still smarting perhaps from the elder Pascal's criticism of his own mathematical work, wrote to a friend that young Pascal had merely repeated the findings of earlier scholars. Moreover, "I do not find it strange that he has offered demonstrations about conics more appropriate than those of the ancients, but other matters related to this subject can be proposed that would scarcely occur to a sixteen-year-old child." Descartes was forty-four at the time.

Since he knew nothing about them, such caustic remarks could not have dampened Blaise's spirits. Meanwhile he began a project that was to show that he possessed an ingenuity far beyond that of a clever boy. As he became more closely acquainted with his father's work, Blaise could not but notice how much time and energy were consumed simply in keeping track of the sums of money collected from the various parishes in the *generalité*. The accounting procedures employed by Richelieu's tax assessors may not have been complicated by later standards, but they did demand a minimum of exact calculation. What if, Blaise reasoned, this essentially mechanical task could be performed by a machine, could be done, so to speak, automatically, so that the human agent could be spared the weariness and boredom such drudgery inevitably brought with it and the process itself made virtually error free? A calculating machine had been dreamed of by many in the past, and even planned by a few, but Blaise Pascal, with the help of a skilled *rouennais* craftsman, actually invented one that added, subtracted, multiplied, and divided numbers composed of as many as eight digits. The contraption, a cumbersome apparatus with its interlocking wheels, bars, and weights, took two years of hard labor to perfect, but by the inventor's twenty-first birthday in 1644 it was finished and workable.

He hoped that it would prove marketable as well, but in this aspiration he was doomed to long-term disappointment. Despite strenuous efforts over the next decade, Blaise could never find a way to produce *les pascalines,* as they were fittingly called, cheaply enough to make them attractive to a wide clientele. But if his bourgeois ambition for profit was frustrated, his desire for fame was not. The limited circle of those who had admired the precocious achievement of the *Essai pour les coniques* now expanded to include other prominent savants and also pragmatic men of affairs, who could especially appreciate the application of science to the solution of a practical problem. It is not without significance that, when he wished to promote his arithmetical machine, Blaise Pascal addressed himself to persons of political rank, like the Chancellor of France and, later, the Queen of Sweden. But most important of all was the impact his success had on the young inventor himself, on his confidence and his sense of who he was and what he could accomplish. "In constantly perfecting my machine," he wrote with justifiable pride,

> I always found reasons to alter this or that aspect of it, and, ultimately recognizing all the potential pitfalls to get it to run smoothly and to keep its moving parts disentangled and to lessen the likelihood of its breaking down too easily by the passage of time or by movement from place to place, I found the patience to construct more than fifty models, some of wood, others of ivory and ebony, still others of copper, before I brought the process to a conclusion in the machine I now present to the public.

A year after writing these triumphant lines, Blaise Pascal turned his creative mind to a consideration of another scientific puzzle. To this one, too, he devoted his efforts over many years, and it also came to his notice because of a specific problem. But, unlike the promotion and perfecting of his rather eccentric calculating machine, his investigations into the nature of the vacuum put him squarely within an area of research of wide interest in France and indeed all of Europe. In the summer of 1646 the royal officer charged with the supervision of military installations traveled to Dieppe to observe the workings of an alleged mechanical marvel, a kind of primitive diving bell, which might, if properly developed, have an important role to play in naval warfare. On his way back to Paris the officer stopped in Rouen to consult Étienne Pascal — whose reputation as a scientist was well known to him — and described the essential features of the apparatus as he had witnessed them. If a mechanism of this sort were to prove feasible, Étienne responded, it would depend on the much-controverted possibility of creating a vacuum. The conventional wisdom held that "nature abhors a vacuum," but this dictum had been recently challenged by experiments carried out in Italy and elsewhere. Calling into conference his gifted son, Étienne Pascal submerged into a bowl full of mercury a glass tube itself full of mercury, closed end upward. The result, as he pointed out to the officer, was that some, but not all, of the mercury leaked into the bowl, leaving the column inside the tube with a sizable gap. What is this lacuna, Étienne asked rhetorically. Is it air? is it a vacuum?

Young Blaise, fascinated, watched this demonstration, though without doubt he had observed it or something like it before. His own instincts and presuppositions, in accord with those of his father, led him to explain the phenomenon as proof of the existence of a vacuum. Nevertheless, careful not to shock the sensibilities of a cautious bureaucrat, he insisted that the long-established doctrine should not be set aside lightly. "It may be," he said to the officer, "that the space in the tube that seems to be empty is really air, which, in order to avoid a vacuum, has penetrated the glass through its pores." Whether or not this was the case could be shown only by inductive analysis, which meant a long series of experiments.

The intellectual challenge quickly assumed for Blaise a significance far beyond the conundrum that had perplexed the royal officer. Consistent with what was coming to be called the scientific method, young Pascal subjected the problem of the vacuum to repeated testing. He employed tubes of various sizes and shapes, and even invented a pneumatic tube — the "Pascal syringe" — into which he poured various liquids besides mercury — water, oil, even wine. Perhaps most important, he introduced into the equation differing heights that the liquids had to travel. Spectacular in this respect were the occasions when the tubes were strapped to the main mast of a ship, forty feet over the waters of the harbor, or attached to a high church steeple in Paris, or — in a *tour de force* in which Pascal was aided by his brother-in-law, Florin Périer — set atop the Puy-de-Dôme overlooking Clermont, nearly 5,000 feet above the sea (November 1647).

Throughout this period of experimentation, young Pascal scrupulously avoided claiming more for his research than it actually revealed. But at the same time he did not hesitate to assert his findings, unconventional as they might have been. "After having demonstrated," he wrote, "that none of the matters perceptible to our senses, and of which we know anything, apparently fill this empty space, my opinion is that, until someone has shown me the existence of some matter that does fill it, it is a genuine vacuum, destitute of all matter whatsoever." Experience, he was arguing in effect, can never give way to theory, fact to mental construct. Pressed, however, by the opposition that quickly manifested itself — most notably from a distinguished Jesuit metaphysician named Étienne Noel, who published several tracts defending the traditional position — Pascal proved quite willing to posit a generali-

28

zation, once he was satisfied that his further research justified it. "I am inclined to impute all these results," he wrote in reply to Noel, "to the weight and pressure of the air, because I consider them only as particular cases of the general proposition respecting the equilibrium of liquids."

It has been said that Descartes suggested the Puy-de-Dôme experiment to Pascal when the two met in late September 1647. More likely Descartes, who prided himself on his knowledge of medicine, and who tended in any case to condescend to the young prodigy from the Auvergne, spent most of their brief encounter advising Pascal on how best to treat his various maladies. However that may have been, the great experiment had a markedly different significance for each of them. For Descartes it necessarily fit into a preconceived system; for Pascal what mattered in the adventure on the Puy-de-Dôme was its factual content, consistent with the long series of experiments performed before. Such was to be the orientation of his thought for the rest of his life.

But even as all these projects and investigations progressed, Blaise Pascal was passing through the first stages of a spiritual crisis.

2 The Ghost of Augustine

W HEN Cardinal Richelieu died in 1642, Pope Urban VIII is said to have remarked, "If there is no final judgment, M. de Richelieu has led an extremely successful life. But if there is, he will have much to answer for." This observation, though not altogether uncharacteristic of the clever and sardonic Barberini pope, must surely be apocryphal. It smacks much more of later commentary on the cardinal and his career than it does of the seventeenth century, when hardly anybody, however eminent or powerful, was prepared to dismiss the reality of the last judgment. Even the Great Condé, the most celebrated soldier of his age and a mocker of religion all his life, received the sacraments on his deathbed. Perhaps the prince's conversion, tardy and dubious as it may have been, owed something to the prayers of his first wife, the cardinal's favorite niece. Modern secular analysis in any event finds it difficult to accept that a statesman of Richelieu's stature, a man who appears to have virtually created *Realpolitik*, could also have been sincere and serious in his religious beliefs. Similar disavowals have been made about England's Elizabeth I and Holland's William the Silent, as though, in their pragmatic wisdom, they had somehow remained beyond the reach of the enthusiasms unleashed by the Protestant Reformation. The assumption is that these pioneers of modernity could not

possibly have committed themselves to the religious mumbo jumbo —
including concern about final accountability before the throne of God
— that preoccupied their less enlightened contemporaries. And yet it
was Queen Elizabeth who, as her death approached, thought to fend
off that day of wrath with the unsheathed sword she kept on her
dressing table. "Ahead of their times" is a descriptive phrase best set
quietly aside along with other misnomers designed to make the past
more palatable to the present. "Ahead of their times" is a contradiction
in terms.

Cardinal Richelieu was no saint, nor indeed was his frequent
antagonist, the highly politicized Urban VIII, but they lived in an age
of saints, and they played important roles in the great Catholic revival
that reached a climax in France during Richelieu's years of power, the
very years Blaise Pascal was growing up. The seeds of that revival had
been sown by Richelieu's first patron, the randy Henri IV — another
personage often described, mistakenly, as "ahead of his times" —
whose conversion to Catholicism, whatever the political advantage he
discerned in it, was genuine and heartfelt, though of course he was no
saint either. The Counter-Reformation came late to France, largely because of the religious wars that had dragged on almost until the end
of the sixteenth century, but also because the reforming decrees of the
Council of Trent (1545-1563) had remained unpromulgated and unen-
forced by the Gallican Church, always suspicious of ultramontane pretensions. Indeed, administrative control of the Catholic Church in
France, under the terms of the concordat agreed to by the monarchy
and the papacy in 1516, was so completely monopolized by the crown
that only when a king took the initiative could France expect to experience the kind of revivified Catholicism that had already transformed
the Church in Spain and Italy, in Austria and southern Germany.

In those countries the painful business of sweeping away the
decay of centuries had solidly begun. The papacy, freshly energized by
the mandate given to it at Trent, reasserted within the Catholic community the moral leadership that had been largely forfeited by the
antics of the Renaissance popes. Bishops were seen now residing in
their dioceses and tending to their pastoral responsibilities. The first
halting steps had been taken to provide a lower clergy with a professional training that emphasized moral as much as intellectual preparation. Some young men emerged from the newly founded seminaries

and went courageously to their deaths trying to preserve or to restore the Catholic faith in hostile places like England. While old religious orders underwent radical reform, new ones, reflecting the demands of a new era, were instituted. Most notable among these latter was the Society of Jesus, which almost overnight became an ecclesiastical colossus, spreading its influence — at once zealous, keenly aggressive, single-minded in its ends and yet supple and humanistic in its means — all across Europe and over the seas to Asia and America. Pious confraternities sprang up everywhere, groups of lay men and women who put to the test their devotional commitments by trying with the corporal works of mercy to soften some of secular society's endemic cruelties. Magnificent baroque churches were built, to be sure, but so were hospitals and orphanages. And undergirding all these institutional developments, this almost frantic activity, was a novel religious sobriety, a dedication to prayer and sacramental piety, a heightened reverence for the contemplative and even, in some cases, for the mystical vocation — a seriousness, in short, about the Christian faith and its implications, for which these renewed Catholics might well have thanked (though of course they did not) the likes of Luther and Calvin.

A common characteristic of this process of conversion was the grip it had taken upon the upper classes, and it did the same in France when it finally appeared there during the reign of Henri IV. In a society so rigidly and unabashedly hierarchical, this was a circumstance of singular importance. Manners and mores were dictated from above; whether or not they trickled down to the populace at large was a question the élites seldom bothered to ask themselves. What caught their attention was that profligate clergymen and scoffers were no longer received in the best Parisian hotels. Freethinkers — *libertins* — learned to keep their opinions to themselves or to express them only within a narrow circle of intimates. Regularity in religious practice became fashionable; indeed, it seemed as though noblemen and affluent lawyers competed with each other in demonstrating extraordinary zeal. This is not to say that such practice was therefore insincere or merely for show. But it should not be concluded either that a kind of revivalist fervor swept all before it; plenty of vice continued to flourish in and around the court of that notorious philanderer, Henri IV.

Yet it was this king who, by many — though by no means all — of the ecclesiastical appointments he made, began the restructuring of an episcopacy more in accord with the ideals of Trent. Energetic new bishops like young Richelieu at Luçon, and others more devoted to exclusively religious concerns than he, transformed dioceses that had long languished in corruption and neglect. If Henri populated his court with swarms of royal mistresses and bastards, he also welcomed there the likes of François de Sales (1577-1622), the saintly bishop of Geneva, and strongly supported him. De Sales's record as a successful missioner among the Huguenots of Savoy was remarkable enough, but even more so were the immensely influential books of devotion he wrote for the edification of the upper classes. Another court familiar was Pierre de Bérulle (1575-1629), who shortly after his ordination was named almoner to the king. De Bérulle belonged to a group of *dévots* who congregated at the house of his cousin, Madame Barbe-Jeanne Acarie, a noblewoman reputed to have achieved the heights of mystical prayer. She and de Bérulle were responsible for bringing seven of Teresa of Ávila's nuns from Spain and thus establishing in France the reformed order of the Discalced Carmelites — a project heartily endorsed by the king. Shortly afterward de Bérulle set up the French Oratory, modeled upon, but independent of, the Roman foundation of Philip Neri, and so he could boast that he had introduced into the Gallican Church the best elements of the Spanish and Italian Catholic revivals. His Oratorians within a few years were staffing seminaries and promoting, especially among the younger clergy, much-needed improvement in preaching and theological study.

The impact of the more roughly hewn Vincent de Paul (1581-1660) was felt somewhat later, during the reigns of Henri IV's son and grandson, but if anything it proved deeper and more lasting than that of any other reformer during this *grand siècle.* There was hardly an apostolic endeavor to which de Paul, strongly influenced by de Bérulle, did not turn his hand. The priests of his Lazarist Order he commissioned to evangelize a peasantry that in many places had lapsed into virtual paganism, while he sent his Daughters of Charity, who included in their number matrons from the most prestigious families in Paris, to minister to the poor and sick in the slums of the city. Meanwhile, the reform displayed its internationalist character through the ever-growing influence of the Society of Jesus. To be sure, the assertive Jesuits had for a brief time aroused the suspicions of Henri IV and had been expelled from the country. But, once returned, their discipline, cohesion, and sheer talent guaranteed them a large role in the unfolding religious drama. Their effectiveness showed itself particularly in the first-rate *collèges* they established, where the sons of the élite classes — de Sales and de Bérulle among them — received their education.

Normandy was not immune from the religious enthusiasm that gripped the whole of France during the first half of the seventeenth century. The revival so woven into the fabric of public and private life during those years was making itself felt in Rouen and its environs by an outburst of mysticism and pious practice. Such manifestations were found, consistent with similar events elsewhere, most often among the élites rather than among the populace at large. Thus Corneille's drama of Christian martyrdom, *Polyceute,* could be appreciated only by the literate few, but those few were precisely the persons who set the tone and the standards for the rest of society.

The family Pascal, however, continued, as had been their wont in Paris, to practice their Catholicism faithfully but without any remarkable fervor. Inevitably Étienne, the quintessential civil servant and amateur scientist, gave the lead. Extremism in any form aroused his suspicions. He considered, with reason, that he belonged to that set popularly called *honnêtes hommes,* cultivated gentlemen with intellectual tastes, who lived by a code of self-defined integrity and personal honor and who, though formally dutiful to their Christian obligations, frequented the fashionable salons with more alacrity than they did the parish church. Nevertheless Étienne and his now-grown children must have been impressed, as was all Rouen, when their *curé,* once a member of de Bérulle's Oratory, relinquished his lucrative benefice in order to don the habit of a penitent hermit. At about the same time, a colleague of Étienne Pascal in the royal bureaucracy announced his "conversion" to a strict evangelical observance, and the resultant drastic change in the conduct of one who was a professional intimate and a neighbor no doubt had its impact upon the tax assessor and his family.

No single cause can explain these and many other instances of the rise of a newly fervent Catholicism, which to a large degree simply reflected the spirit of the times. Yet it was more than coincidence, as Gilberte Périer pointed out, that "there came into Normandy, to the village of Rouville, a pastor who was a very great servant of God. He governed his parish with very solid piety and preached at Mass the most admirable sermons." Rouville lay only a short distance from Rouen, and before long its little church was crowded on Sunday mornings with visitors from the city. The priest's name was Jean Guillebert. He had recently received his doctorate in theology from the Sorbonne. He had for some years enjoyed the revenues attached to the parish at Rouville as a non-resident, an example of how the bad old days stubbornly persisted even in this era of reform. Then suddenly, early in 1643, he deserted the academic halls of Paris to assume his pastoral duties. The result was electric. Guillebert combined extraordinary zeal with an attractive and, indeed, a charismatic personality, and soon members of illustrious families throughout the region were professing themselves his "converts" — they had passed from a life of dutiful but cold religious practice to one of austerity, penance, and fierce enthusiasm. Guillebert for his part made no secret of his own inspiration; he had come to remote Rouville, he said, to preach the pure gospel of Christ at the order of his mentor, the abbé de Saint-Cyran.

Neither Blaise Pascal nor his father nor his sisters ever met the abbé de Saint-Cyran, who nevertheless was destined to exert profound influence over all of them. Not that they could have remained unaware of the unique position this balding, black-bearded priest gradually assumed during the 1630s, right at the center of the great world of Parisian fashion and power, for the Pascals had regularly moved along the edges of that world. Though they never frequented his modest lodgings beneath the shadow of Notre Dame or, later, near the Luxembourg palace, many of the leading personages of Church and state did, and not a few of them emerged as Saint-Cyran's devoted disciples. It was not merely the impression made by his strong character or the consistency and coherence of his philosophy of life that so strongly affected these sophisticated people. Saint-Cyran preached a message of high idealism and self-sacrifice, a paean to a mystical Catholicism shorn of all impurities, just at the moment when the exuberance of the Counter-Reformation had reached its peak in France — at the moment, too, when the intricate entanglement of religion and politics within a tiny governing class seemed to open to one as gifted and dedicated as he almost limitless opportunities to make his influence felt. Such heady possibilities perhaps blinded him to the personal peril these very circumstances could also involve.

35

For his part, Étienne Pascal, the *honnête homme*, maintained an ambivalent attitude toward what he knew of the abbé's program of reform during his sojourn in Paris and, later, in Rouen, that of Saint-Cyran's disiciple, Guillebert. On the one hand, their extreme pessimism about the capacity of human beings to achieve by their own efforts a measure of fulfillment was bound to put off an admirer of Montaigne and the stoic philosophers. Studied denigration of free will had no charms for him, nor did the abbé's strict insistence on the Christian's need to abide unquestioningly by the dictates of a spiritual director. Saint-Cyran's own success *persona ad personam* in this regard was a key element in the development of his system, which eventually flourished more through personal contact and example than through learned argument. In due course Étienne would have cause to appreciate this fact, but at this stage of his life, never having experienced the abbé's special magic, he was too keenly self-motivated to find the usage appealing. His reservations, however, did not rule out admiration for what he had heard from friends about Saint-Cyran's zeal and indifference to creature comforts, about his steadfast devotion to the causes he served; Étienne discerned the same positive qualities in Guillebert. And though he took little interest in academic theology, he could as a committed scientist sympathize with the inductive nature of Saint-Cyran's method of inquiry — the accumulation and analysis of original texts — at least to the extent that he understood it.

Events intervened to preclude any later meeting between Saint-Cyran and the Pascals. About the time they departed for Normandy, Richelieu had had Saint-Cyran arrested and imprisoned in the royal fortress at Vincennes. The abbé's fall was occasioned by a combination of factors, but fundamental to them all was the cardinal's jealousy of Saint-Cyran's growing influence. Too many government officials, rich merchants, and savants, too many grand nobles and their pious wives, too many bishops and prominent religious, and — more disturbing than the others — too many members of the royal family were lionizing Saint-Cyran and treating him as an oracle. More specifically, those *catholiques dévots,* who deplored the cardinal's alliance with the Protestant powers in his struggle against Spain and Austria, might have discovered a leader in Saint-Cyran. Richelieu, whose cunning foreign policy during the Thirty Years' War had earned him in many quarters the sobriquet "arbiter of Europe," could not tolerate even the possibility of a challenge to his authority within the narrow ambit of the French court.

That the cardinal chose a specifically religious issue to bring the abbé to book is one more reminder that neither they nor any of their contemporaries imagined religion to be merely a private matter, nicely differentiated from the realm of politics. To separate Saint-Cyran the *homme d'état* from Saint-Cyran the *homme de religion* is to indulge in a meaningless distinction. The specific offense was Saint-Cyran's teaching about the degree of sorrow necessary for a person to receive absolution when partaking of the sacrament of penance. It went without saying that a penitent had to be sorry he had committed the sins he had just confessed if he expected forgiveness for them. But traditional Catholic theology had further refined this truism by distinguishing between "contrition" (sometimes called perfect contrition), a sinner's remorse stemming exclusively from his love of the God he had offended, and "attrition" (imperfect contrition), a grief motivated as much by shame and self-loathing and fear of punishment as by charity. "Contrition" was held to be the nobler demeanor and something to be universally striven for, but the consensus was that "attrition" sufficed within the framework of the confessional. This view had been sanctioned by the Council of Trent, and, not incidentally, it had been advanced by Bishop Richelieu, some years before his rise to supreme authority, in a catechism he had prepared for use in his diocese.

During the late 1630s a spate of books and pamphlets appeared that argued to the contrary, that no penitent could receive forgiveness, sacramental or otherwise, without evincing genuine contrition. These publications, it was said, were inspired by Saint-Cyran and typical of his excessively severe teaching. One tract, written by a young lawyer named Antoine LeMaître, especially outraged the cardinal and his entourage; it was a scathing indictment of moral laxity in high places, which, the author intimated, was rooted in the careless administration of the sacrament of penance. When Louis XIII's confessor began to hint at the same theme, and the scrupulous king, as a result, lost several nights' sleep fretting over his inability to feel perfect contrition for his sins, Richelieu struck: Saint-Cyran was arrested and incarcerated and his books and papers confiscated. Protests by a host of distinguished persons — Vincent de Paul boldly called Saint-Cyran "one of the most right-thinking men I have ever dealt with" — did no good, nor did the

abbé's eventual offer to submit formally to the teachings of Trent and
— as he expressed it rather awkwardly — to condemn those who condemned the efficacy of attrition. The cardinal remained adamant, and
until after Richelieu died Saint-Cyran continued a prisoner at the
Vincennes, hailed by ever-increasing numbers of disciples as "the martyr of the love of God."

Jean-Ambroise Duvergier de Hauranne — he adopted the more familiar name Saint-Cyran in 1620 when he became titular abbot of the
monastery of Saint-Cyran-en-Brenne — was born in Bayonne in 1581.
His family, Gascon and Basque in its lineage, shared the same bourgeois
antecedents as the Pascals of Clermont, though it was by far the more
prosperous. Nevertheless Alderman Jean Duvergier had thirteen children to provide for, and early on he designated an ecclesiastical career
for Jean-Ambroise, who was tonsured at the age of ten and received
his first benefice at fifteen, the year before he was ordained a subdeacon.
These religious commitments by no means ruled out future secular
ascendancy in an era when priests readily rose to the highest posts in
the kingdom. The young cleric, fully aware of this fact, attended the
Jesuit *collège* at Agen, reputed to be the finest school in the whole
southwest, and then took a master of arts degree at the University of
Paris. Thus well founded in the humanities, he returned to the Jesuits
to begin his formal study of theology (1600). But in order to do so he
had to matriculate at Louvain, in the Spanish Netherlands, because at
this pivotal moment in his life the Society of Jesus lay under the ban of
the king of France.

The University of Louvain was just then at the height of its fame
as a center of theological learning in the Catholic world. Far from being
paralyzed by the confessional wars that had engulfed the Low Countries for forty years, the university had flourished in that bloody cockpit
of criss-crossing armies and reciprocal massacres. Indeed, within its
various faculties and colleges, all of them clerical preserves, debate and
controversy raged with something of the gusto with which Catholic
pikemen and Calvinist musketeers routinely assaulted each other. The
Jesuits were at Louvain, armed with an array of talented researchers
and innovative methods, and so were the Dominicans, always ready
to do battle in defense of what they considered the pure scholasticism
long associated with their order. Distinguished scholars among the

secular clergy joined in the fray as well, local Flemings and Hollanders, to be sure, but also Englishmen who had fled Queen Elizabeth's persecution of her Catholic subjects. The occasional presence of Italian, Spanish, French, and German savants contributed to the international ambience of the university, as did the sonorous rhythms of the Renaissance Latin in which all lectures, readings, and disputations were carried on.

Duvergier spent four years in this rich, lively, and contentious academic atmosphere. The masters with whom he studied could boast of prestigious credentials in their respective fields. If scholasticism, as filtered through contemporary Jesuit commentators, formed the basis of the instruction he received, he was also introduced to biblical analysis and — most significant as things turned out — to "positive theology." Rooted in the Renaissance recovery of ancient texts, this relatively new branch of sacred science departed from that venerable methodology of the schools that proceeded deductively according to the norms of Aristotelian logic. Positive theologians, in contrast, drew their conclusions by way of induction, by reconstructing through the accumulation of long-neglected texts the intellectual tradition of the early Christian centuries. Catholics had been prompted to take on this formal inquiry into the writings of the "fathers" of the Church — the study of "patristics" — not only by the work of the humanists within their own ranks but also, and even more so, by the controversies they had engaged in with the Protestant Reformers. Luther and particularly Calvin had built their vision of the Church upon a patristic as well as a scriptural foundation that could not go unchallenged. Indeed, it could be said, somewhat oversimply, that Protestantism, in all its varieties, purported to base itself upon the New Testament teachings of St. Paul as interpreted and elaborated by the ancient fathers, especially by St. Augustine (354-430), the great bishop of Hippo Regius.

A contemporary of Duvergier as a student at Louvain, and so subject to the same intellectual influences, was Cornelius Jansen, the youngest son of a skilled artisan, born in the flat, boggy land of southeast Holland. The two did not meet, however, until 1609, after both had left the university and had gone to Paris to pursue further study. There they struck up a friendship, with the relatively well-off Duvergier inviting the financially straitened Jansen to share his Parisian lodgings. Then, two years later, they settled into a Duvergier property on the

outskirts of Bayonne. Thus began a spiritual and intellectual partner-
ship that was to last for the next three decades.

During the five years they spent together in Bayonne, the two
young men gave themselves over entirely to study, later accounts of
which were much embellished in the telling by their admirers. They
were bound from twelve to fifteen hours a day to their desks, so it was
said, relaxing only by an occasional game of shuttlecock. Jansen, it was
also said, never bothered to go to bed but merely took brief naps in the
chair in which he sat hunched over whatever text he was scrutinizing
at the moment. Their intent was to penetrate to a deeper and more
satisfying understanding of Christian truth than that which had been
presented to them at Louvain and the Sorbonne. In this endeavor the
attention they gave the Bible was conventionally Catholic, steering clear
of any hint of Protestant *sola scriptura* and seeking out rather the sym-
bolic and metaphorical interpretations so favored by the commentators
of the primitive Church. Indeed, the study of these ancient fathers
became their primary occupation, almost their obsession. Neither of
them in any case was well enough equipped in philology to launch out
into serious biblical criticism.

It is wrong to suppose that during this period of daily intimacy
the two young men pieced together that complexus of doctrines and
mores that later came to be called Jansenism. Their work at this stage
was more humdrum than excitingly innovative, and, except for the then
universally absorbing subject of witchcraft and sorcery, they showed
little interest in contemporary theological debates. Though he was four
years younger than his companion, Jansen from the beginning assumed
the leading role in their collaboration. His was by far the more powerful
mind, and he could also boast a disinterestedness that eluded Duvergier, who for a considerable time yet continued to hanker after the
worldly success his father had hoped he would find through a career
in the Church. Such conflicting aspirations, however, did not prevent
Duvergier from becoming an ever more effective auxiliary in the joint
scholarly enterprise. Certainly, as they pored over the tomes of the
fathers of the Church, both of them, and especially Jansen, grew increasingly disenchanted with the scholastic method. But this state of
mind reflected not so much a negation as an affirmation of the exhilarating discoveries opened to them by an inductive, positive theology. They
accordingly compiled enormous indexes and cross-referenced files of

40

patristic sources. Stacks of notebooks and collections of précis littered their workrooms. Information, ever more information, is what they sought, and, applying themselves relentlessly, information is what they obtained.

In the summer of 1614 Jansen departed for the Netherlands, which he had not seen for five years. His visit lasted eighteen months, during which time he was ordained priest by the archbishop of Mechlin. At the end of 1615 he returned to Bayonne, and he and Duvergier resumed their idyllic, if more than a little eccentric, routine of study and shuttlecock. A year later, however, Jansen was summoned to the deathbed of his father, and, though he intended to return — he left behind a chestful of liturgical vestments, books, and manuscripts — it was not to be: his arrival home coincided with his appointment as president of a newly founded college at Louvain. So the direct daily contact between him and Duvergier ended, but not their mutually supportive relationship, which was sustained by a continuous exchange of correspondence. And in the long and often convoluted letters the two men wrote each other one preoccupation loomed increasingly large: the need to reshape Catholic thought and conduct in accord with the teachings of St. Augustine of Hippo.

It has been said that Augustine's teachings are so subtle and so varied that, like Scripture itself, they can be cited on both sides of any religious argument. However that may be, what appealed most to Jansen and to Duvergier de Hauranne were the tracts and treatises the saint had composed toward the end of his life in his controversies with the Pelagians. Indeed, it was said of Cornelius Jansen — or Jansenius as he was known in the academic precincts he dwelt in from this point till he became a bishop in 1636 — that he had read the whole of the vast Augustinian *corpus* ten times and the anti-Pelagian material thirty times. Pelagius, a fifth-century monk, had advanced a cheerful, worldly theory about sin and redemption that emphasized the intrinsic strength and nobility of the human person. Those created in God's image and likeness were, he argued, capable of wickedness, but they were by no means impelled in that lamentable direction by any natural flaw. If the original sin of pride and disobedience committed by the parents of the race served as a kind of cosmic bad example, it did not inhibit their progeny from performing acts meriting God's favor and reward. The ability to discern the moral good and to choose it was rooted deep in the nature of every man and woman and was reinforced by "the freedom wherewith Christ has made us free."

Against this happy portrayal of the human condition Augustine had reacted furiously and so persuasively that Pelagianism, as formal doctrine, had been driven into the theological wilderness. Ever mindful of the evil that lurked inside himself — too mindful of it, some commentators thought — the bishop of Hippo insisted that only by the direct intervention of God at every stage of the moral process could human beings escape the ravages of their own wickedness. Jansenius, by a well-nigh obsessive study of the saint's own writings as well as of conciliar and papal pronouncements from the fifth century and after, painstakingly reconstructed the intellectual framework wherein such a somber judgment about the ordinary human lot had been vindicated. This project in positive theology he took on, not as an antiquarian or a merely academic exercise, but out of a stern conviction that St. Augustine's diatribes against the Pelagians had lost none of their relevance. All around him Jansenius seemed to see evidence of a religious culture ready to exalt natural virtue and to ignore the heinousness of sin — and not just among scoffers and *libertins érudits* but among serious practicing Catholics as well. Priests in the confessional abetted a subtle resurgence of the Pelagian poison by coddling their penitents, and theologians did the same by positing arguments calculated to indulge the whims and vanity of the worldly. Most dangerous of all, perhaps, and certainly most insidious, was the idealization of the *honnête homme,* whose vaunted self-sufficiency appeared to Jansenius a clear instance of the Pelagian mind-set. Little wonder, then, that society's élites were suffused with a spirit of accommodation to the world, the flesh, and the Devil. Their conduct was the fruit of an exaggerated estimate of puny human beings' ability to withstand the ravages of sin, so that they forgot, in effect, Jesus' admonition, "Without me you can do nothing."

Given the temper of the times, given the fierce resentments that had riven the Church for a hundred years, Jansenius's line of speculation, as it unfolded, invited some of his fellow Catholics to draw invidious comparisons. The great Protestant divines of the sixteenth century had also studied Augustine carefully, and they had seen the spectre of a revived Pelagianism intruding in to the complex apparatus of late medieval Catholicism. And however much they may have differed in matters of detail, the Protestants were as one in asserting the principle of justification by faith alone. To rely upon the power of free will and the merit of good works was a snare and a delusion; only faith, *sola fides,* the trust in himself that Jesus demanded from those who would be his disciples, could deliver humankind from the moral cesspool into which it had fallen. This was the Pauline creed, declared the Protestants, and the Augustinian one as well.

Jansenius agreed implicitly that this was the Augustinian creed, but only up to a point and with deep reservations. The scholarly work he undertook was aimed as much at rescuing Augustine from the Protestant embrace as at combatting the plague of neo-Pelagianism. Yet awkward questions for a Catholic theologian remained. Did not Jansenius's account of the Augustinian denigration of human liberty — there can be no good moral act without the direct application of divine grace — amply support Martin Luther's views on that subject? If Augustine did indeed believe that such grace was irresistible, did it not follow, as John Calvin had maintained, that God out of divine capriciousness had chosen some for salvation and rejected others, without regard to human merit? In other words, was Jansenian predestination really different from Calvinist predestination? But, responded Jansenius, central as were these matters of sin and redemption, of human freedom and divine omnipotence, they had to be judged in the light of the rest of the Augustinian testament. The Protestants blithely overlooked the saint's own deep sacramental piety, his special devotion to the Eucharist, his regard for the priesthood and the episcopate, his support for the contemplative and mystical vocations, his acceptance of hierarchical authority, his single-minded labors in behalf of unity among Christian believers, and, most revealing of all, the holiness of his daily life. Augustine must be taken whole: the greatest father and doctor of the Church, to be sure, the consummate scholar and teacher, but also — and on this point Duvergier had a surer grasp than the more cerebral Jansenius — the pastor of souls and the director of consciences and always the vulnerable and passionate man whose restless heart could find its repose only in God.

Jansenius, it must be remembered, was an academic theologian who, aside from the seminal years with Duvergier in France, spent most of his career within the confines of the University of Louvain. And the mysteries associated with divine grace and human freedom had been raised and controverted at Louvain a generation before Jansenius arrived there as a student. One important reason was simply the fact that many of the texts composed by St. Augustine, including his anti-Pelagian treatises, had been lost or neglected throughout the Middle Ages. The rediscovery, publication, and wide dissemination of them had opened many doors to the new breed of positive theologians, and nowhere more than at Louvain. In particular, the work of Michel de Bay — Baius is the more familiar Latinized form of his name — had been the occasion of years of wrangling within the university community. More than once Baius's espousal of what he claimed to be Augustinian themes led his critics to accuse him of propounding a kind of Catholic Calvinism — exaggerating the doleful effects of original sin, dismissing the function of free will, and finally adopting a position on predestination hardly distinguishable from that of the heresiarch of Geneva. Baius, a supple ecclesiastical diplomat as well as a combative professor, managed to elude the ultimate condemnation of his academic peers as well as that of several suspicious popes, but the seeds of controversy he and his disciples had sown continued to bear fruit.

The very ambiguity of the word "grace" fed the disputes. The classical root meaning of *gratia* was "favor" or "indulgence," and in this sense St. Augustine had employed it to insist, against the Pelagians, that sinful human beings needed the direct and repeated intervention of divine favor if they were to perform any morally good act. But by extension *gratia* could also be defined as "friendship" or "regard." Out of this meaning of the term, the medieval scholastics, led by St. Thomas Aquinas, had fashioned their notion of grace as a potentially permanent state of friendship with God, a kind of Aristotelian quality inhering in the souls of the just, which rendered their deeds good and meritorious. Later classification distinguished these modes of supernatural presence by calling the first "actual grace" and the second "habitual" or "sanctifying grace." And though these may not necessarily have been mutually exclusive, the emphasis of one at the expense of the other could lead, and indeed over the centuries had led, to desperate quarrels among Catholic savants. Augustinian actual grace might appear to presume a divine determinism that left no more room for human freedom than the Protestant Reformers did, while Thomistic habitual grace might seem to involve an exaggerated commitment to human capacity remindful of Pelagianism.

Then in 1588 — the year before Baius died — a Spanish Jesuit named Luis de Molina published his *De concordia liberi arbitrii cum donis divinae gratiae* (On the harmony of free will with the gifts of divine grace), and the academic debate turned into a firestorm. Molina put forward a theory contending, in effect, that actual grace and free will worked jointly and simultaneously to bring about the justification of the individual. He argued that God provides to the fallen human being a "sufficient grace," which enables him to perform good works. This sufficient grace becomes "efficacious" through the application of the individual's choice and consequent effort, a response predictable enough by reason of the very "sufficiency" of the original divine infusion. Ultimate judgment, to be sure, belongs to God alone, and in that sense every soul is predestined. But the God who judges does so with the complete foreknowledge of every detail of every human life. God knows, and only he knows, whether each man or woman will employ for good or ill that freedom of choice which is as much a constituent of human nature as omniscience is of God's nature. Justification therefore results from a mysterious process of cooperation between the God who saves and the human soul that freely accepts — instead of rejects — that salvific action.

Molina had thus shifted the argument away from what God *does* to what God *knows.* Augustine's insistence that each good human act requires a *prior* impulsion of divine grace was set aside by a theory that, in its symmetry and liberality, had a strong attraction for intellectuals brought up in the humanist tradition. Nor was biblical imagery lacking to support it. In the Garden of Eden it had been only the tree of the *knowledge* of good and evil whose fruit Adam had been forbidden to eat, and when the serpent tempted Eve to defy that prohibition, he had promised her that once she and her husband had tasted that fruit they would be "as gods." The moral debacle for the human race that ensued did not, according to the Molinist view, change the essentials of the case: the Creator remained unique in his possession of the knowledge of the good or evil that the creature was capable of choosing and indeed would choose.

Battle lines were swiftly drawn once Molina's book came off the press. The quarrel soon became partisan as it spread out of Spain into the rest of Catholic Europe, growing as it did ever more raucous and bitter,

45

largely because the Jesuits, as was their wont, rallied in a solid phalanx in support of their confrère against all comers. Appeals were inevitably sent by both camps to Rome, but a series of papal commissions failed to calm the waters. Meanwhile, at Louvain the Jesuit standard-bearer was Leonard Lessius — one of Duvergier de Hauranne's tutors — who summed up Molinism in two propositions: that efficacious election to eternal glory occurs even as God foresees human merit acquired through grace ("From all eternity God decided to offer the same sufficient grace to Peter and Judas, but he knew by his knowledge of future contingencies how each of them would respond"); and that sufficient grace becomes efficacious by the free cooperation of the human being, which God has foreseen and willed. It was not only stout defenders of Baius who called such conclusions a denial of efficacious grace and hence rank Pelagianism. Finally, in 1607 — nearly twenty years after the publication of Molina's *De concordia* — Pope Paul V, following the advice, it was rumored, of François de Sales, ordered both sides to cease and desist from the name-calling and recriminations. There was room for differing opinions on the matter, the pope sensibly pointed out, since the Council of Trent, while affirming the need for both grace and free will in the process of justification, had not determined what the relationship of the two might be. This papal writ was renewed twice over the next fifteen years, with mixed results. The arguments were carried on in more seemly language — Paul V had explicitly forbidden each side labeling the other as heretical — but they were carried on nonetheless.

Such was the intellectual inheritance of the intensely serious and pious young Jansenius, as he read and reread the works of St. Augustine. As the years passed, the products of his experience and study became public, in all their robust anti-Molinism, through an impressive list of publications. He displayed no taste for accommodation. The ingenious notion of a particular category of God's unique knowledge of a human being's free choices — the so-called *scientia media* — he dismissed as no better than a screen for Molina's aberrations. Nor had he any greater patience with another subtle attempt to solve the riddle — to differentiate, that is, the influence of grace upon the human act from its influence upon the faculty that produces that act. This transitory impetus of divine aid was called by its champions *premotio physica* (physical premotion), a term obscure enough in itself to suggest how tangled the controversy had become.

46

Jansenius, by contrast, held straightforwardly to what he believed was the genuine Augustinian position. Distinguish, he said, between the grace of Adam and the grace of Christ, between the human state before and after the fall. In the cool and uncluttered pathways of the Garden of Eden, the working of grace depended upon the response of the human will, which was truly free and yet always attracted to God and his friendship. But once Adam had sinned, he and his descendants were thrust into an unequal struggle, in which the lure of self-gratification — concupiscence — is far stronger than that of God's love. In their fallen state men and women enjoy no real liberty because they are driven so hard by their base desires — unless they are liberated by the grace of Jesus Christ, who tames the recalcitrant human will and heals it by his own curative power. "For the law of the Spirit of life in Christ Jesus hath made me free from the law of sin and death" (St. Paul). Such a realization implied no jettisoning of conventional Catholic piety, as the Protestants maintained it did, no retreat into fideism. Its implications in fact were just the reverse. The Catholic believer, to be worthy of the vocation to which he had been called, must live his faith commitment at the highest possible pitch, must embrace with particular ardor any and every means to curb his radical selfishness, with special emphasis on devotion to the Real Presence of Christ in the Eucharist. But fundamental to all else must be the profoundly penitential mode that the believer brings to every phase of his life, mindful of his helplessness to confront successfully the inner drive toward evil. To purge the old Adam is too gargantuan a task to be left to the vagaries of natural virtue or to the false god of human liberty. The very acceptance of the principles of the gospel, with no compromise, no trimming — no attenuation, for example, of the sinner's unequivocal need for perfect contrition — involves recognition of one's moral impotence. Only the grace of Christ, the new Adam, applied rigorously at every moment of every day, can purify the sons and daughters of Eve.

In 1636 the king of Spain appointed Jansenius bishop of Ypres. Two years later he died. And two years after that was published posthumously his huge Latin treatise that brought together all the reflection and arguments and rebuttals that had absorbed the author across his scholarly and priestly lifetime. The book, consistent with the custom of the time, bore a long and convoluted title, but, significantly, everybody referred to it simply as the *Augustinus*.

The profound mysteries that Jansenius dealt with possessed a technical aspect that made them a subject of legitimate inquiry for professional theologians. But they were also of the greatest practical moment to every believer, sophisticated or not, who felt himself drawn toward a purer and more complete religious commitment. This latter circumstance, rather than any particular gift for abstract argument, is what propelled Jansenius's friend and partner to prominence. Duvergier proved to have the talents of a born counselor, confessor, and director of souls, to say nothing of those of an expert publicist. But before he could exercise these talents he had to pass through a grueling moral crisis of his own and to experience a personal conversion. The claims of a purified religion, the attractions of a life of austere piety, the deep satisfaction he had found in theological studies — all these conflicted cruelly with the worldly ambitions that still beguiled him. Shortly after Jansenius returned from Bayonne to the Netherlands for good, this struggle within Duvergier reached its climax. His conversion was, as all such phenomena must be, largely secret and mysterious. But one sign that the contradictory impulses had been tamed was the turning away from the literary projects he had taken on before — bad poetry in honor of royalty, sycophantic tracts in defense of worldly bishops. In 1618, at the age of thirty-seven, he was ordained priest, and two years later one of the worldly bishops he had defended awarded him with a benefice whose handsome income guaranteed him financial security and independence. So Jean-Ambroise Duvergier de Hauranne became the abbé de Saint-Cyran.

After 1621 he lived mostly in Paris. There, displaying both the ardor of the zealous convert and the fastidious manners of the courtier, he moved easily among the upper classes. The queen mother, Marie de' Medici, took an interest in him, and at first Cardinal Richelieu, ever mindful of Louis XIII's religious sensitivities, found him a useful ally. The doctrine Saint-Cyran preached — not least by the consistency with which he abided by it himself — was Jansenius's version of Augustinianism, with its dire warnings against laxity in the face of human evil and, more specifically, against the kind of easy virtue practiced by the *honnêtes hommes*. Far from being put off by his stern warnings about their worldliness, many *notables* of both sexes eagerly put themselves under his direction. His eloquence in the pulpit won him some disciples, his occasional printed pamphlets — circulated ever more widely as the years passed — gained him others. The very intensity of his own prayer life attracted the devotion of still others, as did his refusal to accept a bishopric or promotion to any other office. The public approval given him by Pierre de Bérulle and Vincent de Paul lent him a kind of saintly endorsement. And by the time Richelieu turned against him and thrust him into the Vincennes, Saint-Cyran had established a network of followers as keenly fervent as himself. Noteworthy among them was Jean Guillebert, *curé* of Rouville in Normandy.

Among those who quickly fell victim to the magic of Guillebert's preaching were two brothers named Deschamps, scions of the lesser nobility, who had been famous all over Normandy for their propensity to violence, their zest for the feud and the duel. Once under the sway of Guillebert, however, they shifted their native ardor to the performance of works of charity, especially for the benefit of the sick. They founded a hospital and even had themselves trained as surgeons.

The practice of medicine was still a primitive art in those days, and physicians with better credentials than the two noble brothers could hardly have called themselves professionals in any modern sense. Even so, a little therapeutic skill was better than none, and when, in January 1646, Étienne Pascal slipped and fell on a patch of ice and dislocated his thigh bone, he asked the Deschamps to oversee treatment of the painful if hardly life-threatening injury. The upshot was that the brothers spent the better part of three months as guests in the Pascal house behind the abbey of Saint-Ouen. Étienne gradually mended under their ministrations, but he, and his son and daughter also, soon discovered that the Deschamps cared much more about spiritual health than they did about physical. Overflowing with the vigor they had formerly expended on swordplay and love affairs, the brothers now applied it to winning the Pascals over to the species of conversion they, under Abbé Guillebert's direction, had already experienced. Young Blaise — so brilliant and winning and so anxious for worldly distinction, as they had been — was the special object of their solicitude; here, they decided, was a budding genius who might do great things for Christ. They talked to him by the hour and gave him devotional books written by Saint-Cyran, as well as more scholarly tracts by Jansenius. Little by little they convinced him of the need to move beyond the merely formal brand of Catholicism and to embrace a deeper understanding and practice of the principles of the gospel. What does it prosper a man, they said to him in effect, to understand all the mysteries of mathematics and all the riddles of the physical universe if he does so at the cost of his immortal soul? Blaise was strongly moved by the Deschamps's sustained appeal, and so, in her turn, was Jacqueline. Together they persuaded their ailing father to listen carefully to what his doctors were telling him, not about his battered leg but about his chances for eternal salvation. Étienne, so much the *honnête homme,* was a harder nut to crack, yet he could not but be impressed by the missionary fervor of these once worldly men. And when Gilberte and her husband visited Rouen that summer, they too professed themselves ready to make a faith commitment different not simply in degree from what they had professed before but different in kind. Thus the whole Pascal family placed themselves under the direction of Father Guillebert, which meant that for all practical purposes they had begun to accept the religious vision of the abbé de Saint-Cyran.

Their "introduction to the devout life" — to borrow a phrase that had been recently sanctified by the title of François de Sales's celebrated book — carried with it a noteworthy social weight. Étienne Pascal, after all, was the second most illustrious royal official in the whole of Normandy, his status confirmed in 1645 by promotion to the rank of *conseiller d'état;* his son was already acclaimed as an intellectual marvel; and his daughter, the poetess, was widely known to have been a favorite of the late Cardinal Richelieu. The family's prominence added a certain luster to the movement that, in the environs of Rouen, took its inspiration from Jean Guillebert. What precisely their "conversion" involved, however, was not so evident to the public at large. It did not mean, of course, a passage from unbelief or unbridled free thought, nor did it suggest — at least consciously — the slightest deviation from Catholic orthodoxy. Rather, it imposed upon the converted a depth of religious seriousness that was entirely new to them; a seriousness about the mandates and counsels of the gospel, about their participation in the sacramental life of the Church, about prayer and fasting and works of charity, about the enormity of sin and the consequent urgency for a divinely induced inner purging so that, following Jesus' admonition, they could address God their Father in the silent recesses of their hearts and be heard by him. Perhaps Gilberte Périer's daughter, Marguerite, best described the significance of the change when she described, in a somewhat pedestrian manner, the prior state of her grandfather: "Étienne Pascal was a pious enough man, but he had not yet received the gift of illumination. He did not yet recognize the full extent of the duties of the Christian life. Having conformed himself to the mores of those worthy people who frequented the fashionable salons, he thought he could combine the values of secular success with the practice of the gospel."

How this "first conversion" affected Étienne's son remains nevertheless something of an enigma, mostly because of his sisters' account of it. Gilberte described the phenomenon in the starkest terms. Before he was twenty-four years old, she declared, that is, before 1647,

> the Providence of God having provided an occasion for my brother to read certain books of piety, God so enlightened him through this kind of study that he came to understand perfectly that the Christian religion obliges us to live only for God and to have no other objective in life but to serve him; and this truth appeared so clear to my brother, so necessary and so useful, that he stopped all his researches, so that from this time onward he renounced the pursuit of all forms of knowledge in order to apply himself unreservedly to that unique thing Jesus Christ called necessary.

An off-hand remark by Jacqueline — alluding to Blaise in 1647 as one "who is no longer a mathematician" — seems to confirm Gilberte's estimate of the "illumination" their brother had experienced.

Their assessment of the event conflicts, however, with other incontrovertible testimony, which perhaps can be most conveniently summed up in chronological terms. Blaise did not begin his research into the nature of the vacuum until after the brothers Deschamps had departed the Pascal household in the spring of 1646. Nor did he for a long time yet cease trying to perfect (and to sell) his calculating machine. And if he had given up the study of mathematics by 1647, it is difficult to explain the appearance of his *traité* on conics in 1648, to say nothing of the many more mathematical inquiries that he embarked upon in succeeding years. Whether Gilberte's unequivocal assertion sprang from a faulty memory or — more likely — from a desire to underscore her brother's reputation as a single-minded crusader for a purified Catholicism, there seems less reason to dispute another of her claims: "By a special divine protection, my brother had always been preserved from all the vices of youth; and, what is even more remarkable in one of his temperament and interests, he had never dallied with free thought when it came to religion, having consistently applied his curiosity to the investigation of natural phenomena."

Blaise Pascal's first conversion, occasioned by the brothers Deschamps, was, in short, a defining moment in his life, but it worked itself out more gradually than his sisters remembered. It has to be discerned within a larger context, which included study and reflection as well as Blaise's own deteriorating health and his conflicting ambitions. Also at issue was his beloved Jacqueline's increasing fervor, which, so to speak, leapfrogged his own. He continued his scientific and mathematical researches with undiminished intensity, but he also remained in contact with Abbé Guillebert and so with the school of Saint-Cyran and Jansenius. That both these latter luminaries were dead by now — Saint-Cyran lived only a few months after his release from the Vincennes in 1643 — mattered less than the literary testaments they had left behind for people like the Pascals to ponder. Nor was there lacking a new generation to carry the banner effectively forward. It was said that for every person who tried to unravel the argument enveloped in the dense pages of Jansenius's *Augustinus,* a hundred found inspiration in a tract called *De la fréquente communion,* written by a young doctor of the Sorbonne named Antoine Arnauld.

3 Port-Royal

INSTRUMENTAL in the temporary expulsion of the Jesuits from France in the late 1590s had been a lawsuit conducted in behalf of the Sorbonne by the celebrated Parisian barrister, Antoine Arnauld. Two generations later, when the Society and the Arnauld family were locked in bitter conflict, pundits would slyly dub this legal intervention "the original sin." Arnauld, like his casual acquaintance Étienne Pascal, had secured for himself a place within the administrative nobility. He had also sired a huge brood of children. The youngest, born in 1612 and named for his father, had matriculated in the 1630s at the Sorbonne, where he had been an intimate of Jean Guillebert, shortly to become *curé* of Rouville in Normandy and spiritual mentor to the Pascals. Young Arnauld had posted a brilliant academic record in the faculty of theology, but he had also displayed a sharply combative, if not belligerent, temperament, which had more than once annoyed the established order. The doctorate was awarded him in 1641, the same year he was ordained priest; but a more decisive event had occurred three years before when, on Christmas Eve, 1638, he had addressed himself to the famous prisoner in the Vincennes. In this letter he announced his "conversion" and asked the abbé de Saint-Cyran to become his director. And so Elijah found his Elisha in the person of the young doctor of divinity whom history would later immortalize as "the Great Arnauld."

His tract *De la fréquente communion*, which so impressed Blaise Pascal and indeed generations of serious Catholics, appeared in 1643. It had been, in a sense, a command performance. A lady of high rank who had been converted by Saint-Cyran from a life of easy virtue had confronted her director with the expostulations of her friends, who, citing their Jesuit confessors, had decided that they should receive the Eucharist frequently despite their venial faults and the vanities and frivolities endemic to the fashionable world in which they lived. Holy Communion, they had been told, was the traditional "Bread of the strong," which was intended by Christ not so much as a reward for good living as an aid to live well. No such overly simple formulation could have been more objectionable than this one to the Augustinian precepts as Saint-Cyran and Jansenius interpreted them. The deep and pervasive sinfulness in which all human beings were immersed meant that the conscientious believer should approach the Communion table only after a long period of penance. The canons of the Church required that every Catholic receive the Sacrament of the altar during the Easter season, and this was perfectly appropriate: the six penitential weeks of Lent that preceded Easter afforded an opportunity for proper preparation — proper purging of concupiscence — and so fit the recipient to have placed upon her tongue the sacred Host. Not that this Lenten exercise was in itself sufficient; one's whole life had to be a kind of Lent, a kind of continuous penitential experience that in the end would be the sole authorization for consuming Christ's very Body and Blood — at Easter or any other time. Saint-Cyran, deprived in his prison cell of the necessary books and references, instructed his new convert, Antoine Arnauld the younger, to make this case, and so he did.

The principles enunciated in *De la fréquente communion* struck Blaise Pascal, when he read them, as perfectly consistent with the evangelical counsels that had been explained to him by the brothers Deschamps. Conversations with Arnauld's friend and fellow disciple of Saint-Cyran, the abbé Guillebert, served only to confirm these first impressions. On the heels of his conversion a situation arose that gave Pascal a chance to put to the test the new level of dedication to which that conversion had committed him. In January 1647, Gilberte Périer recalled, "a man came to Rouen who taught a new philosophy that attracted all the curious. My brother, having been enlisted by two of his young friends, went with them to talk to this man. They were very much surprised that in the conversation they had with him this man drew out from the principles of his philosophy many conclusions on matters of faith contrary to the teachings of the Church." "This man" — so horrified was Gilberte at the memory of him that she could only designate him as *cet homme* — was a forty-five-year-old former Capuchin friar, now a secular priest, named Jacques Forton, sieur de Saint-Ange, doctor of theology of the University of Bourges. However obscure his origins and antecedents, Saint-Ange's legal right to this title of minor nobility went undisputed, and the process of his secularization, from religious to diocesan priest, had adhered to the proper canonical form. Nor was he without a certain amount of fame. He had left his fashionable mark upon many a Parisian salon and had published a variety of works that ambled haphazardly between philosophy and theology. He had powerful patrons, too, including Cardinal Richelieu's nephew, who had bestowed the benefice upon him, the parish of Crosville-sur-Cie, near Rouen.

Among the enormities she attributed to Saint-Ange, Gilberte Périer mentioned explicitly only the one that scandalized her most, "that the body of Jesus Christ was not formed out of the blood of the blessed Virgin Mary" but out of some matter expressly created for that purpose. But "there were other similar things," she said, and her brother and his friends, "having judged among themselves the danger involved in allowing this man to instruct the young, resolved first to admonish him privately and, if he ignored their protestations, to denounce him to the authorities." This procedure — plainly consistent with Jesus' instructions in the gospel — was faithfully adhered to by the fervent three, all laymen in their early twenties, all members of distinguished families, all reputed to be up-and-coming scholars, all disciples of Jean Guillebert and, therefore, of the now deceased Saint-Cyran.

Included among the "other similar things" Gilberte Périer objected to were Saint-Ange's peculiar views about creation and about the Holy Trinity. But these in fact were derivative: the basic position from which sprang all his inferences had been put forward in a three-volume work with the arresting title *La conduite du jugement naturel* (The guidance of material judgment). Here he argued a scarcely disguised Pelagianism that appeared to the enthusiastic young converts to subvert all the

Augustinian maxims they had lately embraced. The Trinity, said Saint-Ange, could be demonstrated by natural reason; faith was necessary only for persons of limited intelligence. He stripped away all the mysteries of Christianity — or so his critics charged — and, most radically wicked of all, he seemed to dismiss the need for revelation and even for God's grace to sinful humankind. True to their pledge, the three self-appointed censors first engaged Saint-Ange in private dialogue — a written record survives — and then, when he refused to recant, they delated him to the ecclesiastical authorities. The coadjutor archbishop and administrator of Rouen — a good man, the three young zealots were assured, but not notably courageous — hesitated to take firm action, and so the appellants made their case to the semi-retired archbishop. The upshot was an ambiguous judgment about Saint-Ange's orthodoxy, a judgment, however, severe enough to render it impossible for him to accept the parish of Crosville-sur-Cie. He found another benefice elsewhere.

The misadventures of the sieur de Saint-Ange retain little interest in themselves, but they do furnish more than a glimpse into the nature of Blaise Pascal's religious "conversion." In these disputes he adopted the same aggressive approach that he brought to his scientific investigations. And, like his work on the calculating machine and his experiments relative to the vacuum, his efforts to thwart Saint-Ange's appointment to a responsible office were ordered to a pragmatic solution — as Gilberte put it, to protect the young people of the region from a perverse and false teacher. The moral factor weighed heavily with Blaise, who, under the guidance of his father, had imbibed the lessons taught by the Stoics and Montaigne, but he joined these now to the gospel truths as preached by Father Guillebert and to the virtuous examples of the unsophisticated Deschamps. Yet there had to be for Blaise an intellectual factor as well, and it is difficult to believe that he could have thrown himself into the theological controversy unless it entailed a methodology consistent with his own tenor of mind. In the school of Jansenius and Saint-Cyran the young Pascal appeared to find satisfaction on both these counts. He had no doubt pondered the distinction drawn by Antoine Arnauld in the opening pages of *De la fréquente communion* between conventional scholasticism — an academic exercise, worthy enough, but fraught with occasions for prideful and trivial wrangles — and the theology needed "for the direction of souls." To achieve this moral purpose only positive theology would do, only the inductive examination of Scripture and the fathers and the decrees of the ancient councils. Here was argument that lived and breathed. And here was a congenial strategy for the new convert, like Blaise Pascal, confident in his own powers but confident also that he had now discovered proper direction for his soul. As he would write much later: "If we submit everything to reason, our religion will be left nothing mysterious or supernatural. If we offend the principles of reason, our religion will be absurd and ridiculous."

The author of *De la fréquente communion* was not the only member of his remarkable family to affect the fortunes of Blaise Pascal. Antoine Arnauld the elder had married Catherine Marion, daughter of a lawyer even more distinguished than himself, the advocate-general of the *Parlement* of Paris. Of the twenty children Catherine bore between 1588 and 1612 — ten of whom survived — the oldest was a son, followed by five little girls. In order to assure an adequate dowry for the marriage of the first of these daughters, also called Catherine, it was determined that her sisters next in age should become nuns. This was not an unusual practice, nor did it mean that the children involved should be withdrawn entirely from the fashionable world into which they had been born. "On July 5, 1602," the girl most directly involved recalled a half-century later, "I came to this convent [of Port-Royal] as abbess, when I was only ten years and ten months old." The appointment of a child to such an office, Jacqueline-Marie Arnauld added in her memoir, was due "to the very great disorder, common enough at that time, when there prevailed no discipline in the awarding of benefices, and when in our [Cistercian] order there was practically no serious observance of the rule." Her influential grandfather, Marion, obtained the necessary licence for her from the king; and, after a prudent lie was told about her age, the routine confirmation of it came eventually from Rome. Jacqueline, young and unformed as she was, rather fancied the idea of being an abbess, of being in command — her gifts in that regard would presently come to full flower. Meanwhile she passed through the various stages of investiture — more worldly *fêtes* than religious ceremonies, as she ruefully remembered them — until, as a sign of completion, she assumed her new name: Mère Marie-Angélique de Sainte-Madeleine, or simply Mère Angélique Arnauld.

The Cistercian convent of Notre Dame de Port-Royal, established in 1204, lay about twenty miles south and west of Paris, near Chevreuse, in a narrow valley with thick woods growing up steeply all round it. Administratively subject to the nearby abbey of Vaux-le-Cernay, it flourished for more than three centuries under both royal and papal patronage. An extensive complex of buildings was gradually constructed around a spacious quadrangle, from the splendid Gothic church at one end to the three-storey residences of the nuns at the other. Outside the compound's low wall, plots of flowers, as well as orchards and gardens of herbs and vegetables, stretched out toward hills covered with oak and pine. Less attractive was the spongy nature of the soil, which after a heavy rain turned into a marsh-like breeding-ground for ague and other illnesses. Nevertheless, during its heyday Port-Royal supported not only sixty choir sisters but also the service personnel necessary for the functioning of so considerable an enterprise. Like all medieval monastic institutions, the convent was sustained by income from the lands ceded to it by pious patrons. And like all medieval convents, Port-Royal was intended to be the abode of women dedicated to the contemplative life. The classic vows of poverty, chastity, and obedience, together with a strict observance of the ancient Benedictine rule — including the mandate to chant daily the various hours of the divine office — were the means whereby the nuns fulfilled their vocation. Unlike members of the more flexible Catholic sisterhoods of later times, the nuns of Port-Royal sought Christian perfection by keeping their vows within the prayerful serenity of the cloister rather than in, say, nursing or teaching within the hurly-burly of the world.

Such at least was the ideal. But the ideal had gone aglimmering at Port-Royal as it had in so many other foundations of religious at the end of the Middle Ages. By the time Mère Angélique arrived there, only twelve nuns were in residence. The house was considered respectable when compared to many others — to Maubuisson, for instance, where the abbess was the promiscuous sister of one of Henri IV's mistresses. But the fervor and regularity of the past had, at Port-Royal, given way to a trivial routine of idleness, gossip, and individual eccentricity, carried on by a gaggle of spinsters corralled into the religious life by their bourgeois families. A small but significant symbol of the gradual relaxation of the rigorous Cistercian spirit was the practice, adopted by the increasingly lethargic ladies of Port-Royal, of singing Matins at four o'clock in the afternoon instead of at four o'clock in the morning. True enough, Monsieur and Madame Arnauld saw to it that the one professed sister leading a genuinely scandalous life was removed from the premises before their daughter entered into office. They also sought to put in order the convent's tangled finances, bearing in mind, no doubt, the generally accepted view that an abbess could spend one-third of a foundation's revenues on herself. But such efforts did not rest easily in Angélique's memory. "My mother feared God, but at that stage in her life she still cared more for the honor of the world than for the honor of God."

During her first years as abbess it did not occur to *"la petite Madame de Port-Royal"* that she should in any way alter her own adolescent style of life or impose any changes upon that of her mature subjects. Indeed, she enjoyed as much as they — perhaps more — the celebrations of the Carnival, the card playing, the gossiping, the diet of rich meats and sweets, the ministrations of a whole squad of servants, the walking out of the convent in the evenings and the frequent and unregulated visits of relations and friends, which might include mild flirtations. But these diversions were not enough to reconcile the child-abbess to her dreary lot; the prospect of life as a nun, even as the ruler of other nuns, became increasingly "insupportable." Madame Arnauld, though perhaps too much in thrall to "the honor of the world," was nevertheless scandalized by her daughter's frivolity, a point she argued with special urgency when, at the end of 1607, illness brought Angélique back to the family home in Paris for a period of convalescence. The girl professed herself grateful for her mother's solicitude, but she took no solace in the admonitions addressed to her. Then, a few months later, back at Port-Royal, she experienced a sea-change, one with immense consequences for the future.

When the festivities connected to the Carnival were over and the Lent of 1608 had begun, Angélique wearily resigned herself to do some spiritual reading every day as a penitential practice. The book that fell to hand was a collection of sermons, "which, though they were very simple, I found beautiful, and they aroused in me a certain amount of devotion." Then, out of the blue, there appeared at the convent gate a Capuchin friar who asked permission to preach to the sisters. Mère Angélique agreed, thinking that a sermon might be an acceptable Lenten entertainment, especially since there had been virtually no preaching at Port-Royal for more than thirty years. Accordingly "we went to hear the sermon of this Capuchin, during which God so sharply touched me that, from that moment, I found myself happier to be a religious than I had been unhappy being one before. And I do not know what I would not have wanted to do for God if the power that his grace gave me had continued to exert itself within me." Her first thought, once the service was over, was to approach the friar and tell him what had happened to her, but upon reflection she decided "that he was too young for me, since I was only sixteen and a half years old, and that I should confide in someone else." Angélique therefore contented herself with joining the other sisters in offering thanks to this priest who had wandered into their midst. "And it was due to God's Providence that I refrained, for this man was highly dissolute, as I learned afterward. He had in fact made a fool of himself in several convents and, a few years later, actually apostatized."

That the agent of Mère Angélique's conversion proved to be disreputable did not lessen its impact upon her. During the months that followed she struggled to come to terms with her new spiritual status. She discovered a delight in prayer she had never known before, but she also suffered from doubts about her unaided capacities. "I continued to be strongly moved by a desire to serve God, and yet I had little insight into what I ought to do in this regard, never having received any instruction." This last point, the recognition of her need for sustained and expert supervision if she were to achieve the higher reaches of the call to holiness, came to be the dominant principle in Mère Angélique's own religious orientation and in the regime she ultimately imposed upon Port-Royal. It was a principle quite in tune with the ethos of the Counter-Reformation, in which vital emphasis was given to the necessity of spiritual direction imparted by well-trained confessors and preachers. Teresa of Ávila had insisted upon it, and the widespread influence of the Jesuits, no less than that of François de Sales and of the coterie surrounding Madame Icarie in Paris, testified to its effectiveness. At Pentecost, 1608, another Capuchin visited Port-Royal. He was an older man, severe of demeanor, and, said Angélique, "I immediately concluded that he was the person I needed. I opened to him the desires of my heart, and he encouraged me." And when she confided in him her qualms about continuing in an office awarded her for worldly reasons, he charged her to assume the task of restoring her convent to its pristine condition even as, by God's grace, she purified herself. Shortly afterward the old friar heard her general confession, a sacramental experience that confirmed for Angélique the commitment she had made. The reform of Port-Royal had begun.

There was resistance, though not from Mère Angélique's putative Cistercian superior, the abbot of Vaux-le-Cernay; he lacked interest in promoting a monastic rule that he did not bother to observe himself, and he was in any case too indolent to interfere. A goodly number of the sisters, however — including, Angélique readily admitted, the best elements among them — saw no reason to alter their way of life merely because this twit of a girl was passing through a phase of adolescent enthusiasm. Only with the passage of time did they come to realize that their young abbess had changed radically and permanently and that she possessed a will of iron to which no obstacle seemed insurmountable. In the ardor of her conversion the nuns of Port-Royal appeared to her as sheep without a shepherd, a sad situation to be corrected by herself and by the succession of spiritual directors to whose guidance she intended to subject the community. So one by one the provisions of the rule were reimposed: strict adherence to the obligations of the vow of poverty, which meant in effect surrender of the right to hold personal property; an austere diet based upon abstinence from meat and delicacies; sanctification of the day through contemplative silence and liturgical prayer — the psalms and hymns of the divine office sung at the prescribed hours; and, fundamental to all else because without it a sense of community could not be restored, the maintenance of cloister, so that the nuns would no longer come and go as they pleased or invite their friends and relatives for chats and strolls.

But the strongest resistance to the reform of Port-Royal came from the family Arnauld. Monsieur and particularly Madame Arnauld wanted their child to be conventionally pious, to fill with dignity and integrity the honorable post they had secured for her. But when Angélique suddenly and unexpectedly displayed all the characteristics of a *dévote*, they were seriously alarmed. Solid bourgeois religion, properly Gallican, they understood and appreciated; anything beyond that smacked to them of fanaticism. Angélique gave them a strong indication of her troubling state of mind when she demanded that new documents confirming her appointment as abbess be applied for from Rome, replacing those that had been obtained orginally under false pretenses. A confrontation was inevitable, and it occurred on September 25, 1609, ever afterward hallowed in the annals of Port-Royal as *"la journée du guichet."*

Antoine Arnauld was genuinely fond of his second daughter and proud of her, and he often visited her, as did other members of the family. Whenever they arrived at Port-Royal on an outing — papa and *maman* with a half-dozen children in tow — they assumed they had full run of the convent compound and all its buildings; it was to be a day of games and a picnic, sanctified at the end, perhaps, by some perfunctory prayers in the nuns' chapel. Nor did little Angélique, at first, assume anything different. Such casual freedom of access, however, was in stark contradiction to the rules of cloister that, since her conversion, she was determined to enforce. So on that fateful September day — "the day of the wicket-gate" — Mère Angélique denied entry beyond the walls to her parents and her siblings; if they wished to speak to her, she said, they must do so in the cramped "parlor," a small, bleak room set aside for this purpose next to the gate. Her father responded to this, to him, humiliating mandate with a paroxysm of rage, her mother with a flood of tears, her sisters and brothers with bewilderment. Mère Angélique herself, her heart pounding, was as affected as they were, but she would not relent.

At the end of this emotionally draining encounter, she had won her point. Antoine Arnauld — who was, after all, a lawyer — agreed, no doubt reluctantly, that his daughter was within her legal rights to insist that the venerable rules of St. Benedict, the acceptance of which four centuries earlier had defined the status of Port-Royal, enjoyed a contractual predominance. Even the imperative of honor due father and mother had to bend when the child entered into mystical marriage with the divine Bridegroom who demanded total dedication, human preferences and connections notwithstanding. By establishing this principle in the face of the presuppositions of a patriarchal society, Mère Angélique had declared her independence and that of the other women of Port-Royal. Nonetheless, she must have found poignantly consoling the endorsement her family ultimately gave the stand she had taken: her mother, widowed in 1619, her widowed elder sister, and her four unmarried sisters all took the veil at the reformed Port-Royal, as did six of her nieces. Three of her four surviving brothers — the most eminent of them, Antoine, had not yet been born on *la journée du guichet* — became closely associated with the mission of Port-Royal and were unapologetically their formidable sister's disciples, as were four of her nephews. The flighty young girl had ripened into a *mulier fortis*.

Over the years that followed, Port-Royal flourished as never before. Far from alienating prospective postulants, Mère Angélique's program of fervent austerity attracted them in ever increasing numbers. Before long eighty nuns were crowded into the compound that formerly had housed only a dozen. The rush of recruits was perhaps predictable, given the appeal that a crusading spirit naturally has for the idealistic young and, moreover, given the temper of a time of religious revival. It was in any event a mixed blessing for the abbess, who had to integrate the supremely important cultivation of her own inner life with an intimidating array of administrative chores. That she proved equal to these differing obligations was testified to by the fierce devotion her subjects gave her and by the wide approval the reformed Port-Royal won in the highest social and political circles. Indeed, her reputation rapidly became such that she was invited to exert her reforming influence on other convents much in need of it, including the notorious Maubuisson.

Though it may be difficult to say precisely when Mère Angélique began to consider the possibility of transferring the convent to Paris, or rather — what came to be her real intention — of establishing a second house in the capital, the reasons for the idea are relatively easy to discern. The material fabric of Port-Royal had been deteriorating for decades. Its fixed revenues in an era of inflated prices could not keep pace with necessary repairs, to say nothing of maintenance for an expanding population. In Paris new benefactions and endowment might be favorably solicited if, as informed sources said, admiration for what Mère Angélique had accomplished in the countryside was shared by all the best elements of society, including the pious young king, Louis XIII. Then, too, she had to face the reality that Port-Royal, tucked away in its little valley, which in rainy seasons turned into a virtual swamp, was not a healthy place, especially when so many people were crammed into it. Finally, the lack of support from her Cistercian superiors led her to wonder whether it would not be well to separate Port-Royal from its old canonical connection. With this intent in mind, she approached François de Sales and proposed that she associate herself with the Visitation order of nuns that he had recently founded. The bishop of Geneva, shortly before his death, gently dissuaded her.

By 1624 — the year Cardinal Richelieu was appointed first minister — Mère Angélique had arrived at a different solution. Having taken care to secure the formal permission of the abbot of Vaux-le-Cernay, she announced her plan to move with her community to Paris. It took a year before the archbishop there gave his approval; he had first to be reminded that among the practical measures inspired by the Council of Trent had been the relocation of religious houses from remote areas to the rapidly expanding cities. Meanwhile, Madame Catherine Arnauld, delighted at the prospect of the return of her daughters from the wilderness — there were four of them now at Port-Royal — scoured the city for an appropriate site. After examining more than a hundred *hôtels* she settled on one called Clagny, at the edge of the Faubourg Saint-Jacques, on the left bank. Once she had seen it, Mère Angélique agreed that the property provided an ideal setting, though with her practiced eye she noted the need for enlargement of the building. On July 19, 1625, Madame Arnauld signed the necessary papers, and so Port-Royal de Paris assumed its status as sister house to what was to be known thereafter as Port-Royal des Champs.

But Mère Angélique wanted more than a mere change of venue for her community; she wanted constitutional change as well. In 1627 Pope Urban VIII granted her petition that Port-Royal be removed from Cistercian jurisdiction and be placed directly under the charge of the archbishop of Paris. At the same time she enlisted the intercession of the queen mother to persuade the king to restore the ancient practice whereby the abbess would be chosen through election held at three-year intervals by the professed nuns themselves. Louis XIII graciously agreed to waive his prerogative of appointment, and in 1629 the pope sanctioned his decision. In a related matter, however, Mère Angélique was disappointed. The authorities refused to grant her wish that at least a skeletal conventual presence be maintained at Port-Royal des Champs. Only much later did they relent, with the result that she spent the next twenty years, with hardly an interruption, in Paris.

They proved to be years of spiritual growth for her and her sisters in religion, but they abounded with threats and alarums as well. Many of the troubles arose because Mère Angélique's zeal for reform was not always shared by those from whom she sought advice and direction.

Ever since the day her own conversion had been occasioned by a sermon preached by a rag-tag friar, she remained firmly convinced that the health of the community depended upon the guidance of a spiritual director, always, as a matter of course, a man. Independent she may have been, but, in the masculine world in which she lived, independence and assertiveness were possible for a woman only up to a point. And in the crucial matter of selecting male counselors, she was not always wise or lucky. Indeed, her early years in Paris were embittered by frequent clashes with directors in whom she had put her confidence, only after a while to discover them burdened, as she decided, with feet of clay. Then, during the Lent of 1635, she invited a special preacher to deliver a series of sermons at Port-Royal.

It was through her elder brother, Robert Arnauld d'Andilly — he took the elaboration of his surname from the location of a piece of property the Arnauld family owned in Poitu — that Mère Angélique had first met the abbé de Saint-Cyran, in 1623 or 1624. Though he is known to have preached at Port-Royal once or twice during the interval, there is no evidence that she was particularly impressed by him during this early acquaintance. Perhaps indeed, despite his reputation as a budding reformer, she rather frowned on him at first as representing one of the worst features of the bad old days; he was, after all, an absentee abbot who enjoyed the revenues of his monastery without residing there. Long after her own reservations had been put to rest, Soeur Marie de Sainte-Claire — née Marie-Claude Arnauld, Angélique's blood sister — continued to lead a faction within the convent wary of the abbé's influence. But Saint-Cyran could count upon the devotion of d'Andilly and that also of Madame Arnauld — now, in her widow's weeds, herself a professed nun at Port-Royal — as well as of Soeur Agnès de Saint-Paul (née Agnès Arnauld), Mère Angélique's closest confidante. The half-dozen or so sisters for whom Saint-Cyran acted as confessor no doubt also were his advocates. Mère Angélique at any rate eventually found in him the director she had been waiting for all her religious life. She ruefully recalled years afterward his visit to Port-Royal des Champs, shortly before the community's removal to Paris.

He told me he had seen many abbesses reform their convents, but only a few who had also reformed themselves. I found myself among the larger group, even if God had given me the grace to strive to be among the smaller. From that time on I revered the wisdom of this holy man, though at first I did not sufficiently appreciate that holiness, and so did not enjoy the happiness that God seems to have offered me if I had then placed myself under his direction.

By 1637 even Soeur Marie de Sainte-Claire had succumbed to the spiritual mastery of Saint-Cyran, and from that time on Port-Royal could fairly be called the focal point of the reform of religion envisaged by him and Jansenius all those years before in Bayonne. Not that austerity or serious dedication to the vows and to community life needed to be inculcated; these had long ago been attained through the efforts of Mère Angélique and her auxiliaries. What Saint-Cyran's sermons and instructions provided was a theological framework for the nuns and indeed for all the *dévots* who increasingly looked to Port-Royal for inspiration. They were already caught up in a sublime religious experience, already converted; the abbé's teaching on sin and grace and related matters confirmed their aspirations.

Never mind, he declared with a sweep of his hand, that the grace enjoyed by Adam and Eve gave them greater freedom than their descendants; those descendants, by the grace of Jesus Christ, are now more surely in the hands of God and less prone, as their first parents were, to depend upon their own strength. The natural corruption, the concupiscence, and the moral languor that flow from original sin and bind the human race to earth and to ultimate dissolution can be escaped not by any merits of our own but only by those of Christ. Our humility must reach toward the supreme humiliation experienced by the Savior. We must pray for grace constantly, at every turn of the moral road, else we shall fall into the void out of which we shall be powerless to deliver ourselves. "The death that stems from sin," he told the nuns on one occasion, "never occurs unless we choose it. I am consoled by this truth, because it means that I shall not experience the death of my soul if I do not will it. But it is always God who forms this will, who accomplishes the good all the more freely, although determined by his own omnipotence. It is God's grace that brings about full knowledge and full consent." So much for the vaunted human liberty of the Molinists — and by the tone and gesture he employed his congregation would have understood the implication: so much for the laxists, the slackers, the *libertins*, yes, the *honnêtes hommes* as well, and so much for the Jesuit confessors who curried the favor of their proud penitents.

But what of the Molinist accusation that such an economy of salvation amounts to Calvinist predestination? Here the polemical ground grew slippery and the verbal formulation more subtle. Christ surely died "to buy back all human beings," said Saint-Cyran, and therefore "predestination is nothing more than the eternal love God has for some of Adam's children, the love he bears to those he has decided to save from among the totality of humankind, which has merited damnation." In fact, the greater the individual's sin — the apostle Peter's denial of Jesus, for instance — the more striking the working of this principle. Nor should it be an invitation to despair; if clearly the number of those God has decided, on his own incomprehensible terms, to love and to save is severely limited — many are called, Jesus said, but few are chosen — one must, to be sure, live one's earthly life in fear and trembling. But, the abbé insisted with an unusual rhetorical flourish, live also with hope and tranquility in the knowledge that "Jesus Christ has come for our sakes, to make us do the things which are impossible for us to do when left to our human devices. There will always be more angels on our side than against us." Though we cannot know who will be saved and who damned, there are "signposts in the predestined soul": perfect surrender to and a holy dependence upon God's will; the prolonged exercise of a sincere piety; the practice of penance, personal and sacramental; the humble acceptance of the grace of the present moment; and submission to the dictates of a director.

It is significant that the "signpost" mentioned last in this list was actually first in the order given by Saint-Cyran. He brought no false modesty to his estimate of the importance of the director of souls, and therefore of himself, in the program of reform he advocated — in what may be called, from the inception of the alliance between him and Port-Royal, the Jansenist scheme of things. Even during the harsh years of his imprisonment, from 1638, he carried on this function with undiminished zeal. This he did through the continued circulation of his writings, through his correspondence, and, thanks to the collusion of the sympathetic governor of the Vincennes, through the personal contacts he managed to preserve. As far as Port-Royal itself was concerned,

he dispatched there one of his most devoted disciples. The priest Antoine Singlin, a sometime Parisian linen draper who had fallen under
the influence first of Vincent de Paul and then of Saint-Cyran, had none
of the charismatic gifts of the master, but his simplicity and directness,
the transparent holiness of his personal life, shone through his sermons
and won the hearts of many, nuns and layfolk, who heard him Sunday
by Sunday in the chapel of Port-Royal.

Mère Angélique — grown portly now, a kindly matron and stern
matriarch, quite majestic in her religious habit of long white gown and
black veil, with a scarlet cross emblazoned on the front of the outer
scapular — continued her sway through the perilous days of the 1640s.
In so doing, however, she was not without the lively support of the
rest of her family. To administer the spiritual and temporal affairs of
the convent, she and her sister Agnès virtually alternated as abbess and
mistress of novices, the gentler and natively more introspective Mère
Agnès fashioning a modest following of her own. Add to them the
abiding impact within the cloister of seven other Arnauld women —
their mother, sisters, and nieces — and the emergence, after Saint-
Cyran's death, of their youngest brother, Antoine, as the intellectual
leader of the movement, and it becomes tempting to describe Port-
Royal as a spiritual family firm.

And during the 1640s, even as the Jansenist party appeared to prosper,
the days for that very reason did become more perilous. The
governmental pressures that had put Saint-Cyran behind bars continued to be felt after Cardinal Richelieu died. If anything they were
made heavier by the posthumous publication of Jansenius's *Augustinus*,
which, if rapturously received by Port-Royal, raised the hackles of many
a conventional theologian at the Sorbonne. The official censor there
alleged that he had found expressed in the book views on grace and
free will that were obviously linked to the Calvinist heresy. One witty
Parisian remarked that the censor was as unfair to Jansenius as Jansenius had been to St. Augustine. But the Jesuits, especially stung by
Antoine Arnauld's implications in *De la fréquente communion* that their
Molinist theory was a species of laxism, were not in a laughing mood,
and their influence at court and among the ruling class generally was
by no means diminished. The new first minister, Cardinal Mazarin,
kept his counsel, but, since his hold on power was less secure than that

of his predecessor, there seemed all the more reason to expect that he would be just as vigilant as Richelieu had been when it came to the formation of factions outside his direct control.

Religious contention and political uncertainty, therefore, were both much in evidence when Blaise Pascal returned to Paris in the summer of 1647. Due to the exertions of his scientific investigations and, perhaps, to the added emotional strain involved in the controversy with Saint-Ange, his always tenuous health had deteriorated markedly. Headache, severe stomach pain, periodic paralysis in his legs — these and other symptoms indicated an illness beyond the skill of provincial physicians. Étienne Pascal, when posted to Rouen, had kept the lease on the house in the rue Brise-miche, and here his son took up residence. And not alone: his younger sister accompanied him.

Whatever treatment and medicine the Parisian doctors prescribed, the result was moderately successful, and Blaise's condition improved enough for him to see through the press his Latin treatise on conics as well as a pamphlet laying out the preliminary conclusions of his re-search on the vacuum. Meanwhile he came into immediate contact with Port-Royal, a quite predictable circumstance since Father Guillebert was still his director. Even so, it was Jacqueline who took the lead. Shortly before their departure from Rouen, and at the surprisingly advanced age of twenty-one, she had received the sacrament of confirmation, "preparing herself for it," her sister Gilberte reported, "by studying some of the little tracts of M. de Saint-Cyran. One can say that she truly received the Holy Ghost, for from that hour she was entirely changed." Once in Paris she frequented the services at Port-Royal and heard the sermons of Father Singlin, "who described the Christian life in a man-ner that fulfilled completely the aspirations she had felt since God had touched her." She confided to her brother that she wanted to consecrate herself to Christ as a nun of Port-Royal, and he enthusiastically en-dorsed the idea.

Blaise had also listened to and been impressed by the sermons of Antoine Singlin, and, like Jacqueline, he had paid homage to the for-midable Arnauld sisters, Mère Angélique and Mère Agnès. But his explanation of the religious experience he had had in Rouen reflected the man of science as well as the recent convert, to a degree that was not altogether welcome to the Port-Royalists. Reason, Blaise said cheer-fully to one of them, common sense even, shows what flummery the opponents of Saint-Cyran talk when they argue against his principles, though of course one's faith brings one to the same conclusion. This sort of breezy self-confidence made Mère Angélique and her associates uneasy about Blaise Pascal, and it produced for years a constraint in the relationship between him and them. They might have been re-assured had they been privy to the dour testimony he offered to his sister Gilberte in a letter written to her shortly after he had met them. "It is our sins," he wrote in April 1648,

> that keep us wrapped up in corporeal and terrestrial things. And these entanglements are not only the punishment for these sins but also the occasion for doing the same evil again. So it is neces-sary, if we are to rise from our fall, that we make use of this earthy place where we are buried. This is why we have to take full advantage of the benevolence through which God allows us to have always before our eyes an image of the good we have lost and to surround ourselves with the captivity to which his justice has reduced us.

Toward the end of that year Étienne Pascal, his term of office completed, returned from Normandy. Jacqueline asked his permission to join the community at Port-Royal; it would never have occurred to her to do so without his consent. The old man — he was sixty-one now and ailing — refused, tearfully pleading that he could not face his last years without the company of his beloved daughter. His son interceded with him, but to no avail. An awkward compromise was worked out whereby Jacqueline would live in religious seclusion within the Pascal household, with Blaise acting as liaison between her and Port-Royal.

But even as these private arrangements took shape public events had begun to intrude. As they have so often in the city's tumultuous history, the barricades were going up in the streets of Paris.

4 Bereavement and
the Lure of the World

A N AURA of unreality still clings to the memory of the Fronde, that
series of civil disturbances that rocked Paris and parts of provincial France between 1648 and 1653. The very word has a comic-opera
ring to it: *fronde* means a slingshot and had then specific reference to
the sport of mischievous Parisian urchins who, to the irritation of the
magistrates, used to pelt passing carriages with stones. If the Fronde
had enjoyed the slightest success in achieving its goal — to roll back
the centralized power of the monarchy so much advanced by the administration of Cardinal Richelieu — perhaps the chroniclers would
have paid it more serious heed.

Not that the *frondeurs* were so casually dismissed at the time. The
first upsurge of resistance to the crown issued from members of the
Parlement of Paris — not of course a "parliament" in the English sense
of the word but rather the most important of the thirteen sovereign
French courts whose function it was to "register" and thus lend legal
finality to all decrees and edicts. Under Henri IV and Richelieu the
Parlement had become more or less a rubber stamp for royal initiatives.
The potential weakness of the monarchy during the regency for the
child-king, Louis XIV — his father had died in 1643, only months after
his great chief minister — tempted the *parlementaires* to gamble that

there might be a reprise of the anarchic conditions that had prevailed during the minority of Louis XIII. The lawyers and administrative nobles who composed the *Parlement* of Paris brought their challenge to a climax by refusing to endorse the royal budget of 1648 and, during that summer, by putting forward twenty-seven propositions aimed at sharply reducing the crown's ability to tax and to assert its control over the provinces. The regency at first appeared ready to acquiesce, then reversed course and arrested the leading *parlementaires,* then found itself, at the beginning of 1649, confronted by those fabled Parisian barricades. Military intervention failed, and by the spring the *Parlement* seemed to have won the concessions it was seeking.

But in fact the regency was not so weak as its opponents supposed. Anne of Austria, the queen mother, and Richelieu's successor as first minister, Cardinal Mazarin, made a formidable team. Indeed, they were widely rumored, though never proved, to have been lovers. Anne in any event, despite her title a Spanish princess by birth — and the struggle between Spain and France dragged on even after the general settlement that ended the Thirty Years' War elsewhere in Europe — had to tread warily lest she be labeled a sympathizer with, if not an agent of, the perennial enemy. Nevertheless, she understood — as her mother-in-law, Marie de' Medici, had not — how best to exploit the awe in which her young son, as heir to St. Louis IX, was held by the vast majority of the French people. As for Jules Mazarin, Richelieu's protégé (né Giulio Mazzarino, formerly soldier and diplomat in the service of the Papal States), he may have lacked something of his master's stature, but he was a worthy successor nonetheless, a handsome, charming man, a practitioner of the politics of realism, as befitted his Italian heritage, shrewd, and above all patient. His dismissal from office had been one of the demands of the *parlementaires,* and he prudently went off into exile in Germany. But not for long.

By January 1650, it was clear that the *parlementaires* had overplayed their hand; or perhaps the narrowness of their support — their original alliance with the Parisian lower orders had soon melted away — and the raw self-interest that impelled them had doomed their efforts from the start. There was to emerge at any rate no French equivalent to the oligarchy of merchants and professionals that was at this moment developing in England to serve as a counterbalance to the nobility and the monarchy. The second stage of the Fronde endured the same kind of dénouement. In their quarrel with the *Parlement* the queen mother and the cardinal had enlisted the support of the old landed aristocracy, the *noblesse d'épée*. Once the cause of the lawyers collapsed, these noblemen saw an opportunity to regain the prerogatives that had been ruthlessly torn from them by Henri IV and Richelieu. Under the leadership of the Prince of Condé, the king's cousin, this Fronde of the Nobles prospered for a while, won a few skirmishes; but in the end it, too, petered out, a victim of conflicting ambitions and jealousies. A last desperate attempt to ally those natural antagonists, the lords and the bourgeois *parlementaires* — the first Fronde and the second — predictably came to nothing. Condé's flight into the refuge of the Spanish Netherlands followed by the triumphal entry into Paris of Louis and his mother (October 1652) clearly signalled that political feudalism had breathed its last. At the beginning of the following year, Mazarin returned to resume charge of day-to-day affairs, nor was the authority of the monarchy seriously challenged again in France until the Revolution of 1789.

A succession of failed *coups d'état* rather than a full-scale insurrection, the Fronde nevertheless made life anxious and even dangerous for those caught in its wake. This was especially the case in Paris and its environs, where most of the fighting took place. Those who could leave the capital did so, among them the three Pascals, who departed for the Auvergne in May 1649. They lived with Gilberte and Florin Périer for the next eighteen months, safe from the sporadic violence that punctuated the short span of the first Fronde. Little evidence survives of their activities during their time in Clermont, though it may be surmised, from what went on before and after their temporary exile, that Blaise continued to try to harmonize his scientific investigations and his enduring worldly ambitions with a religious enthusiasm that continued to wax and wane. Jacqueline for her part followed as best she could a nun's regimen in her sister's home, as she had been doing in her father's. Gilberte, the busy housewife and mother, marveled at the intensity of her sister's solitariness and prayer life; Jacqueline scarcely left her room except to go to church or, under direction, to visit the sick poor. She remained in communication with Port-Royal through letters regularly exchanged with the mistress of novices, Mère Agnès Arnauld.

The three returned to Paris in November 1650, in time to witness —

from a house on the rue de Touraine, in the Marais district — Conde's futile campaigns.

What they may have thought of the prince's military adventures remains unknown, though it is unlikely that they had much sympathy for them. Blaise at any rate was engaged at the time in a battle of his own, a literary battle related to his research on the vacuum. In the early summer of 1651 a Jesuit attached to the *collège* in Montferrand published anonymously a thesis in which he asserted that "certain persons, lovers of novelty," had claimed credit for original experiments carried out in Normandy and the Auvergne, which in fact had been performed elsewhere in Europe years earlier. This publication was dedicated to the president of the *Cour des aides* in Clermont, the very judicial body on which Étienne Pascal had served two decades before, and to this grand personage, no doubt well known to his father, Blaise Pascal addressed a public response.

His tone was both haughty and aggrieved. "You see, Monsieur," he wrote on July 16,

> that in specifying the provinces of Normandy and the Auvergne, it is my experiments of which the thesis speaks. Nor can I conceal from you that this Jesuit father, whose acquaintance I have not the honor to enjoy, whose name I do not know, of whom I have no memory of ever seeing, with whom I have nothing in common directly or indirectly, nine or ten months after I have left Clermont, when I am a hundred leagues away and when nothing is further from my thoughts, I am shocked that this father, I say, should choose me as a subject for his homily.

"And not 'me' only: the *'certaines personnes'*" accused of plagiarism must include Pascal's brother-in-law, Florin Périer, who — it will be recalled — performed the definitive experiment on the Puy-de-Dôme. Périer, a minor royal official, could not afford to stand guilty of dishonesty in the eyes of the esteemed president of the *Cour des aides* of Clermont, and Blaise Pascal was anxious to exonerate Périer as well as himself. In order to do so he reviewed the research done previously in Italy and Poland, admitted its relevance, but maintained also that the consequences of his own experiments (and Périer's) had been "very

74

good and very useful." Certainly others had before challenged the conventional wisdom about nature's abhorrence of a vacuum, "but without thorough induction this insight remained mere conjecture." Therefore, from 1647, "I projected a series of experiments, which reached their climax the next year with M. Périer's enterprise at the summit and at the base of the Puy-de-Dôme." Other prominent researchers, "including Galileo," have made their contributions, but so, protested the young Pascal, have I. And, characteristic of his mind-set, he did so, not by arguing to sustain a preconceived system of thought, but by laying out an accumulation of observable data.

Not that Blaise Pascal hesitated, in presenting his case, to invoke the prerogatives of his class and his heritage. My father, he assured the president of the *Cour des aides*, joins me and my brother-in-law in advancing these claims to originality. Blaise must nevertheless have felt a pang in urging this contention, for when he did so Étienne Pascal was clearly a dying man.

The exact date of his demise was September 24, 1651. Gilberte Périer, who was about to go into labor — she bore a son three days later — was not present at her father's deathbed, and Jacqueline immediately sent the sad news to her and her husband in Clermont. Nearly a month later, on October 17, Blaise Pascal also took up the pen, but what he wrote his in-laws was more a pious tract than a family letter. It was longer than 5,000 words, and its extraordinary importance lies in the glimpse it provides into Blaise's religious attitudes between his first and second conversions.

He began by saying, rather whimsically, that Jacqueline had not really finished her letter, since she recounted only the specifics having to do with their father's last illness. "I might well repeat them here, so deeply have I carved them into my heart and so very consoling are they." But, he continued, it might be better to say something instead about "the result I discern from this experience, that his death was so Christian, so happy, so holy, so desirable indeed that, aside from one's natural sentiments, there is nothing for the Christian to do but rejoice." Such joy should rise spontaneously within us, because in the evils that befall us "we find consolation not in ourselves, nor in any human considerations, nor in whatever has been created, but only in God." Creatures are never "the first cause of the accidents we call evil that happen to us." We who are bereaved by the death of our father will find no "solid relief" unless we acknowledge that what has occurred is a result "not of chance, nor of some fatal necessity of nature, nor of the interplay of the elements or parts of the human condition"; it is rather "an event indispensable, inevitable, just, holy, and useful for the well-being of the Church and for the exaltation of the name and of the glory of God, an intervention of Providence decreed from all eternity to take place in the fullness of time, in such a year, on such a day, at such an hour, in such a place, in such a manner." What is left for us is "to unite our will to that of God himself, to will in him, with him, and for him the thing that he has eternally willed in us and for us."

The ancients did not understand this truth: "Neither Seneca nor Socrates has anything persuasive to tell us." They thought that "death was natural to man," and they based their teaching on this "false principle," which led them inevitably to "base" and "puerile" conclusions. "It is far different with Jesus Christ," and we who believe in him "enjoy the inestimable advantage of knowing that death is nothing other than a punishment for sin, imposed upon man in order to expiate his crimes." What is our life, "the life of Christians, but a perpetual sacrifice that can be brought to fruition only by death." Christ entered the world "and offered himself to God as a holocaust and a victim"; all that he is, all that he did — "his birth, his life, his death, his resurrection and ascension, his real presence in the Eucharist, his eternal seat at the right hand of the Father" — point to his "unique sacrifice." And "what has been achieved in Jesus Christ must be achieved also in us, his members."

So it is that "death without Jesus Christ is horrible, detestable, an abomination of nature." But with him "it is entirely different; it is amiable, holy, a joy to the faithful, because all is sweetness in Jesus Christ, even death." Bear in mind that Christ's death was and is a perpetual sacrifice and that the climax of any sacrificial ritual is the death of the victim. As Scripture says, only through his sufferings, which culminated with his death on the cross, could Jesus enter into his glory. It can be no different for us.

From the moment we enter into the Church, which is the world of the faithful and particularly of the elect — where Jesus Christ entered from the moment of his Incarnation by a privilege reserved to the only Son of God — we are offered and sanctified in a sacrifice fully accomplished only by death, whereby we are delivered from all vices, from the love of this natural life, from the contagion that always threatens to infect us.

Therefore we must not mourn like the pagans, who have no hope. "We did not lose my father at the moment of his death. Indeed, we had lost him, so to speak, on the day he entered the Church, on the day of his baptism. From then on he belonged to God." Now, through earthly death, freed at last from the ravages of sin, "God has deigned to complete and to crown his sacrifice." Étienne Pascal has accomplished "the only thing for which he was created; the will of God has been fulfilled in him, and his will has been absorbed into God's." It is "the special privilege" afforded to Christians to understand that the human body "is not a chunk of spoiled meat, as a deceitful nature would have us think, but rather the inviolable and eternal temple of the Holy Ghost." So the fathers of the Church have taught us to honor the relics of the saints who have gone before us, their very flesh and bones.

Yet, despite this salutary teaching, the "natural horror" of death clings even to us believers. Why should this be so?

Let me tell you what I have learned from two very great and very holy men. The truth that unlocks this mystery is that God has created every human being with two loves, one for God and the other for himself, with, however, this corollary: that the love of God should be infinite, that is to say, should be without any object except God himself, while the love one has for oneself should end in God. A person in this state not only loves himself without sin, but, in fact, he cannot not love himself without sin.

Self-love therefore was natural in Adam and Eve, and laudable. But when they lost their innocence — and lost it for all their descendants — "it became criminal and violent." The consequence is that "the prospect of death for innocent Adam had a natural horror attached to it, because it would have meant the end of a life conformed to God's will." But for a guilty Adam, and for all of us who have rejected the infinite love of God, the reality is far otherwise. "It was right to loathe death when it separated a holy soul from a holy body, but it is also right to delight in death when it separates a chosen soul from an impure body."

Adam rightly loved his own innocent life, and Jesus Christ, the second Adam, did the same, "as is apparent from the agony of anticipation he suffered in the garden the night before the crucifixion." But the death we must undergo is of "a contrary kind; it punishes a culpable body and purges a vicious body, and therefore we ought not to fear it if we have even a little faith, hope, and charity. One of the grand principles of Christianity is this, that what Christ has achieved must also be achieved in the soul and body of every Christian; that as Jesus Christ took suffering upon himself during his mortal life and died, was raised to a new life, mounted up to heaven to sit at the Father's right hand," so must the Christian soul "suffer and die to sin in penitence and in baptism, so that it may depart the earth, at the hour of death, and rise to heaven, to God's right hand. Then, at the last judgment, the body too shall rise, and thus we can say that death is the coronation of the beatitude of the soul and the beginning of the beatitude of the body." For we must abide by the sage instruction of St. Augustine: "If our bodies were to die and be raised to glory at the moment of our baptism, then we would obey the mandates of the gospel only because of our love of life; instead, the grandeur of faith shines most brilliantly when the promise of immortality is stretched out against the shadows of death."

This is the common faith we profess, "and I believe nothing more is necessary through my puny efforts to contribute to your consolation. I would not presume to offer you succor on my own, but since these are lessons I have learned, I offer them with the assurance that God will bless these seeds and give them growth." Another lesson "I have learned from a holy man is that in our affliction one of the most solid and useful charities toward the dead is to do the things they would want us to do if they were still in the world, and to abide by the good advice they have given us. By this practice we almost make them come to life in us." Indeed, "as the heresiarchs are punished in another world for the sins to which they have led their followers, in whom their poison still lives," so the blessed dead "are rewarded, outside their own merit, through those to whom they have given their counsel and their example."

May God fortify us in our resolutions. No doubt the recommendations Blaise has offered the Périers "you would have followed without my having suggested them." As for Blaise himself, "had I lost my father six years ago, I myself would have been lost, and although I believe that now my dependence upon him is less absolute, I know his presence would have been expedient for me for another ten years and useful for the rest of my life." But we have to hope "that God, having taken him away at such a time, in such a place, in such a manner, has without doubt done the best to promote his own glory and our salvation." It would have been feckless to have begged God to spare Étienne Pascal; "we know plenty of instances in which distinguished persons have pleaded in such a vein, with the result that their prayers, having been answered, have brought about nothing but misery for them." As for what is to happen next in this valley of tears, human beings, afflicted by "the serpent concupiscence," are too weak "to be able to probe safely into future contingencies. Let us then hope in God, and not weary ourselves with rash and indiscreet predictions. We should hand over to God the conduct of our lives, so that trouble should not domineer over us."

There is much that is intriguing in this document. Whom did Pascal refer to, for example, when he invoked the authority of "two very great and very holy men"? Saint-Cyran and Jansenius, perhaps; more likely Guillebert and Antoine Singlin, or even the brothers Deschamps, back in Rouen. Similarly, who was "the holy man" who maintained that abiding by the counsel and example of the dead amounted in a sense to revivifying them? And who were the distinguished acquaintances of the Pascals whose successful prayer for sick relatives resulted in "misery"? Equally mysterious is the explicit assertion that had Étienne Pascal died six years earlier Blaise's first conversion would not have occurred — "I myself would have been lost" — when the testimony of Gilberte Périer clearly indicates that the son's adhesion to serious religion preceded that of the father. But, however that may be, the overall message rings with the Augustinian bias: the deep moral pessimism — the human being by fallen nature merely "a chunk of spoiled meat" — the need for constant penance, the staunch reverence for the sacraments of baptism and the Eucharist, the notion of the Church as "the world particularly of the elect," and, most remarkably, the ingenious explanation of how original sin had radically altered one's love of oneself from a good to an evil and, consequently, had determined the Christian's proper attitude toward death.

79

Not that Pascal's screed displays any theological sophistication. It is a manifesto born out of pious earnestness rather than out of argument. One would never suspect from reading it that quarrels over the meaning and consequences of original sin had been raging in learned circles for a hundred years, that from Luther and Calvin to Baius and Molina the differing alternative explanations had been laid out and fought over, not only in university common rooms but on battlefields as well. Thus, for example, Pascal's bland assertion that immortality was "natural" to human beings in the state of innocence begged one of the most important questions raised during a century of intense debate and was — though he would have been chagrined to have been told so — of dubious Catholic orthodoxy. Aside from a perfunctory reference to the Church fathers and the citation of a familiar verse or two of Scripture, there is no evidence in his letter that Pascal yet possessed any of the ordinary tools of theological discourse. Nor should it come as a surprise that he wrote like a man who had learned his divinity so far from the sermons he had heard, like those of Singlin delivered at Port-Royal, for that was the only divinity he so far knew at this moment of his life. He had received merely the barest religious instruction from a father — his sole teacher — who had always insisted that the realms of faith and reason must be kept strictly apart. And the death of that father prompted the son to seek consolation and to offer it to others, not in doctrinal subtlety, but in the hallowed language of the converted heart.

All the more remarkable, therefore, in the light of so robust a confession of faith, was Blaise Pascal's *volte-face* with regard to his younger sister's religious aspirations. He who had before been her ally in trying to persuade their father to allow her to enter Port-Royal now, with the father dead, changed his mind and begged Jacqueline to forgo the convent and stay with him. No doubt the overriding reason was the deep affection he had for her who had been his playmate and his soul mate throughout their lives. He had lost his beloved father, and, if he were to lose his sister as well, he would be doubly orphaned. The family ties plainly bound him more closely than they did her; she had in fact committed her heart to another family altogether.

Then, too, the brother's own religious fervor depended less than did the sister's upon the mystique of Port-Royal — a difference between

80

them at this stage perhaps of degree rather than of kind. Blaise at any rate may have recalled with distaste an instance of Port-Royal's unbending severity that had occurred during their recent sojourn in Clermont. Jacqueline had taken for her confessor there a local Oratorian of good reputation who, among other edifying suggestions, proposed that she employ her poetic gifts in translating into French one of the hymns of the breviary. She chose the *Jesu, nostra redemptio* from the office of the feast of the Ascension, and the priest, much impressed by the beauty of her verse, urged her to incorporate such literary work into her spiritual routine. But Jacqueline, struck by scruples, contacted her mentors in Paris, who replied with chilling vigor. "This talent for poetry," Mère Agnès Arnauld wrote, "is not something for which God will ask of you an accounting. You must bury it." Blaise Pascal, still an inventor and a physicist and a mathematician, was not likely to have sympathized with so stark a repudiation of natural genius.

More surprisingly, brother and sister also bruised each other over money. Étienne Pascal's estate was substantial at least on paper, though far from lavish. Much of it was in the form of debts owed, not all of them collectable. Toward the end of October 1651 — just after Blaise had sent his long letter of condolence to Clermont — Jacqueline signed over her share in the property to Blaise, who, in return, legally guaranteed her an ample yearly income. Gilberte, for whom her father had provided at the time of her marriage, did not figure in this settlement. Of course all parties realized that if and when Jacqueline became a nun and swore a vow of poverty she could not take her annuity with her, which would then revert to her heir, that is, to her brother. It is impossible to say to what extent Blaise was moved to agree to this arrangement in hopes that it would induce his sister to delay entry into the convent for a while or, perhaps, forever. Jacqueline at any rate was not to be swayed, though she did not tell her brother so. Gilberte, who came to Paris at the end of November, was witness to the strains in the household on the rue de Touraine. Jacqueline confided to her that she intended to present herself as a postulant to Port-Royal at the new year, but, to spare his feelings, she told Blaise that she would go there only for a brief retreat. Not till the eve of her departure — January 3, 1652 — did Gilberte inform their brother of the impending separation. "He retired very sadly to his own rooms without seeing Jacqueline, who was waiting in a little parlor where she was accustomed to say her prayers." The next morning "I turned back into the corridor when I saw she was ready to leave. We did not say adieu for fear we would break down."

So Jacqueline Pascal, twenty-six years old, forsook the world and became Soeur Jacqueline de Sainte-Euphémie in the convent of Port-Royal de Paris. Her brother remained bitterly estranged from her for many months, and only with great reluctance did he give his consent — the canon law required the agreement of the postulant's nearest male relative — to her clothing in the nun's habit the following May. Nor did this end the period of resentment and disenchantment. Over the next year a wrangle dragged on over Jacqueline's patrimony. In order that she might be a benefactress as well as a member of the community she had joined, Jacqueline was anxious to have her share of the family property handed over to Port-Royal as a dowry, a scheme Blaise at first strongly resisted. Mère Agnès and Abbé Singlin tried to mediate the dispute, but without success.

Then Mère Angélique Arnauld took up the cudgels. She was fully aware that Pascal adhered to what she called "a healthy theology" and that he had in fact been instrumental in the conversion of his sister. But she had an abiding suspicion of "worldly" intellectuals, and, when Blaise waited upon this imposing woman, with her intimidating reputation for sanctity and wisdom, and meekly greeted her as "ma mère," she lectured him firmly about the need to spiritualize his priorities. Port-Royal, she said, had need of the financial support a dowry for Soeur de Sainte-Euphémie would bring, but the community would welcome her without it if her brother remained adamant. "I am obliged to say this to you, and I plead in God's name that you decide nothing out of merely human considerations: if you are not prepared to perform this act of charity in the spirit of charity, you should not do it at all. You see, Monsieur, we have learned from the transcendent teaching of M. de Saint-Cyran to receive nothing for the house of God that does not come from God. Everything that is done for some other motive than charity is not a fruit of God's spirit, and consequently we ought to have no interest in it."

On June 5, 1653, Blaise Pascal and Mère Angélique formally signed and had notarized the document that settled the matter of the dowry in Port-Royal's favor, and the next day Jacqueline made her solemn profession. Nevertheless, reconciliation between brother and sister did not follow immediately. Some relief of the bitter feelings, however, did arise from an unexpected quarter later that same year. Gilberte, who had supported Blaise in the quarrel over the dowry, brought two of her daughters to Paris for medical treatment. One of them, Marguerite Périer, suffered from an exceedingly painful fistula in the tear duct of her left eye. When their mother returned to Clermont in January 1654, she left both girls at Port-Royal as *pensionnaires,* or boarders, and thus in the care of their aunt and of the other nuns. Blaise Pascal, who was uncommonly fond of his nieces and especially of Marguerite, was thus willy-nilly drawn into closer contact with the convent and his sister.

Not that he was yet ready to embrace the ideals of Christian living that Port-Royal represented. Indeed, when the Périer women arrived in Paris, he was away from the city, still nursing the wounds that issued from his quarrel with Jacqueline. But that was only a detail when compared to the deeper intellectual level where lay an indefinable reluctance to conform to the rigid style of life the teaching of Saint-Cyran demanded. His sister Gilberte nevertheless tried to offer a mournful and somewhat intricate explanation. "My poor brother," she began, "suffered from continual illness, which only increased as time went by." Because of this unhappy circumstance, she maintained, not altogether persuasively, he came to prize the science of personal perfection more than the sciences of physics or mathematics. The clinical description she furnished was, to be sure, somber enough.

> My brother, among other infirmities, could not swallow any liquids that were not warm, and even then he could only take them a drop at a time. But since he had all sorts of other maladies — dreadful headaches and severe indigestion among them — the physicians ordered that he purge himself every other day for three months. The upshot was that he had to swallow medicines, heated, drop by drop. All this resulted in a condition painful in the extreme, though my brother never uttered a word of complaint.

These treatments brought some relief but by no means a complete cure. So the doctors recommended a psychological therapy: let Blaise give up those occupations which caused him stress "and find occasions to divert himself. My brother was reluctant to accept this counsel, because he could discern the moral dangers involved." But in the end he abided by the medical advice, "believing himself to be obliged to do everything possible to restore his health and imagining that upright diversions could not but help to promote it. So it was that he turned for solace to the world."

One can almost, over the centuries, sense Gilberte Périer's shudder of revulsion as she recorded her brother's flight into *"le monde."* She was of course writing long after the fact, and long after she, and Blaise too, had wholly embraced the formulae of Port-Royal. It was no joy to her to remember this transitional moment. Not that she thought her brother ever guilty of riotous living: "By the mercy of God he always remained free from the ordinary vices." But that same God, she knew with the wisdom of hindsight and the ardor of conversion, "had called him to a greater perfection," and it pained her to recollect that for a while he had eluded this divine summons.

Gilberte thus ascribed the period of her brother's "worldliness" solely to the exigencies imposed upon him by his delicate health: a chronically sick person needs, and perhaps deserves, diversion more than does a healthy one. Yet there were other factors also at work. The pious sentiments the death of Étienne Pascal elicited from his son were no doubt genuinely felt, but they were not strong enough to soften the sting of loss and the gloomy intimation of mortality inevitable at such a season. Then came the estrangement from the even more treasured Jacqueline and the separation from her, the soreness of which was kept keen by the tedious squabble with Port-Royal over her dowry. At the beginning of 1652 Blaise Pascal found himself alone for the first time in his twenty-nine years, found himself without the constant emotional support that his father and sisters had up till then wholeheartedly given him. Lonely, depressed, financially straitened — an unfamiliar state of affairs exacerbated by the continued commercial failure of the calculating machine — he remained as yet unable or unwilling to search for relief in his religion, and he felt vaguely guilty that this was so.

Little wonder that he sought new friendships and the strengthening of old ones, that he intensified his scientific investigations — four significant treatises were composed during this time — and that he moved his residence restlessly from the rue de Touraine, with its familial associations, to the rue Beaubourg. Shortage of money as well as loneliness may explain his long stay (October 1652–May 1653) with the Périers in the Auvergne, where he tried with scant success to collect some of the debts owed his father's estate. While he was there, a tantalizing rumor coincidentally made the rounds — recorded by Pascal's niece Marguerite and repeated by his sometime pupil, the playwright Jean Racine — that Blaise was busily courting a well-fixed but nameless *femme savante* who lived in Clermont. The evidence for this romance is too slender to be convincing — as is Marguerite's assertion that her uncle was dissuaded from pursuing the lady by the pleas of his sister Jacqueline — but if indeed something of the kind occurred, it may well have stemmed, on Pascal's part, as much from considerations financial as amorous.

On the basis of some letters he wrote a few years later to a noblewoman of Poitu, the suggestion has been advanced that Pascal hoped to marry her. But the content of the correspondence that has survived smacks more of the intentions of a spiritual counselor than of a lover. And by the time he was writing to Charlotte de Roannez, Pascal had experienced his second and definitive conversion, a circumstance that renders a courtship with her or with anyone else most unlikely.

It is certainly the case, however, that Blaise Pascal's relationship with Charlotte's older brother, the duc de Roannez, was uniquely important during the so-called "worldly period" and remained so afterward. Arthus Gouffier enjoyed the courtesy title of marquis de Boisy until 1642 when, upon the death of his grandfather, he inherited his duchy. Born in 1627, he was four years younger than Pascal (and six years older than his sister Charlotte). His family was of the *noblesse d'épée* of Poitu, of which province he was appointed, by hereditary right, royal governor in 1651. He had distinguished himself — and had demonstrated his loyalty to the crown — during the campaigns that resulted in the final defeat of the Prince of Condé and the collapse of the Fronde. Besides this traditional soldierly occupation, the young nobleman also displayed an entrepreneurial spirit and an abiding interest in the commercial and industrial development of his province, undertakings not unlike those of contemporary Puritan magnates in England.

His acquaintance with Blaise Pascal went back a number of years. In accord with the practice of many of the great noble families, the ducs de Roannez maintained a residence in Paris. The *hôtel* Roannez was located in the rue de Cloitre-Saint-Merri, hardly a stone's throw from the house on the rue de Brise-miche leased by Étienne Pascal before and during his term as the king's tax collector in Normandy, the house to which his son and daughter returned from Rouen in 1647. This physical proximity presented an opportunity for the two men to become friends and even intimates.

Such youthful intimacy would hardly have ripened, however, without shared interests and aspirations. Roannez was at this stage of his life by no means unattracted by the pleasures automatically accorded to the young men of a privileged caste, but, even so, he did represent a new species of the old nobility. His lively spirit responded to the exciting intellectual and moral currents that, since the end of the Wars of Religion, had energized the upper reaches of French society. Like any great baron of the realm, he maintained a considerable entourage, which included many noteworthy persons as well as an inevitable sprinkling of quacks, hangers-on, and dilettantes. But Blaise Pascal assumed a special, indeed a commanding, position among the duc's familiars, not only because of their long-standing acquaintance, and not only because of his unique genius, at once playful and profound, which had set him at the forefront of European savants. He also displayed, as his father had done, the virtues of the *honnête homme*, without, however, having succumbed to the seductive charms of the Parisian salons. Politically, to the degree that he bothered to think about public policy, Pascal stood safely and solidly for the established order. Nor did the duc, himself always alert to an opportunity for financial gain, lack sympathy for Pascal's sometimes frantic efforts to have his scientific endeavors turn a monetary profit.

There can be no doubt, however, that religious concerns more than anything else bound the two men together. Both had been deeply affected by the all-encompassing Catholic revival and had felt the influence of the devout humanism of de Sales, the scholarly and contemplative apostolate of de Bérulle, the selfless charitable missions to the urban and rural poor of Vincent de Paul and Louise de Marillac. They could not but admire the fashionable eloquence and the unwearying promotion of quality education undertaken by the Jesuits. And, with the greatest impact of all, they had both come into contact with the high idealism and stern righteousness of Saint-Cyran and Port-Royal. Indeed, with regard to all these common and yet conflicting characteristics, Pascal had adopted a stance not unlike that assumed by the duc himself: a conventional Catholic Frenchman who had undergone half a conversion to a purer level of spiritual seriousness, a pilgrim soul seeking to sort out of a predictable welter of youthful ambitions and uncertainties a genuinely loving relationship with a wrathful God, still, however, unsure of the precise path to follow.

When in September 1653 the duc de Roannez determined to pay a lengthy visit to his estates in Poitu, he invited Blaise Pascal to accompany him. They traveled at a leisurely pace the two hundred miles or so from Paris, through Chartres and Tours and across the Loire valley to Poitiers. The land abounded in an autumnal glow of lush vineyards, of pear and apple orchards, of flocks of sheep and herds of cattle munching the brownish grass on the hillsides. There still lingered in the long memory of the province the romantic lore linked with the enigmatic Eleanor of Aquitaine, who had given over Poitu as a dowry to an English king and to four violent centuries of English occupation. Scars from more recent violence were visible, too, reminding *poitevins* of the Calvinist army that, under the fierce and imperturbable Admiral Coligny, had ravaged the countryside and bombarded Poitiers itself. After that, after the Edict of Nantes had finally brought an end to the confessional struggle, Richelieu had been a reforming bishop here, at Luçon, and now the young duc de Roannez was Louis XIV's provincial governor. His guest from Paris, the eminent mathematician Monsieur Pascal, was a short, slender man of thirty, his face displaying a thoughtful composure but displaying also the pallor of chronic ill health, so dominated by strong dark eyes and an aquiline nose that the wisps of moustache and eyebrows were barely visible, his brown hair receding at the forehead and falling long and curled to his shoulders, his garb rich and stylish and yet sober, his habitual demeanor that of a gentleman-scholar. Pascal remained in Poitu with the duc until the beginning of 1654.

Two other notables were members of Roannez's suite during this provincial interlude. Antoine Gombaud, chevalier de Méré, was a native *poitevin* with property of his own in the region. As befitted one of his rank, he had served as a soldier in his youth, but now, at forty-three, he was best known as a fashionable man-about-Paris whose literary pretensions far exceeded his literary accomplishments. He had come to fancy himself, moreover, as a kind of arbiter of the manners appropriate to the *beau monde*, the overall effect being a personality that mingled charm with condescension. Thirty-five-year-old Damien Mitton had sprung from humbler origins, but, like so many middle-class apparatchiks of his generation, he was already marked out for high office in the royal administration. By repute he had been a religious sceptic until his marriage, after which he had conformed to a regular, if somewhat tepid, practice of Catholicism. Both he and Méré, enthusiastic disciples of Montaigne, were never tardy with the *bon mot* and the sparkling aphorism expected of those who aspired to be counted among the wits and sophisticates of high society. That both of them were widely suspected of being addicted to gambling would not necessarily have tarnished their reputations in that circle.

Though she did not say so, it may well have been his close association with gamblers and gambling that prompted Gilberte Périer to look back upon her brother's "worldly" indulgences with such repugnance. This wickedness — as Gilberte surely would have judged it — was a common pastime with the social élite which, at this moment in his life, Blaise Pascal was busily cultivating. Scraps of correspondence left behind by Méré attest that during their months together in Poitu Pascal had at first bored him and Mitton to distraction, but that later "this mere mathematician who knew nothing else" had become a much more agreeable companion. The reason for this change of attitude seems to have been that Pascal offered to apply his expertise in "mere mathematics" to the solution of some puzzles inherent in certain games of chance.

Méré presented Pascal with two specific problems. The first and easier of them pertained to a simple dice game. A pair of dice contains thirty-six possible combinations of numbers (one and one, two, three, four, five, six; two and one, two, three, four, five, six; and so on). The odds, therefore, against a particular combination — say double sixes — turning up from a single roll of the dice stand at thirty-six to one. But in a *series* of throws — agreed to ahead of time by the players — those odds should fall gradually and predictably. At what precise point in the series, Méré asked, should one begin to bet that a pair of sixes will appear? Pascal responded by drawing up an algebraic formula that showed that only between the twenty-fourth and twenty-fifth throws did the original relationship $1^{35}/_{36}$ convert to less than $1\frac{1}{2}$ and thus alter the odds to favor the appearance of two sixes or indeed of any other prearranged pair of numbers.

Méré's second query, though just as prosaic as the first, involved more complexity. Suppose Jean and Jacques, each wagering thirty-two francs, agreed to a game to be won by whoever of them rolled the dice to a higher total three times. Then, for whatever reason, they decided to terminate the competition after three throws, Jean having won twice and Jacques once. How, in this circumstance, should the stake money be divided? "Jean should say," Pascal answered, "'I am certain of winning thirty-two francs even if I should lose the fourth throw. Since the chance of winning the fourth throw is equal between me and Jacques, I should receive forty-eight francs and he sixteen.'"

But what if, in the same game, play is stopped after two rolls of the dice, both won by Jean? "'If I would have won the next toss,'" Pascal had Jean say, "'all sixty-four francs would have been mine. But even if I were to lose it my share of the stake would have been forty-eight francs, as in the previous case. Therefore only sixteen francs remain to be divided by chance — eight for me and eight for Jacques — allotting me a total of fifty-six.'"

Thus, as the golden autumn of 1653 turned into a grey winter, did the duc de Roannez and his three friends while away some of their leisure time, and no doubt they interspersed such discussion with many a roll of the dice and flip of the coin. For Pascal, however, these recreations afforded an opportunity to consider applications of far broader consequence. He began to work out an arithmetical theory, capsulized in an ingenious numerical triangle, whereby the possible outcomes of certain restricted activities could be predicted — restricted, that is, to activities the results of which were equally possible. It was no accident that this technique arose out of observations related to gambling, because the conventions imposed by games of chance presumed an equal likelihood of outcome. Pascal never believed that application of his triangle could forecast the direction of all or most future contingencies, but he did claim for it — when, during the following summer, he described its function in a series of letters addressed to the distinguished mathematician Pierre de Fermat — a usefulness in that limited range of actions to which it was suited. Fermat agreed: "I am delighted," he wrote to a friend, "to find opinions of mine consistent with those of Monsieur Pascal, for I esteem immeasurably his genius, and I judge him very capable of reaching to the heart of any inquiry he undertakes." So a first halting step toward a theory of probabilities and a science of statistics had been taken around a baize-covered gaming table in a chateau in Poitu.

5 The Night of Fire

B Y THE TIME Blaise Pascal returned to Paris from Poitu, at the beginning of 1654, he was already in the grip of a deep spiritual malaise. Outwardly, to be sure, his style of life appeared to be what it had been since his father's death. He was frequently in attendance at the *hôtel* Roannez, and his friendship with the duc continued to mature. Still fretful about his finances, he expended a good deal of energy seeking opportunities to augment his dwindling capital. He purchased shares, for instance, in a company Roannez had set up to drain marsh-land in Poitu, an investment, however, that brought little if any return. Meanwhile he persevered in his various mathematical inquiries, and he was especially gratified when invited to lecture on his work-in-progress to members of the Parisian Academy, the successor to Père Marsenne's institute to which Étienne Pascal had belonged twenty years before.

Yet no professional recognition, no money-making scheme, successful or otherwise, could still the unease that increasingly defined Pascal's daily existence. These months witnessed the gradual reconcil-iation with Jacqueline, a joyful development in itself. But his contacts with her — and with his Périer nieces now resident at Port-Royal — heightened his inner dissatisfaction. The contrast between his sister's serenity and his own restlessness served as stark notice that acceptance of God by the human intellect did not necessarily entail an embrace of him by the human heart. As she quietly and persistently pressed upon him the ideals of Saint-Cyran, Soeur Jacqueline de Sainte-Euphémie saw all too plainly the dark side of her brother's predicament. He is, she reported to Gilberte Périer, "seized with a contempt for the world and a disgust almost insupportable." Yet very soon both of Pascal's sisters were to recognize Blaise's distress as the darkness just before the dawn.

At some point during this winter of discontent Pascal tried to capture on paper the source of his unhappiness and the solution to the "disgust" that so disheartened him. The little tract he wrote was to bear the significant title "On the Conversion of the Sinner."

"The first stirring," it began, "that God inspires in the soul he truly condescends to touch leads to a knowledge and an extraordinary insight by virtue of which the person looks in an altogether original way into himself and into reality." This "new light" reveals the "painful" inner presence of "an anxiety that pierces through the happy tranquility the soul formerly found in those things which gave it pleasure." Yet, despite this intuition, so firm is the hold of "the vanities of the world" that "exercises of piety remain irksome, even bitterly so."

A genuine dilemma has thus presented itself. "On the one hand, gratification of the senses stimulates the soul more deeply than does the hope for invisible recompense. But, on the other, the intrinsic worth of the invisible excites it more strongly than do the conceits of the sensible." "Disorder and confusion" result from this conflict at first, until the person comes to terms with the fact that "perishable things are perishing or have already perished," until he appreciates "the certainty that all he has loved is in the process of dissolving into nothingness, that each instant strips away a portion of the security he has enjoyed in his possessions, that all he holds most dear is slipping away from him, moment by moment, and that, finally, a day will surely come when he will stand denuded of those external consolations in which he had put his trust." His heart had clung to "the vain and empty," and so his soul must face the prospect of "loneliness and abandonment," because he has failed "to bind himself to the one truly self-subsisting good that could sustain him both during and after this life."

With an introspection that his contemporary, René Descartes, might have appreciated, Pascal accepted as indisputable his own immortality. From this fundamental discernment it was but a short step

> to judge as nothingness every thing that must in the end return to nothingness: the heavens and the earth, one's own spirit and body, one's kinsmen and friends and enemies, wealth and poverty, disgrace, prosperity, honor and ignominy, good reputation and bad, health and sickness and life itself — anything, in short, that endures less long than the soul does is incapable of satisfying the soul, which earnestly desires to be established in a felicity as durable as itself.

World-weary as he may have been, Pascal did not conclude his musings on conversion with this catalogue of despair. Indeed, such a recognition of the ultimate emptiness of created things can be the occasion of "a holy humility" within the chosen soul, which can then "begin to mount above the pride of the commonality of men" and, newly liberated, "condemn their conduct, detest their maxims, weep over their blindness." The sovereign good emerges out of the maelstrom of human contradiction, manifesting two essential qualities: first, it stands more worthy of love than all else combined; and second, the human experience of it cannot be lost without human consent.

Of course, before the scales fall from the eyes of the unconverted, he may fancy the delights of this world as lovable beyond all reckoning. But even then he knows there is no permanence in such things, which despite his utmost efforts and wishes inexorably pass away. Out of a realization of his own immortality the sinner must then give vent to

> an elevated sense so transcendent that it does not pause at the peak of the heavens, nor with the angels, nor with any created beings, however admirable. The soul then rises beyond all creatures until its swelling heart beats at the very throne of God, in whom it finds repose at last. Here it confronts that Absolute which incorporates in itself all that is lovable and which cannot be forfeited unless one chooses to forfeit it.

So the drama of conversion approaches its climax. "Reason, aided by the light of grace," obliges the person to admit that only by his own evil, self-indulgent choices does he relinquish the blessings of a boundless love and cheat his own immortal destiny. But this recognition, this bending of the intellect — and here can be heard the soft voice of Jacqueline Pascal — is not itself enough. The lure of sin, the temptations of the world, the flesh, and the Devil lurk around every corner. "It is one thing," wrote her brother plaintively,

> to begin to know God and to want to reach him. It is quite another to bring these aspirations to fulfillment when the soul remains ignorant of how to do so. If his yearning for conversion is genuinely sincere, the sinner will imitate a traveler who has lost his way. He will have recourse to those who have precise knowledge of the road to take and who can therefore conduct him securely to the God whom for so long he had neglected.

What better guide could there have been for such a journey than the ghost of the Abbé de Saint-Cyran?

In late September or early October 1654, Blaise Pascal changed his residence once again, moving himself and his diminished possessions this time from the rue Beaubourg across the Seine to the Faubourg Saint-Michel. These new lodgings, on the rue des Francs-Bourgeois (now 54 rue Monsieur-le-Prince), lay hard by the Luxembourg palace and so not far from the house in which Étienne Pascal had briefly settled the family two decades earlier. But nostalgia for a vanished childhood had not brought Blaise back to the left bank. What attracted him to the rue des Francs-Bourgeois was its proximity to the convent of Port-Royal de Paris, where, after a ten-minute walk down a gentle hill and past Anne of Austria's basilica of the Val-de-Grace, he could expect to come into the consoling presence of Soeur Jacqueline de Sainte-Euphémie and of the beloved Périer nieces.

Indeed, so often did her brother appear at the convent's visitors' grille and engage Jacqueline in lengthy conversation that — as she confided to their sister Gilberte — "it would take a volume to recount all the visits one by one; so much so, I almost thought I had no time to do any other work." What Blaise had to say during these many conversations, however, Jacqueline was able to reduce to one sad tale.

He comes to see me and opens his heart to me so poignantly that I cannot but pity him. He acknowledges that in the midst of his grand occupations and of all those activities that can contribute to making him love the world — activities to which one might reasonably suppose him strongly attached — he really wants to leave all this behind him. Pricked by the continual reproach of his conscience, he has been stung, he says, by a strong aversion toward worldly follies and amusements. And yet he feels no attraction toward the God he has abandoned. Not that he harbors the doubts of an unbeliever, but he realizes it has been his own natural powers, and not the finger of God, that have prompted him to concede the existence of a better state of things. In the detachment he now feels from the situation in which he has placed himself, he understands that, although he entertained the same feelings about God as before, he also believed himself capable of accomplishing everything on his own. It followed, then, that he would have been bound during these years by horrible attachments, which inevitably led him to resist the graces God wanted to give him.

"Although he entertained the same feelings about God as before" — the feelings, that is, or rather the convictions Blaise had held since his first conversion in 1646. But, Jacqueline insisted, such mere assents of the intellect did not suffice. On the contrary, they were snares and delusions, because they encouraged the believer — and especially the learned believer — to try to satisfy the demands of both God and the world, to indulge in the moral compromises characteristic of the *honnête homme.* In thus pretending to square the circle her mathematician brother had brought upon himself only bitterness and disillusionment. He had come to despise the allurements of worldly success and fame and diversion, and yet he hesitated to question the prowess of his mind, so that God's grace could work fully within him. A pitiable state, thought Jacqueline, but one not without happy potential. "This confession," she wrote Gilberte, "surprised me as much as it gave me joy. And ever since he confided it to me, I have conceived a hope that I never had before. I think it my duty to inform you of it and so obligate you to pray God in our brother's behalf."

For Jacqueline this new "hope" possessed as much urgency as

poignancy. Her love for Blaise included a debt she was anxious to honor. She remained ever aware that it had been he who, back in Rouen, had originally felt the impulse of conversion and then had opened the same possibility to her. "God used you," she had told him in 1652, "to secure for me the first movements of grace," which had ultimately led her to safe harbor at Port-Royal. "Properly speaking," she added later, "I am your daughter, and I shall never forget that fact."

Whether or not a result of his sisters' prayers, Blaise Pascal quite suddenly solved the quandary that had been troubling him at least since the time of his father's death. It happened as he sat brooding in his rented rooms on the rue des Francs-Bourgeois, late in the evening of Monday, November 23, 1654 — *la nuit de feu*. Only after his death, nine years later, did the secret emerge, when a servant noticed what appeared to be extra padding sewn into the dead man's discarded doublet. Closer examination revealed that the "padding" was really a piece of parchment and, wrapped inside the parchment, a faded sheet of paper, upon both of which was written, in Blaise Pascal's hand, an account of his "night of fire." Or rather not so much an account as a testament to the experience of divine power that had overwhelmed him and completely altered the direction of his life. Here was an avowal of the second and definitive conversion, a pact between God and himself, the *mémorial* of which Pascal carried concealed on his person till the day he died.

The event itself, so deeply private, must forever remain shrouded in mystery. A lesser puzzle is why Pascal wrote two copies of the *mémorial* and kept both of them permanently at hand. The texts are substantially the same, though there are a few significant differences in content between them and a considerable one in form. Clearly the paper text — written hurriedly, smudged, crowded with excisions and insertions, scarcely legible in places — was composed first, composed indeed at the very moment of illumination. Beneath a small cross crudely scrawled at the top of the sheet the words tumbled forth with a fiery intensity.

The year of grace 1654.
Monday, 23 November, feast of Saint Clement,
    pope and martyr and others in the martyrology.

The eve of Saint Chrysogonus martyr and others.
From about half-past ten in the evening
    until about half-past midnight.
Fire.
The God of Abraham, the God of Isaac, the God of Jacob.
Not of the philosophers and intellectuals.
Certitude, certitude, feeling, joy, peace.
The God of Jesus Christ.
My God and your God [in Latin, accusative case].
Your God will be my God.
Forgetfulness of the world and of everything except God.
One finds oneself only by way of the directions taught
    in the gospel.
 The grandeur of the human soul.
Oh just Father, the world has not known you,
    but I have known you.
Joy, joy, joy, tears of joy.
I have separated myself from him._____
They have abandoned me, the fountain of living water
    [in Latin].
My God, will you leave me?
May I not be separated from him eternally.
_____

This is eternal life, that they know you the one true God
    and J.C. whom you have sent.
Jesus Christ._____
Jesus Christ._____
I have separated myself from him. I have run away from him,
    renounced him, crucified him.
May I never be separated from him._____
One preserves oneself only by way of the lessons taught
    in the gospel.
Renunciation total and sweet.
And so forth.

The parchment text introduces a few minor verbal changes and grammatical corrections, as well as one curious omission: "They have abandoned me the fountain," the words "of living water (*aquae vivae*)"

96

having dropped out. This quotation from Jeremiah (2:13) is not so identified in the parchment or the paper, nor is Jesus' definition of eternal life given at the Last Supper (John 17:3). Other biblical references, however, are supplied in the parchment, though in a truncated form so as to suggest that they have been cited from memory. Thus, for example, after quoting part of Ruth's beautiful pledge to Naomi (1:16) — "Wherever you go I will go, wherever you live I will live, your people shall be my people and your God my God" — Pascal simply wrote "Ruth" on the parchment. Also, instead of the simple cross inscribed at the head of the paper text, there appear at the top and the bottom of the parchment more carefully drawn crosses, each of them surrounded by little dash-like lines that imply rays coming forth from them.

More significant than these relatively trivial alterations and additions is the appendix Pascal fixed to the end of the parchment. Gone is the pregnant "and so forth" of the paper text, and in its stead are three supplementary lines.

> Total submission to Jesus Christ and to my director.
> Eternally in bliss, in exchange for a day of hard training
> in this world.
> May I never forget your words [in Latin].

The last line echoes Psalm 119:16 (118 in the Vulgate) — always a favorite of her brother, according to Gilberte Périer — while the first two, especially the words *"soumission totale à mon directeur,"* have about them the ring of Port-Royal.

In form, the parchment text differs sharply from that inscribed on the sheet of paper. The latter presents the reader with a script scribbled with feverish emotion; the former, by contrast, has a studied look to it, carefully composed, perfectly legible, beautifully crafted. Two words are printed in capital letters, "FIRE" and "GOD" ("forgetfulness of everything except GOD"). Certain other words received emphasis by reason of size or the density of the ink; among these are Christ's name as well as the "grandeur" attributed to the human soul and the "total" renunciation of the world and its pomps that Pascal has now undertaken. The parchment text, in short, stands as a measured and reflective confirmation of the original *mémorial*, the two of them now bound together and secretly lodged next to their author's heart.

In attempting to reconstruct what happened to Blaise Pascal on the night of November 23-24, 1654, it is useful to recall — especially in this present age, so widely indifferent to it — how, during the sixteenth and seventeenth centuries, the Bible defined not only the terms of religious controversy among Christians but also the norms of personal piety. It has been asserted that John Calvin knew the whole of the Bible by heart, and not only in order to smite his confessional opponents. If this claim is an exaggeration, it is surely an excusable one, more excusable than the allegation that devotional emphasis on the Scriptures was a Protestant preserve.

Pascal's *mémorial* is in fact suffused with biblical imagery and reference, quite beyond the explicit instances alluded to above, and it would be impossible to unravel the obscurities in the document without placing it within that context. Once he had identified the specific date and the precise time of his illumination, Pascal wrote the word "FIRE," and then he immediately invoked "the God of Abraham, the God of Isaac, the God of Jacob." The allusion was clearly to the third chapter of Exodus. Moses, having fled from Egypt, was tending the flocks of Jethro, his father-in-law, which task brought him to "the far side of the wilderness to Horeb, the mountain of God." Here, as he rested, Moses "saw the shape of a flame of fire coming from the middle of a bush, but it was not being burnt up." Filled with wonder, he approached this extraordinary phenomenon, and then he heard a voice calling his name. "Here I am," Moses answered. "Take off your shoes," came the response, "for the place on which you stand is holy ground. I am the God of Abraham, the God of Isaac, and the God of Jacob." A terrified and bewildered Moses, having covered his face in fear, then heard what his mission was to be, to lead God's people out of the bondage of Egypt. But, said Moses, what am I to reply if I am asked who has sent me — "what am I to tell them?" "I Am who I Am. This is what you must say to the sons of Israel. I Am has sent me to you, the God of Abraham, the God of Isaac, and the God of Jacob."

And this God was also "the God of Jesus Christ," and the words of the Savior recorded in the New Testament leapt into Pascal's mind even as he pondered this scene from the Old. When Jesus wished to refute those of his contemporaries who denied the resurrection of the dead, he too recalled that moment of truth on Mount Horeb: "I am the God of Abraham, and the God of Isaac, and the God of Jacob" (Matt.

22:32), Jesus quoted to the Sadducees, and these patriarchs, their earthly mission completed, nevertheless have survived until now, he said, for "God is God, not of the dead, but of the living."

So when Pascal wrote upon the *mémorial* the word "FIRE," it was the burning bush on Horeb — the bush that burned and yet was not destroyed by the flames — that he was confronted with. "Here I am," Moses had said. And, echoed Pascal, here I am, *me voici,* all these centuries later, and what name am I to give to you, the Lord of hosts? The answer came resoundingly: I am the God of Abraham and of your fathers, and of Jesus your brother; I am the God, not of the philosophers nor of those who deal in complex dialectic and in subtle abstraction, but of the holy people I have marked out from Abraham's time forever, as numerous as the sands on the seashore — the God who has chosen to dwell within the history of humankind. When Pascal contrasted the living God of the patriarchs with the conceptual Deity of the philosophers, he had passed over to the "holy ground" where the divine fire illumines without consuming, where the presence of God is discerned with an intensity and a directness that mock the arguments of the savants.

An elaboration of this followed promptly by way of a second scriptural allusion — this one of four Latin words in the accusative case — which in the *mémorial* was linked closely to the first. Upon the parchment text Pascal added the explicit reference to John 20:17. Mary Magdalen, on the morning of the Sunday after the crucifixion, went to the garden where the body of Jesus had been interred. She met there a man whom she assumed to be the supervisor of the garden, and, when she found Jesus' tomb empty, she asked this man to allow her to take charge of Jesus' dead body, which, for some reason she did not know, had been spirited away. The person to whom she addressed this appeal proved to be Jesus himself. "Woman, why are you weeping?" he said. "They have taken my Lord away, and I do not know where they have put him." Then, suddenly, Mary recognized Jesus, who said to her: "Mary, tell my brethren that I am ascending to my Father and your Father, to my God and your God" — *Deum meum et Deum vestrum,* object of the verb *ascendere,* as Pascal's copy of the Latin Vulgate correctly rendered the last phrase. And these words immediately called into his consciousness the tag of Ruth's promise to Naomi: "Your God," he quoted in French, "shall be my God." And who was Ruth? She was

the ancestress of King David and therefore also of Jesus, so often referred to in his lifetime as the son of David.

Here, at these scriptural evocations, is to be discerned — to the
extent that it can be discerned at all — the essence of Pascal's moment
of ultimate conversion: the FIRE of the burning bush, the related appeal
to the God of the patriarchs, echoed by Jesus himself, the experience of
Mary Magdalen in the garden of burial, and, finally, the remembrance
of Ruth's vow, which, in human terms, had put in train God's visitation
to his people in the person of his divine Son. Neither Moses nor Mary
Magdalen recognized at first who it was that spoke to them — "I must
go and look at this strange sight," Moses had said, "and see why the
bush is not burnt." Similarly Blaise Pascal had not appreciated the
reality that had confronted him at his first conversion eight years before.
Or rather — so it seemed to him now — he had tried to absorb that
experience the way a philosopher and a savant would have absorbed
it, as if it were an idea, a notion, conforming to the demands of the
limited human intellect, and had tried to adapt it to the standards of
the *honnête homme* and the successful man of the world. It was not that
he now judged these considerations unworthy or unuseful; they had
become for him simply irrelevant. For how could one compare, say,
Descartes's bare, cold idea of the First Cause of a thinking substance to
the rapturous apprehension of Mary Magdalen in the garden, when,
looking directly into the face of the risen Jesus, she said to him out of
her full heart, "Rabboni!"

This kind of realization is what has brought Pascal "certitude"
and "joy" and "peace," and brought him, too, to the conviction that he
must now follow the path of "forgetfulness of the world and of everything except God" and that only by adhering to "the directions of the
gospel" could the potential "grandeur" of his soul be achieved. He
turned for inspiration again to the Gospel of John, this time to the
seventeenth chapter and the end of Jesus' priestly prayer at the Last
Supper: "Oh just Father, the world has not known you, but I have
known you." In the fifteenth chapter of John, Jesus assured his apostles
that they were his friends, that he was the vine and they the branches.
The knowledge of such intimacy has consumed Pascal in this instant
with "joy, joy, joy, tears of joy."

And yet he grasped the doleful fact that he had routinely "separated" himself from a loving God, and he thought of the denunciation

leveled by Jeremiah (2:5-13) against the people chosen like himself, reaching its climax with the chilling utterance: "They have abandoned me, the fountain of living water." Was not the fearful recompense that God in his turn will abandon his people? "My God, will you leave me?" cried Pascal, echoing the terrible words of Jesus on the cross: "Eli, Eli, lama sabachthani — My God, my God, why have you forsaken me?" (Matt. 27:46). From this fiery moment Blaise Pascal would for the rest of his life quake at the prospect that God might justly abandon him, so that his constant prayer would be, "May I not be separated from him eternally." Once more he invoked the assurance recorded in John's Gospel (17:3) — "This is eternal life," to know God and the Christ whom God has sent — without forgetting, however, that in the past "I have separated myself from him. I have run away from him, renounced him, crucified him."

And then a sacramental *cri de coeur* only a Catholic would have written: "May I never be separated from him," which was a word-for-word translation from the prayer said just before the reception of Communion at Mass. Only "renunciation total and sweet" to the dictates of the gospel could "preserve" him from separation and dreadful abandonment, or, as that same liturgical prayer expressed it, "May the recognition of your Body, Lord Jesus Christ, which I all unworthy presume to receive, not bring me to judgment and condemnation."

But the analysis of the *mémorial* in biblical terms, crucial as it may be, cannot by itself explain the full significance of "the night of fire." Many mysteries remain. One of them arises from what appears to be a small difference between the paper text and the parchment. The line that reads in the former "Certitude, certitude, feeling, joy, peace" becomes in the latter — written, it will be remembered, after some reflection on Pascal's part — "Certitude, joy, certitude, feeling, sight," with a second "joy" inserted at the end and slightly above the line, as though in afterthought. The change in word order and omission of "peace" present a lesser puzzle than does the addition of *"vue"* immediately after *"sentiment."* This last word can indeed be translated "sight" or "feeling" or "perception," but it also admits of narrower connotations, like "consciousness" or — perhaps better in this context — "love."

Or perhaps best of all a combination of these meanings. What Pascal has experienced has been a "love," an overwhelming affection that nevertheless brought with it also a species of knowledge, for *sentiment* always includes in its definition an element of the cognitive. Not, to be sure, the knowledge of "the philosophers and the intellectuals," which he already possessed in a fuller measure than most, but rather an intensely heightened perception, a boundlessly deepened consciousness of the kind Moses and Mary Magdalen had gained by "sight" in their personal encounters. Involved here, therefore, were a "certitude" far removed from that of the abstract mathematical demonstration and, in consequnce, a "joy" that surpassed ordinary understanding.

Did Pascal find in these two hours of *sentiment* and *vue* a confirmation of the opening lines of his little treatise "On the Conversion of the Sinner," composed shortly before (or, it is possible, shortly afterward): "The first stirring that God inspires in the soul he truly condescends to touch leads to a knowledge and an extraordinary insight into himself and into reality"? What has been translated here as "an extraordinary insight" reads in Pascal's French *"une vue extraordinaire."* Here is an affective knowledge that issues from a direct confrontation between persons. Not "person" in the philosophical sense, a general and therefore necessarily vague delineation. It does not seem farfetched to recall that *vue* can also be the past participle of the verb to see. The *personne vue* — the person seen — by Moses on Horeb was "the God of Abraham"; the *personne vue* by Mary in the garden was her beloved "Rabboni." "Jesus Christ, Jesus Christ," cried Blaise Pascal. "May I never be separated from him."

Yet it would be wrong to conclude that Pascal emerged from his searing conversion experience disdainful of the disciplines that had nourished his intellect since childhood. Indeed, it might be argued that the kind of direct knowledge he arrived at then was not inconsistent with the mind-set of a scientist who performed innumerable discrete experiments before theorizing about the vacuum and of an inventor who tinkered with no less than fifty models before he succeeded in producing a workable calculating machine. Pascal at any rate continued his researches virtually till the eve of his death. He did not see himself lapsing into fundamentalism, nor did he think his new moral status incompatible with his life-long habits. He had learned at his father's knee to distinguish sharply between the realms of faith and reason — reason understood as the capacity to probe successfully into the finite. At issue, rather, after November 23-24, 1654, was a question of priorities. As long before as 1647 Jacqueline Pascal had contended that her brother had ceased to be a mathematician. She meant by that claim, not that he had given up his intellectual pursuits, but that, after his first conversion, he could no longer be *defined* in terms of mathematics or of any other worldly endeavor. He had become a Christian believer, and his faith took precedence over all else. During the stressful years that followed Blaise had wandered back and forth between his sister's confidence and his own doubts and hesitations. "The night of fire," however, settled the matter forever.

6 Conversation at Port-Royal des Champs

A FTER Blaise Pascal died, and the *mémorial* he had written describing his "night of fire" had been discovered, several stories circulated purporting to explain that mysterious event. One of them recounted how Pascal, on an outing with friends, had been involved in
a serious carriage accident on a bridge over the Seine near the Parisian
suburb of Neuilly; though he was not injured, claimed an anonymous
source, this brush with death led Pascal to reevaluate his spiritual
condition and "to live afterward in total solitude." Another theory, this
one recorded by Marguerite Périer, credited her uncle's definitive conversion to the effect of a sermon he heard preached by Abbé Singlin,
Saint-Cyran's disciple and successor as spiritual director of the nuns at
Port-Royal de Paris.

Neither of these accounts, however, contributes much to an understanding of the phenomenon of November 23-24, 1654. Certainly
Pascal, ever since he and Jacqueline had returned to Paris from Rouen
in 1647, had often heard Antoine Singlin speak at Port-Royal, and he
had come to admire deeply the priest's translucent holiness and sincerity if not his eloquence. But the sermon in question was delivered on
the feast of the Immaculate Conception of the Virgin, December 8, 1654,
a full fortnight after the *nuit de feu*. Perhaps Marguerite grounded her

explanation upon a line in a letter written on that day, December 8, by her aunt to her mother, in which Jacqueline joyfully informed Gilberte of their brother's newly intense religious commitment and in which she added with evident satisfaction, "Everything is now under the direction of Monsieur Singlin." This last declaration was wholly consistent with what Blaise had carefully written at the bottom of the parchment text of the *mémorial:* "Total submission to Jesus Christ and to my director." The estimable Singlin was indeed to fulfill this latter role, but neither he nor Jacqueline nor anyone else was given an inkling of what had transpired on the rue des Francs-Bourgeois during those fiery two hours. To the end Blaise Pascal kept his precious secret and, not incidentally, the independence that underlay it.

As for the report that Pascal, after the accident on the bridge at Neuilly, had withdrawn into "total solitude," this was simply not the case. On the contrary, he continued to live outwardly much as he had before. There is no evidence, for example, that he gave up any domestic amenities. His residence in the Faubourg Saint-Michel was presided over by a sister of that Louise Default who had managed Étienne Pascal's household for so many years. Besides this good lady, her husband, and her two daughters, Pascal regularly enjoyed the service of a footman and a cook. The house itself, located between two tennis courts and abutting a pretty garden graced by flower beds and fruit trees, was the kind of urban haven one of Pascal's status and class understandably took for granted. Indeed, his sister Jacqueline remained troubled that Blaise appeared to be "so jolly a penitent," and that he had clearly not given up association with worldly friends like those — Méré and Mitton — who had been his companions during the recent trip to Poitu. She probably was appeased to some extent once she had learned that the influence of the converted Blaise had led the closest of those friends, the duc de Roannez, to pledge himself to a life of penance and pious retirement from the ordinary obligations and associations of the *noblesse* to which he belonged.

But there can be no doubt that Soeur Jacqueline de Sainte-Euphémie was particularly pleased that her brother, the "jolly penitent," had in January 1655 gone on retreat to Port-Royal des Champs.

It may be recalled that when Mère Angélique Arnauld removed her nuns to Paris in 1625 she had hoped to maintain a presence at their former site. But the ecclesiastical authorities of the day did not agree, with the result that the original convent of Port-Royal stood empty and gradually fell into a desolation of weeds and swamp and crumbling buildings. Technical jurisdiction over the place, however, along with the properties that made up its endowment, remained with the nuns, which meant in effect under the control of the two Arnauld sisters, Angélique and Agnès, who took turns winning election as abbess of Port-Royal. It was indeed an Arnauld family connection that ultimately provided the old convent, after twelve years of disintegration and solitude, an exhilarating new lease on life.

Catherine Arnauld, elder sister of Angélique and Agnès, had married a man named LeMaître. This union was unhappy and of short duration, and Catherine in due course left her husband and, with her sons, moved back to her parents' home. The oldest of these boys, Antoine LeMaître, born in 1608, matured quickly into a brilliant advocate, whose legal skill and eloquence marked him out as a man destined for a great career and won him the admiration of many potential patrons, including Cardinal Richelieu. But Antoine — like his uncle, Robert Arnauld d'Andilly, his grandmother Arnauld, his aunts, and his mother — fell under the spellbinding influence of the Abbé de Saint-Cyran, who convinced him to renounce his worldly if legitimate aspirations and to embrace the rigorous forms of Augustinian piety. The public conversion of such a one to principles that soon would be labeled Jansenist — once *Augustinus* (1640) and *De la fréquente communion* (1643) had been published — set off alarm bells in the highest circles. Then, in 1647, Antoine LeMaître gave substance as well as notoriety to his new allegiance by joining the pamphlet war over contrition and writing the single most biting indictment of official "laxity." The circulation of this tract — it may be recalled — so angered Richelieu that from that date he began to consider how best to suppress Saint-Cyran's influence.

At the beginning of 1638, therefore, young LeMaître had not only determined that he had been called to a life of holy retirement, far from the law courts and fashionable salons where he had formerly been a luminary; he had also become a *persona non grata* with the all-powerful first minister of the crown. Given these circumstances, his aunts were able to offer him a refuge, first in a small house built within the compound of Port-Royal de Paris and then, in July — when Saint-Cyran was arrested — more prudently at the deserted convent of Port-Royal des Champs, twenty miles away. Here he was soon joined by two of his brothers, the soldier Simon and the aspiring priest Isaac, known respectively — in the confusing nomenclature favored by the Arnauld family — as de Sericourt and de Saci, and later by his widowed uncle, Robert d'Andilly. Related as they were by blood, these men were also united in their loyalty to Saint-Cyran and their desire to practice the kind of intensely penitential life commended by their master. Thus came into being *les solitaires* of Port-Royal des Champs.

Over the years that followed, the original Solitaries attracted like-minded men, twenty-five or so altogether, representing all classes and conditions — though most of them were prosperous bourgeoisie like the Arnaulds — some of whom stayed only for a period of spiritual refreshment and then moved on, so that there were usually about a dozen in residence. They developed for themselves a quasi-monastic rule that allocated time for liturgical and private prayer as well as for study and manual labor. To satisfy this last resolution they concentrated on refurbishing the old convent complex: repairing buildings, draining the nearby marshes, and planting gardens and orchards that became the envy of the region. As far as intellectual work was concerned, the Solitaries did not produce much original scholarship, occupying themselves as they did mostly with translations of patristic texts. Some of them, however, notably LeMaître himself and Pierre Nicole (soon to become famous in his own right), proved to be gifted teachers, and their schools for young boys — the *petites écoles* as they were called — attained during their brief existence a solid reputation for excellence and innovation, as well as the faithful attachment of prestigious alumni like the dramatist Jean Racine and the historian Louis-Sébastien Tillemont.

For a while Richelieu's suspicions of their religious and political orthodoxy and, perhaps more, those of his confidant, the Capuchin friar, Joseph du Tremblay, continued to hang over the Solitaries, who, early in their corporate existence, found it expedient to disperse to a provincial town some distance from Paris. But soon after the death of Père Joseph, the enigmatic and somewhat sinister "grey eminence," they returned quietly to Port-Royal des Champs, and from 1640 they were left more or less undisturbed till the late 1650s.

Richelieu himself died in 1642, and Mazarin's regime was not strong enough to indulge in all the antagonisms of its predecessor. A sign that tensions had relaxed somewhat appeared in 1648 when Mère Angélique, having won the concession denied her twenty-three years before, returned to the ancient convent where she had once reigned as child-abbess. The triumph was to be short-lived, but it must have been delectable at the time. On a brilliant morning in mid-May, she, accompanied by nine other nuns, came home again to the little valley where she had first felt the touch of God's hand. As bells rang merrily and enthusiastic tenants and neighbors crowded forward to greet her, she saw all around physical evidence of revival in restored buildings and the flowers and fruit trees and the overall look of neatness and decorum. Such had been the result of the labors of *les solitaires,* most prominent among whom were her own nephews, who conducted her now into the newly decorated chapel for the singing of a solemn Te Deum to celebrate the reunion of the two Port-Royals.

As for the Solitaries, they now withdrew to a collection of farm buildings set on the top of a hill behind the convent and its compound. In this austere location, dubbed simply "the Barns *(les granges),*" they carried on as before, with no flagging in their prayer lives or their ascetical practices, and if anything with a heightened dedication to the work of the *petites écoles.* Predictably, Mère Angélique did not encourage direct communication between her sisters in the valley and her disciples on the hilltop. One link, however, was established in that Father Singlin, as Saint-Cyran's heir, acted as spiritual director to both communities des Champs, as well as to the nuns back at Port-Royal de Paris. The logistical difficulties involved in such an arrangement soon became obvious, and when, in 1650, Isaac LeMaître de Saci was ordained priest, Singlin delegated to him the sacramental ministry to *les solitaires* or, as they were now known in the vicinity, *les messieurs des granges.* This arrangement brought with it at first a certain strain, because Antoine LeMaître, still the dominant figure among the Solitaries, was willing enough that de Saci should offer Mass and preach to the community, but the prospect of making his confession to his younger brother gave him serious pause.

But by the time Blaise Pascal, in the wake of his fiery conversion, went into retreat at *les granges* — January 1655 — Antoine had long since set aside his scruples in this regard. Father de Saci's credentials as confessor and spiritual guide of the Solitaries had been accepted by all concerned.

"Our new convert," as Jacqueline Pascal described their brother to Gilberte Périer, "decided that it was necessary for him to make a retreat away from home." After confiding to the duc de Roannez the fact of his elevated spiritual status, Blaise made his way to the country house of one of Roannez's noble friends. "But," reported Jacqueline, "since he could not find there the solitude he wanted, he obtained a room or rather a cell among the Solitaries of Port-Royal. From there he has written me of his joy at being treated and lodged like a prince — but a prince in accord with the teaching of St. Bernard, in a solitary place where one can profess and practice as much poverty as discretion allows." Pascal joined the Solitaries in their recitation of the divine office, "rising at five in the morning without feeling the least infirmity, and, convinced that God wished it, he added fasting to sleeplessness, as though in defiance of all the rules the physicians have imposed on him." Here, too, he was given the spiritual direction that the followers of Saint-Cyran considered so important: "Monsieur Singlin, who has remained in Paris during this time, has provided our brother a director whom he did not know before but with whom he is now totally entranced, an incomparable man, who is besides a member of a good family."

Jacqueline's slightly snobbish description of LeMaître de Saci actually tells little about this priest who was the first to guide Blaise Pascal on this leg of his spiritual journey. He appears to have been a prudent counselor at any rate, a man of deep faith and commitment, but also a phlegmatic man who displayed little of the fire and passion characteristic of the Arnaulds. Indeed, his secretary long afterward remembered him saying that too much ardor could be a sign of worldliness. Charm he possessed in abundance, and poise, and above all a capacity to accommodate himself to the individual peculiarities of those who sought his guidance. With a carpenter he listened serenely to anecdotes connected to carpentry; with Pascal he listened with similar aplomb to tales out of philosophy.

Most of what passed between the two remained of course strictly private. But one exchange was recorded many years later when de Saci's secretary composed his reminiscences. Nicolas Fontaine apparently took extended notes of this conversation at the time, because his account not only captures the essence of many of the themes that would be developed in Pascal's later writings but also accurately reflects the Pascalian literary style. It has therefore become the convention to include the pamphlet-length *Entretien avec M. de Saci* in the canon of Pascal's *Oeuvres complètes*.

Blaise Pascal's reputation had preceded him to Port-Royal des Champs. Here was a man, Secretary Fontaine recalled, "who had won admiration not only in all of France but in all of Europe." His researches and inventions were the talk of intellectuals everywhere. "This admirable man, finally being touched by God, submitted his elevated spirit to the sweet yoke of Jesus Christ, and this heart so noble and so grand humbly embraced a life of penitence." De Saci himself agreed with his secretary's glowing estimate, without, however, admitting that the recently converted savant brought with him any new spiritual insights. "M. Pascal," he said, "is extremely admirable in that, not having read the Fathers of the Church, he has by the penetration of his own spirit discovered the same truths that they had discovered. He says he finds these things surprising, because he never encountered them anywhere before. But for us, we are accustomed to seeing them on every page of our books." De Saci on this recorded occasion followed his ordinary counseling mode — fit the exchange to the client's perspective — and courteously inquired about his new disciple's recent studies. "M. Pascal told him that the authors he was examining most assiduously were Epictetus and Montaigne, and he spoke very highly of them. M. de Saci, who had never thought it right to read such writers, nevertheless asked M. Pascal to explain them to him."

Had de Saci and Fontaine known in detail what had happened to Pascal only a few weeks before, they might have been surprised that he chose to expound on the views of two philosophers. But the secret of "the night of fire," and its repudiation of the God of the savants in favor of the God of Abraham, remained securely with him who had experienced it. All the more reason, therefore, to see Pascal's choice of authors as evidence of a crucial stage in his religious and intellectual development. He remained a savant — a philosopher in the broad sense — whether he liked it or not. His conversion pierced him to the roots of his being, but it did not, it could not, lead him to disparage the powers of a mind that had unlocked so many secrets of mathematics and physics and that had gained him the reputation which so impressed Fontaine. What he did now see clearly was an analogy between the scientific work he had done all his life and the spiritual work his newly found zeal pointed him toward in the future. It was not reason itself he had disdained in his experiments relative to the vacuum or in the construction of his calculating machine, but reason misused. The truth in these and related matters had emerged from the application of his strict scientific method — inductive, direct, individual, experimental — which paid no heed to conventional wisdom or to elaborate systems, like that of Descartes. Would not the truth about God and the spiritual life and the problem of good and evil and all the other eternal verities find expression in a mind similarly disposed? After his conversion, after his mystic confrontation with the divine, Pascal did not doubt that this would be so. Already, as he spoke earnestly with Father de Saci, there was forming in his consciousness an apologetic that would not deny rationality but would confine rationality to its proper sphere, just as he had always done in his scientific researches. Already the seeds of the *Pensées* were being sown.

Epictetus and Montaigne were perfect foils for the first step in this process. The Greek Stoic preached a species of natural virtue grounded in the intrinsic nobility of the human person. His pagan God manifested himself in the orderly and sensible way in which he had arranged the universe and in the capacities for self-fulfillment with which he had endowed his creatures. The French essayist — to whose work Pascal had been introduced by his father and perhaps reintroduced by his gambling friends Méré and Mitton — testified to an abiding scepticism about the competence of the human mind and a cynicism about the human predicament in general. Born a Catholic, and nominally faithful to his birthright during the harsh days of the Religious Wars, Montaigne viewed the world with a dry and withering pessimism that found no solace in religion. A Greek recluse of the first century and a brilliant, chronically ailing, cosmopolitan French *politique* of the sixteenth: these were the opponents Blaise Pascal selected to lend focus to his new apologetic.

Strictly speaking, Pascal, though he probably did not know this to be the case, had never read the works of Epictetus, because Epictetus wrote nothing. But a particularly fervent disciple had carefully copied down the teachings of the master and had preserved many of them in two treatises, recently translated into French, with which Pascal was familiar. He began his exposition by explaining to de Saci that "Epictetus is one of those worldly philosophers who has understood better

111

than others the duties involved in the human condition." Epictetus insists above all that one must recognize God "as one's principal object," that one should accept as fact that "God governs all things with justice," and that therefore one must "submit oneself to God with a good heart and strive to conform one's will to the very great wisdom with which God directs all things." Such a psychological orientation, declared Pascal, "will put a halt to all complaints and murmurings and will prepare a person to endure serenely all contingencies, even the most troublesome." Genuine detachment of the sort recommended by Epictetus brings with it genuine contentment, a view with which no doubt de Saci could identify. "Never say, 'I have lost this or that'; say rather, 'I have returned this or that which was never really mine.' Do not say, 'My son has died or my wife has died.' Say rather, 'I have given them back again.' "

This line of argument was perhaps more easily put forward by the likes of Epictetus and Pascal, who never had a wife or child and so never had to mourn their passing; nor, for that matter, had de Saci. Pascal's point at any rate applied to all the goods of this life, including the most intimate relationships: "Seeing that God has permitted you the use of such things, take care to treat them as though they belonged to another, much like a man makes use of a room in an inn when he is on a journey." Or put the Stoic lesson in the form of an epigram: "You ought not," said Pascal, "to desire that those things that happen should happen as you wish them to; rather you ought to want them to happen as they in fact do." For Epictetus has taught clearly the lesson that all the world's a stage. "Remember that you are here as an actor, that you play a role in a comedy such as it has pleased the divine playwright to assign to you. If it is a large role or small, long or short, enjoy it. If he wishes that you should play the difficult part of the outcast, you ought to do so with all the simplicity you can muster. And so it should be with everything else." Thus stood the admirable principles, as Pascal judged them, of Epictetus's ethical system. "Keep before your eyes every day the inevitability of death and of evils that appear the most unbearable, and then you will never descend to mean and trivial thoughts, you will never desire anything in excess."

"So you see, Monsieur," Pascal said to de Saci, changing now the thrust of his account, "the brilliance of this great philosopher who has so well understood the duties imposed upon all men and women.

Indeed, I hazard to say that he would have merited god-like veneration had he understood at the same time his own powerlessness, seeing that it is necessary to be God himself to teach men both these truths." Unhappily Epictetus has proved himself to be too much "earth and ashes, for, after having grasped so well what one ought to do, he invalidates his conclusion by presuming one can do what one ought." At this point de Saci must have nodded in vigorous agreement with what appeared to echo the lessons of St. Augustine as taught by Saint-Cyran and Jansenius. And the meeting of minds could only have strengthened as Pascal proceeded remorselessly: "Epictetus says that God has given man the means of fulfilling all his obligations; that these means are completely within our power; that it is necessary to search out happiness through our own resources, because God has given them to us for this very purpose." True enough, the philosopher acknowledges that "neither goods nor life nor reputation are under our control, and so these cannot lead us to God." But then he jumps to the false conclusion that the human intellect and will are totally unfettered and therefore that through the proper employment of them "we can render ourselves perfect, that man through these capacities can know God, love him, obey him, please him, can be cleansed of all vices and acquire all virtues, can, in short, make himself holy and thus a friend of God." Epictetus — and by implication the whole Stoic school — in asserting these principles manifests "a diabolical pride" that is compounded by, among other foolish errors, a quirky kind of pantheism, a denial that pain and death are genuine evils, and the notion that "a severe enough persecution can be construed as a call from God to commit suicide."

This last in Pascal's recitation of Stoic misconceptions may well have touched a chord within de Saci. He and all *les messieurs des granges* were aware that dark clouds of persecution, from both the secular and the ecclesiastical establishments, were lowering around Port-Royal and all those now, early in 1655, disdainfully referred to as Jansenists. Not that any of them would have contemplated the extreme solution recommended by Epictetus. Indeed, they would have fastened instead, as Pascal did, upon what seemed to be the root of such an outlandish view, the "diabolical pride" that pretended to a self-sufficient human autonomy. Here was a pagan version of Pelagianism proclaimed centuries before Pelagius.

The second of the authors under discussion advocated a philosophy that seemed at first blush the reverse of that of the Stoics, but for Pascal it was rather a parallel aberration. "As for Montaigne, of whom, Monsieur, you also want me to speak, he was born in a Christian country and professed the Catholic faith, and in this circumstance he is compatible with us." But, not unlike Epictetus, Montaigne searches for a morality outside Christian revelation — in his argument he employs Catholicism only as an expedient *deus ex machina* — and, quite unlike Epictetus, his view of the human condition is such that "he places everything in a doubt so general and so universal that he is carried away by it, so that, if he doubts, and even doubts if he doubts, his uncertainty rolls back upon itself into a perpetual and restless circle." De Saci, innocent though he was of the details of contemporary philosophy, may well have known enough to wonder whether Pascal's strictures might also apply to another French thinker of note, René Descartes. If so, Pascal quickly disabused him. "It is in this doubt," he continued, "which doubts itself, and in this ignorance which knows nothing and which he calls his master-formula, that one finds the sum and substance of Montaigne's teaching." He cannot even state his opinion affirmatively, for if he says that he doubts, he betrays himself by averring that he does indeed doubt. Look, Pascal told de Saci, at the title page of Montaigne's *Essais,* and you will see emblazoned there the celebrated device of evenly balanced scales beneath which is printed the motto *Que sais-je?* So acute and perverse is this indecision that it can be expressed only by an interrogatory: not "I do not know" but "What do I know?" "Contradictories are judged to rest in perfect equilibrium and so in a state of pure scepticism."

This studied indecisiveness Montaigne has brought to his analysis of every department of life and thought. "When he says that he would be as willing to submit a lawsuit to the first passerby as to a judge learned in all the statutes of the realm, he does not suggest thereby that he would alter the established judicial order; he has not enough ambition for that. Nor does he mean that his counsel would be preferable to any one else's; he simply believes that no good will come of such an initiative in any case. Montaigne aims to demonstrate the vanity of all the most cherished civic assumptions and opinions. If the number of laws is diminished, then perhaps the number of lawsuits would decrease as well, seeing that such difficulties increase to the degree that they are adjudicated, seeing that legal obscurities are multiplied by legal commentaries." Montaigne's method, as described by Pascal, always leads to the same dreary end: "By one example or another, he points to the feebleness of all convictions; like a soldier he stands upon the battlements of universal doubt, so that he can accept with equal indifference victory or defeat."

In the religious controversies of his own time, to be sure, Montaigne put "the same irresolute and wavering attitude" to good use. Heretics and unbelievers received no comfort or support from him, and his mode of dealing with them was his usual sceptical one, mocking, for example, the absurdity of the Protestants' "claim that they alone understood the true sense of the Scriptures," and the atheists' impudence in denying the existence of a sovereign Being "when they cannot even explain the simplest natural phenomena." Not without admiration did Pascal offer de Saci and Fontaine a witty summary of Montaigne's savage critique of the contradictory opinions about soul and body, space and time, infinity and change, "in which Montaigne amply demonstrates the vanity of all those who pass for the most enlightened and the most resolute." Indeed, "in the end the Essayist examines carefully all the sciences, including geometry and physics and medicine, then turns to history and politics and ethics and jurisprudence, treating all of them in such a way that one remains convinced from his analysis that our conscious thoughts are no better than a dream from which we awaken only at death and during which we have no more principles of truth at our disposal than when we are asleep."

De Saci had no comment about Pascal's handling of Epictetus's system — at least Fontaine recorded none. But the priest found disturbing even the qualified approval accorded to Montaigne. "I am obliged to you, Monsieur," he said. "I am sure that had I read Montaigne over a long period I would not have understood him nearly as well as I do as a result of this conversation." It may be, he continued, that this man possessed "a good spirit," but he wondered whether Pascal had not exaggerated Montaigne's merits. "You can readily understand that having lived my life the way I have, no one has ever encouraged me to read this author, all of whose works lack the qualities St. Augustine urged us to seek out in our reading, humility and piety. One might indeed pardon the philosophers of old, the so-called Academicians, who called everything into doubt. But what need has Montaigne to amuse himself by renewing a doctrine that Christians now know to be folly?" What Augustine said about the Academicians might well be applied to Montaigne: "He places everything that he calls faith to one side; so we, who have the faith, ought likewise to set aside everything he says."

Pascal responded to this gentle rebuff by observing smoothly that if he knew and could interpret Montaigne with some skill, the same could be said of de Saci vis-à-vis St. Augustine, "with no advantage to poor Montaigne." But, as Fontaine remembered it, Pascal "was so brimming over with his author, that he could not restrain himself." Perhaps he was brimming over also with that zest for inquiry and debate which had already disquieted some of the devotées of Port-Royal, notably de Saci's venerable aunt, Mère Angélique Arnauld. His desire at any rate to conform to his new director's serene and settled point of view could not prevent his mind from probing into the intellectual challenges raised by his conversion. If there was to be war with the philosophers, he would fight it with a strategy of his own choosing.

"I confess to you, Monsieur," he said, "that I cannot behold without joy how Montaigne indomitably batters the pride of reason with its own weapons, the bloody revolt of man against man who, when he tries to raise himself by his own maxims and without God, instead lowers himself to the level of the beasts." But the trouble with Montaigne was that he did not follow up "this useful humiliation" of human pride by providing a means of moving from the knowledge of fatal moral weakness to a cure for it. "On the contrary, despite being a member of the Church, he acts like a kind of pagan." Therefore link him with Epictetus, a pagan in name as well as in fact, and you have "the two great defenders of the two most celebrated sects in the world, sects dependent solely upon reason," which, left to its own resources, must willy-nilly choose the exaggerated rationalism of the Stoic or the scepticism of the incurable cynic. Epictetus teaches us what we ought to do without providing any mechanism to accomplish it; the result is a deadly pride. Montaigne, on the other hand, shows us how weak we really are; the result is an indolent acceptance of radical evil.

Pascal knew full well that de Saci neither wanted nor needed instruction in pagan philosophy, that indeed he was repelled by it. But Pascal, who wanted de Saci's approval as well as his understanding, was arguing on a different tack. "It is true, Monsieur," he admitted, "that you have admirably helped me to see how little utility Christians can draw from these philosophical studies." The key word in this admission was "Christians," which meant for de Saci, and now for Pascal as well, those who had embraced a deeper commitment and a higher knowledge, those who had been converted to the Christian vocation as preached by Saint-Cyran and practiced by Port-Royal. "Let me tell you very simply my thought on the usefulness of reading such books. I find in Epictetus an incomparable art, which, unintentionally, can upset the tranquility of those who seek the truth in the external things of the world. Similarly, Montaigne is incomparable in confounding the conceit of those who, outside the faith, pride themselves in having achieved the ultimate justice." There is no question that both of them can seduce the intellectually unwary: "This is why the rules about reading them must be drawn up with care, discretion, and proper regard for the condition and moral state of those to whom one recommends them." And of course the genuinely converted have no need to seek such enlightenment in the scribblings of pagan philosophers; but may it not be incumbent upon the converted in their discourse with atheists and *libertins,* even with luke-warm Catholics and the all too numerous *honnêtes hommes,* to point out how arid are these two mutually exclusive moral systems? And how can this be done without some direct acquaintance with them? It is never a question, Pascal continued, of combining Epictetus and Montaigne into a kind of synthesis, because the vice of the one cancels out the virtue of the other. "These two worldly sages place contraries in the same subject; for one attributes grandeur to human nature and the other feebleness to the same nature, and these cannot subsist together. Whereas faith teaches us to place these characteristics in different subjects. All that is vile and infirm belongs to nature, all that is wise and masterful belongs to grace. *Voilà* the new and astonishing union that God alone can reveal, and that he alone can bring about, surely an image and an effect of the ineffable union of two natures in the one person of the God-Man, Jesus Christ."

At this juncture in his "conversation" with an ecclesiastic — presumably a professional theologian — the brash disciple thought it appropriate to offer a gesture of apology to the master. "I must ask your pardon, Monsieur, in bringing theology into this discussion rather than restricting myself to my philosophical subject. I did so unintentionally. And yet it is difficult not to do so, because to treat of partial truth is to confront the center of all truths." De Saci waved aside this rather lame

117

excuse and merely remarked that Pascal's "reflections, so wise and uplifting," reminded him "of those skillful physicians who, by the adroit manner in which they mix elements in themselves poisonous, thereby concoct healing medicines." If this was not a wholehearted endorsement of the new apologetics taking shape in Pascal's *pensées*, neither was it a repudiation. And so it was, concluded Secretary Fontaine tactfully, "that these two beautifully spiritual persons concurred finally on the subject of the study of Epictetus and Montaigne, though they reached the same conclusion by somewhat different routes: Monsieur de Saci at a single stroke, thanks to his clear view of Christianity; and Monsieur Pascal only after having interested himself for a long time in the teachings of these philosophers."

By the end of January 1655, Pascal had returned to Paris. Little is known of his movements or of his precise activities during the year that followed, though it is safe to assume that much of his time and energy was devoted to theological inquiries — including treatises on grace and a short life of Christ — destined to come to light only later. Certainly he maintained his intimacy with the duc de Roannez; rumor had it that it was Pascal who persuaded Roannez to affirm his conversion by giving up the prospect of an advantageous marriage, much to the fury of the duc's family. Nor did Pascal cease to cultivate Méré and Mitton, who, though never fervent converts like their mutual friend Roannez, nevertheless showed increasing sympathy for the partisans of Port-Royal.

Gilberte Périer, however, remembered that now her brother's style of life changed dramatically. He kept his lodgings in the rue des Francs-Bourgeois, "but from this time on he dispensed as much as he could with the service of his domestics. He made his own bed, took his meals in the kitchen and fetched his own dishes, and, in short, left to the staff only those things he could not possibly do himself." The tapestries and decorative hangings in his bed-chamber he decided were unnecessary superfluities, and so he stripped the walls bare. He routinely repressed the enjoyment of any sensual pleasure, however legitimate, and even when the conventions of society dictated otherwise he displayed "a marvelous skill" in avoiding their influence. "We never heard him praise the food he was eating, and when occasionally he was served some choice delicacy and was asked if he liked it, he would simply reply: 'Only memory would allow me to answer, and just now I do not remember, and I assure you I am not paying any particular attention.'" Indeed, he bristled with impatience when someone in his presence, "in accord with the ordinary practice of the world," applauded the taste of a piece of meat, " 'because,' he said, 'this was the mark of one who eats in order to gratify his taste, which is always wrong.'" For himself Blaise disdained the use of all sauces and seasonings, "specifically those blended out of the juices of oranges or sour grapes of which he was naturally so fond," and strictly limited the quantity of food he ate "to the needs of the stomach and not of the appetite." Gilberte recorded one curious side-effect of all this austerity at the dining table: "I was astonished that my brother could ingest the most disgusting medicines without distress, and he laughed at me and said he could not understand it either, unless it was because he took them under direction and not voluntarily."

But such mortification of the senses had its counterpart at an intellectual level as well, or so Gilberte believed. "My brother had by nature an extraordinary disposition of mind, but he added to this a set of rules, peculiar to himself, by which his talent to communicate was further augmented. These were not rooted just in attractive thoughts that gave off a false brilliance and in reality signified nothing." The art of persuasion, as the converted Blaise Pascal aimed to practice it, refrained from "all grandiose language," employed "few metaphorical expressions," and possessed nothing of "the rude, the obscure, or the superfluous." "He conceived of eloquence," Gilberte continued, "as a means of saying things in such a manner that all those who listened to him could do so with pleasure and without pain." To accomplish this end, "he made the human heart and the human spirit his special study, so that he came to understand fully the springs of human motivation. When he shared his thought about something, he put himself in the place of those who were to listen to him." And he was ruthlessly honest: the inconvenient truth was not blurred or omitted; "what was little he did not describe as great, what was great he did not describe as little." Finally, so complete a master was he of his mode of expression "that he was able to say exactly what he thought." His writing style revealed parallel virtues: "simple, equitable, strong, engaging, and natural, all at the same time," and all about to burst upon the public — recalling the moment must have given a tug to Gilberte's heart — in the form of the *Lettres au provincial.*

119

Indeed, the occasion for the appearance of that remarkable work of religious controversy, the *Provincial Letters,* was at hand. The setting was once again Port-Royal des Champs, almost exactly a year after Blaise Pascal had made his retreat there and had engaged Father de Saci in "conversation." In the interval, though busy about his Parisian life, he had kept in touch with *les messieurs des granges,* and Soeur Jacqueline maintained that during this period her brother invented an ingenious method of speed-reading for the pupils in the Solitaries' *petites écoles.* Blaise at any rate had returned in January 1656, and this time, in the barns overlooking the old and refurbished convent, he met Antoine Arnauld, Mère Angélique's youngest brother and LeMaître's and de Saci's uncle (though he was younger than the former and only a year older than the latter), the man already coming to be known as "the Great Arnauld," the heir of Saint-Cyran, the embattled chief of the Jansenist party.

7 Les Provinciales

EVER since the publication of his *De la fréquente communion* in 1643 — the year also of the Abbé Saint-Cyran's death — Antoine Arnauld had been recognized as the intellectual leader of those French Catholics who claimed to represent the pristine teachings of St. Augustine. At the end of 1655, when he was forty-three, the stocky, balding Arnauld could reflect upon a dozen years of fluctuating fortunes for him and his partisans. Indeed, he could look back further than that, to the formative years of his childhood so dominated by his mother and older sisters — his father had died when Antoine was seven — and to his fateful meeting, in young manhood, with Saint-Cyran, who had offered him a kind of spiritual paternity. Forsaking, like his uncle, LeMaître, the prospect of a brilliant career in the law, Arnauld had astonished a generation of theologians at the Sorbonne with his intelligence and dialectical skill — astonished and yet to some degree distressed teachers and colleagues by the very relentlessness with which he drove his principles to their logical conclusions. There appeared in him, as it does in all those who would lead a revolution — or perhaps in this instance the better term is *coup d'état*, since Jansenism in its beginnings was restricted to a small portion of the ruling élite — a single-mindedness that brushed aside opposing argument as the self-interested posturing of a corrupt establishment.

The tangle of competing interests and jurisdictions within that establishment, however, determined that the fate of Arnauld's movement would depend on much more than the persuasiveness of its polemic. The removal by death of Cardinal Richelieu's firm hand (1642) had brought to the tiller of the state the supple but weaker one of Cardinal Mazarin, who in any case was less concerned than his predecessor had been with matters strictly religious. And yet the phrase "matters strictly religious" is in fact something of a misnomer; neither Mazarin nor any of his contemporaries considered religion a private affair to be left to the whims of those who chose to practice it. The horrors that accompanied religious disunity had been burned into the consciousness of French men and women, not only by the civil wars of their own recent past but by the agonies being endured at that moment in the German-speaking lands to the east. Mazarin may have had little interest in the subtleties involved in disputes over grace and free will, but he drew no distinction between church and state, between the common weal and confessional uniformity. King and faith and lawful government stood or fell together: *un roi, une foi, une loi.*

But *le roi* at the moment was a child, Louis XIV, which meant that the cardinal had to guide affairs through the regency headed by his ally, the queen mother. No dictatorship is as strong as its pretensions, and this was particularly the case in a hereditary monarchy during a king's minority. Queen Anne and Mazarin were to learn this painful lesson at the end of the decade, with the outbreak of the Fronde. The bourgeois *parlementaires* and the great nobles, like the Prince of Condé, still could exert real power and so still had to be appeased or at least circumvented by the central regime. And the same could be said of the ninety or so bishops, who were all appointed by the crown, to be sure, but who also represented their own class interests and exercised considerable economic and social as well as ecclesiastical authority within their far-flung dioceses. The Estates General had not met since 1614 (nor would it meet again until the eve of the Revolution in 1789), but the first two estates, the clergy and the nobility, maintained at least a modicum of organization and the capacity to affect public policy.

Port-Royal could count among its converts a small but not insignificant minority of such persons; perhaps the most notorious and outspoken among them was yet another member of the Arnauld family, Antoine's older brother, Henri, who was bishop of Angers. A sprinkling of dukes and countesses and rich advocates, as well as fifteen or so other bishops, were similarly disposed. As for the lower clergy, the numbers who embraced Jansenist principles were not large, but their reputation as preachers and scholars was outstanding, and their zeal for the cause seemed to some to compensate for the thinness in their ranks. By and large they were secular priests rather than ordained members of the religious orders, a circumstance that tended to heighten the age-old tension between these two groups. Among the religious it was, predictably, the Jesuits — Molinists almost to a man — who raised the fiercest objections to Jansenist views, while the traditional antagonists of the Jesuits in theological debate, the Dominicans, assumed a softer and yet vigilant attitude. But most significant in the long run was the stern opposition of the aging Vincent de Paul, who, if he had admired the virtues of Saint-Cyran, did not find them duplicated in Saint-Cyran's heir; he denounced Arnauld's *Fréquente communion* in the strongest terms, declaring, with pardonable exaggeration, that this insidious book had undermined Eucharistic devotion in half the population of Paris. This was a crucial intervention, not only because de Paul had long been a confidant of the queen mother but also because he was already widely regarded with reverential awe as a saint. Hardly less weighty at the time was the adverse judgment about Port-Royal rendered by Jean-Jacques Olier, the much respected *curé* of Saint-Sulpice on the left bank and the founder of the celebrated seminary that evolved out of that parish.

Another vested interest ultimately had to be heard from. The increasingly acrimonious pamphlet war that dragged on during the 1640s could not, in the end, declare a victor. A dispute over the relationship between divine grace and free will was, at root, a doctrinal one, and the arbiter in such matters in France was the theology faculty of the University of Paris, the Sorbonne. Antoine Arnauld, himself a doctor of the university, proved so formidable a controversialist that at first few of his colleagues had the stomach to challenge him, and indeed he could count on a certain number of supporters among them. Suddenly, in the summer of 1649, came a dramatic turn of events. Nicolas Cornet, the venerable seventy-seven-year-old syndic (censor) of the Sorbonne, known to be close to Mazarin as he had been to Richelieu, presented to the assembled doctors of divinity seven propositions — five drawn from Jansenius's *Augustinus* and two from Arnauld's

Fréquente communion — and recommended that they be formally censured as heretical. A stormy debate over the motion followed during succeeding months, much of it turning on arcane points of ecclesiastical law and academic privilege. The weight of the argument, however, moved remorselessly against the Jansenist position. Then, the next year, an Assembly of the French clergy endorsed Cornet's condemnation of *Augustinus,* though it declined to do the same to *Fréquente communion;* thus the seven proscribed propositions were reduced to five.

The distinction was of small comfort to Arnauld and his followers, convinced as they were that Jansenius's masterwork presented a uniquely precious compendium of the teachings of St. Augustine. But worse was to follow. Four French bishops petitioned Rome to confirm the clergy's condemnation, while eleven others, in a letter drafted at Port-Royal, wrote in rebuttal. So it was that the Holy See, the last court of appeal, finally entered the fray. Not, however, without a great deal of reluctance. From the beginning of the Jansenist dispute the popes had reacted with extreme caution and reserve, warily hiding behind a screen of legal technicalities and precedents. In 1643 Urban VIII, under pressure from the Jesuits, had indeed issued a mild rebuke when *Augustinus* had been published, first in Flanders and then in Paris and Rouen, but the bull *In eminenti* mentioned neither the book nor its author, and contented itself with renewing the condemnation of Baius and complaining that any publication on the subject of grace and freedom contravened the strictures imposed by Paul V forty years earlier. Urban's successor, Innocent X, was similarly disinclined to risk the prestige of the papacy by involving it in such subtle quarrels, but he could not remain indifferent to so bitter a controversy rending the enormously important Gallican Church, nor could he ignore appeals directed to him explicitly in his office as the supreme guardian of the Catholic deposit of faith.

Nor were such appeals made lightly. King, clergy, *Parlement,* and the French Catholic élite as a whole exulted in their "Gallican liberties," and, while acknowledging the primacy of the pope, they were ever ready to resist undue "ultramontane" interference in their affairs. It may be that the appeals of 1650 would never have been dispatched to Rome had France not fallen at that moment into the crisis of the Fronde. Innocent X at any rate, mindful of this national sensitivity — and mindful, too, that in the dangerous post-Reformation world he lived in he dared not alienate the French Church — proceeded with the utmost circumspection. In April 1651, he appointed an *ad hoc* committee of five cardinals, who in turn enlisted the services of a squad of thirteen learned consultors. This body met formally fifty-one times over the next two years, a schedule of remarkable rigor for the usually relaxed Roman curia. Swarms of lobbyists competed furiously in their efforts to influence the outcome. In mid May 1653, the cardinals' committee submitted its report to the pope, who, on the last day of that month, approved it and issued a constitution, titled *Cum occasione*, confirming the earlier French condemnation of the following five propositions of Jansenius:

1. Some of the commandments of God are not possible for righteous persons to fulfill, even when they desire and endeavor to accomplish them according to the powers they possess; and the grace which would render these commandments capable of fulfillment is lacking to these persons.
2. Even in a state of corrupt nature inner grace is always irresistible.
3. To deserve reward or to forfeit it in the corrupt state of human nature does not demand a human liberty which excludes necessity, but only a liberty free from external constraint suffices.
4. The Semi-Pelagians admitted the necessity of an inner predisposing grace for each particular act, even for faith in the beginning, and they were heretical in maintaining that this grace was such that a person's will could either resist it or obey it.
5. To say that Christ died and shed his blood for all mankind is a Semi-Pelagian doctrine.

In 1644, at the instance of the queen mother (prompted no doubt by Vincent de Paul), an attempt had been made to induce Antoine Arnauld to go to Rome and plead his case — and, by implication, that of Saint-Cyran and Jansenius — in person. But old Pope Urban died that summer, and Giambattista Pamfili was not elected as Innocent X until the end of September, so nothing came of the proposal. Arnauld nevertheless had chosen that occasion to give public assurances of his filial loyalty to the Holy See and of his willingness to submit unreservedly to its dogmatic decisions. Now, nine years later, he did the same, but he also introduced an ingenious distinction that, his enemies quickly charged, amounted to an evasion. One must distinguish, Arnauld declared, between the substance of Innocent X's finding and the accuracy of its application. While granting that the five propositions as stated in the papal document were indeed heretical, Arnauld denied that they could be found in *Augustinus*. As a matter of right or law *(droit)*, the pope was, as always, correct; but the pope's teaching authority did not extend to the question of fact *(fait)*. Jansenius had not in reality held or taught the five propositions, which had been falsely and maliciously attributed to him by Molinist Jesuits and other Pelagians and Semi-Pelagians. Upon this discernment of the difference between *droit* and *fait* Arnauld prepared to take his stand.

His opponents at home gave the maneuver short shrift. In March 1654, the Assembly of the Clergy, as hostile to the Jansenists as its predecessor four years earlier, declared that a fair reading of *Cum occasione* made plain that the pontiff had intended to address the *fait* of the matter under dispute as well as the *droit,* that in fact the objectionable propositions were to be found in *Augustinus.* Confirmation of this conclusion appeared in a Roman Brief at the end of September. By then the last rebels of the Fronde had been defeated, and Mazarin was securely back in power. After his recent bitter experience the cardinal was in no mood to tolerate dissidence of any kind. Let the ladies and gentlemen of Port-Royal conform, or the full weight of the restored monarchy would crush them.

The new year of 1655 therefore began somberly for Antoine Arnauld and his associates, and it promptly gave rise to a genuine crisis. On January 31 — a few days after Blaise Pascal had returned to Paris from his first retreat at Port-Royal des Champs — the duc de Liancourt went to his parish church of Saint-Sulpice to make his sacramental confession. The duc was widely known as a fervent adherent of Jansenist principles; his granddaughter, like Pascal's nieces, the Périer sisters, was a *pensionnaire* at Port-Royal de Paris. On this day his confessor refused him absolution and further informed him that if he presented himself at the communion rail the Eucharist would be denied him. The reason for the prohibition, the priest said, was Liancourt's notorious association with *"les messieurs de Port-Royal,"* two of whom were then living in his Parisian residence. The priest added that the decision had been made by the pastor of the parish and the priest's own superior, Jean-Jacques Olier.

Such a challenge could not go unanswered. Within a month Arnauld had published a provocative pamphlet, *Lettre d'un Docteur à une*

126

personne de condition (Letter of a doctor [of theology] to a person of rank), in which he portrayed the events at Saint-Sulpice as part of a calculated strategy to defame submissive children of the Church who had willingly conformed to the condemnation of the five propositions. But in reasserting the distinction between *droit* and *fait*, this tract provoked several hostile rejoinders, including one written by François Annat, the young king's Jesuit confessor. The Jansenists are heretics, Annat stated flatly, because they have adopted Calvinist theories about grace, because they deny "that interior grace, necessary for our will in order that it can choose what God demands of it, is never lacking, even when it sins." In July Arnauld responded sharply in a *Seconde lettre à un Duc et Pair*, a book of two hundred pages, which went over the same ground as before but which also cited a favorite Jansenist example of the absence of efficacious grace at a moment of moral crisis: when Peter denied Jesus on the first Good Friday, he did so because "interior grace" (in Annat's words) was lacking to him.

Arnauld's enemies gleefully pounced upon this illustration, which, they charged, clearly endorsed the first and second of the five condemned propositions. If Peter sinned by reason of a default in divine aid, he sinned out of a compulsion rooted in his own corrupt nature; if he had acted virtuously instead, he would have done so under an analogous duress, since the force of divine grace is irresistible. In either case Peter's freedom to choose good or ill has been repudiated. So much for the evasive distinction between right and fact, cried the chorus of critics; the *doctrine* preached by the Jansenists is no different from John Calvin's predestinarianism.

The current now began to run very strongly against Port-Royal and against Antoine Arnauld in particular. In May, the French bishops, succumbing to pressure from Mazarin, produced a formulary that stated that the five propositions were heretical and that they were in fact to be found in *Augustinus;* this instrument was to be subscribed to by all the clergy, secular and religious. In early November Arnauld's *Seconde lettre* was denounced to the Sorbonne. A commission of six doctors was appointed to examine both the question of *fait* — did Arnauld propose a particular view on grace and free will — and of *droit* — was that view at odds with Catholic orthodoxy. With the commission's report on December 10 the debate within the faculty began. It lasted for over a month. Arnauld requested, and was refused, a special hearing, and had to content himself with challenging the legality of a procedure that, he charged, allowed the vote to a suspiciously large number of mendicant friars. Though supporters in the faculty argued his case with skill and ardor, the result was never in doubt. On January 14, 1656, the *Seconde lettre* was condemned on the question of fact by a vote of 130 to 71. The next day Arnauld issued a statement protesting that his terminology, and therefore his doctrine, merely reproduced that of Chrysostom and Augustine.

But this appeal to antiquity did not deflect the theologians of the Sorbonne from their purpose; they immediately moved their deliberations from the question of fact to the question of substance *(droit)* — in this instance whether the tract, with its example of Peter's sin, fell under the same censure as did the first proposition. By this time, Arnauld, fearful now of the police, had prudently retired to Port-Royal des Champs. On his infrequent visits to Paris he was careful to disguise himself; he wore a wig and exchanged his soutane for a fashionable garb bristling, as one old friend recalled, "with cuffs and tassels." Meanwhile the debate in the Sorbonne proceeded at a quicker pace, mandated by an impatient Cardinal Mazarin, while Arnauld along with his associates grew ever more apprehensive. Conference followed tense conference among these increasingly desperate men, including at this ominous moment — January 18 or 19 — Blaise Pascal, who had returned to Port-Royal des Champs for another spiritual retreat. Neither he nor any of the *solitaires* doubted that the second vote would echo the first and that as a result of it Arnauld would be expelled from the university and the Augustinian cause might well be ruined. Arnauld prepared still another statement for public release, but when he read it to his assembled comrades they glumly shook their heads. "I see that you find this text inadequate," Arnauld said, "and I agree with you." Then he turned to Pascal and said, "But you who are young, you ought to do something." A few days later the same company had read to them by its author his *Lettre écrite à un Provincial par un de ses amis sur le sujet des disputes présentes de la Sorbonne.*

"Monsieur, how wrong we were! I only had my eyes opened yesterday. Until then I thought that the arguments in the Sorbonne were about something of real importance and fraught with the gravest consequences for religion." Thus begins the first of the eighteen *Provincial*

Letters Pascal published anonymously at short intervals between January 27, 1656, and March 24, 1657. He also wrote the opening lines of a nineteenth and contemplated a twentieth, some notes for which ultimately appeared scattered through the *Pensées*. Each pamphlet, written in scintillating French, ran to eight or ten pages of print. Although a complete edition was published at Paris and another at Cologne in 1657, and a year later a Latin version appeared, translated by the most capable of the Solitaries, Pierre Nicole, there is no reason to suppose that Pascal realized on that day at Port-Royal des Champs when he read the first *lettre* to his friends to what lengths this project would take him. His use of the vernacular, along with the brevity and pungent rhetoric he employed, underscored the real objective of the *Lettres*. Pope, king, bishops, university: all the traditional sources of power in church and state were circling menacingly round the hapless Jansenists. Appeal to these authorities had been tried and had failed. The moment had arrived — at least so it seemed to Antoine Arnauld — when a last appeal should be tried, this time to the relatively small literate public, to the *honnêtes hommes* of Pascal's own class and attainments. Such persons, who would have shunned wearisome theological tracts, particularly those written in Latin, might be expected to appreciate a brisk and stylish exposé skillfully composed in their own language.

The *Provincial Letters* were neither academic nor, strictly speaking, theological. In substance they belonged to the genre of popular polemic — "popular" understood in a qualitative rather than a quantitative sense. In tone they manifested their author's supple intelligence and his surprisingly abundant gift for humor, ranging as they did between gentle irony and savage sarcasm. Like all able controversialists, Pascal demonstrated the ability to strike his opponents at their weakest points. Not much space was reserved for nuance or labored distinctions. Pascal was in any case neither trained nor even well read in standard theological literature; he had to depend in this regard upon resources supplied to him by others, particularly by Arnauld and Nicole. But at a deeper level the author of the *Provincial Letters* rejected the idea that theology was an inquiry by human reason into revealed truth and so a matter of scientific speculation properly left to academic specialists. Ever since his conversion on the "night of fire" he was convinced that his knowledge of the divine depended upon prayer and experience; and the divine he knew was the God, not of the savants, but of Abraham and of Jesus Christ.

The first ten *Provincial Letters* were addressed by a Parisian to an imaginary friend, a gentleman living in the country; hence their title. Numbers eleven through sixteen were directed "by the author of the letters to a provincial to the Reverend Jesuit Fathers," the most adamant of the Jansenists' foes. In the last two *lettres* — seventeen and eighteen, both published during the early months of 1657 — Pascal narrowed his target to François Annat, who stood out in Pascal's mind as more sinister and formidable than the other French Jesuits. In content the first three *lettres* and the last two might be roughly categorized as doctrinal, since they dealt with the tortured question of grace and freedom; those that came in between treated of moral matters, specifically with the laxity — as Pascal judged it — of Jesuit ethical teaching and practice. It would be wrong, however, to attempt too rigid a classification.

But whether the subject be doctrinal or moral, Pascal's method in the early *Provincial Letters* was ridicule. In order to defend Arnauld, he poked fun at the doctors of the Sorbonne and at the pompous manner in which they debated trivialities and tangled themselves in meaningless terminology. In order to convict the Jesuits of pandering to the lowest instincts of their penitents, he chose the most outlandish examples possible. Writing in the first person, he invented dialogues in which he played the role of a somewhat naive interlocutor, a kind of everyman, whose search for the truth has been constantly frustrated by encounters with academic pretension and jesuitical sophistry. Wherever he turned in this intellectual wasteland he had to listen to pettifogging statements designed to enhance the reputations of *soi-disant* theological experts or — in the case of the Jesuits — to further their order's campaign to control every aspect of the Church's life. Another invariable characteristic of these exchanges, as the writer pointed out to his friend in the provinces, was the assertion of the "learned" that the ordinary Catholic could not really comprehend the issues under dispute and should therefore refrain from inquiring about them. More than once an unaffected question earned a "rude rebuff." This was a shrewd, controversial stroke, given the character of the audience for whom Pascal was writing. "'The difference between us professionals,'" he had one of his doctors say, "'is so subtle that we can barely explain it ourselves; you would have too much difficulty understanding it.'" And another: "'You do not know very much about all this.'" And a Jesuit: "'You do not even

130

know what the terms signify, and yet you talk like a doctor of divinity.' "
The contrast drawn in these early *lettres* between the straightforward
and unassuming demeanor of the Jansenist narrator and the humbug
consistently indulged in by the specialists he encountered was central to
Pascal's art; but just as artful was the insinuation that these persons, for
all their pretensions, were more to be laughed at than confuted.

So the portrayal in the opening *lettres* of what was, Pascal knew
full well, a life-and-death struggle as far as Port-Royal was concerned,
nevertheless accentuated the ludicrous. The nameless writer, having
brushed aside the question of *fait* and the adverse vote the Sorbonne
had already recorded against Arnauld — "this point is unimportant,
because it involves no question of faith" — described to his friend how
he scurried from doctor to doctor, from Molinist to Thomist to Jansenist and back again, trying to ascertain what the commotion was all
about. When the Sorbonne proposed to scrutinize Arnauld's comments about St. Peter's fall, "you and I both thought that this meant
examining the basic principles of grace, for instance whether it is not
given to all men or whether it is efficacious, but we were quite mistaken. I have become a great theologian in a short time, as you will
see."

To "become a great theologian," the narrator explained, did not
entail penetrating to the essence of the intellectual problem at hand and
then treating it thoroughly and fairly. It involved instead garnering
enough votes "to crush Monsieur Arnauld," to cap the earlier negative
vote with a second, definitive one, even if to do so necessitated dishon-
estly packing the university's register of electors with unlicensed out-
siders. Bandying words, however, was even more the mark of "a great
theologian." The present dispute turned upon the understanding of
"efficacious" as distinguished from "sufficient" grace: did St. Peter,
when he denied Jesus, have at his disposal divine aid "sufficient" to
ward off "efficaciously" the cowardly weakness inherent in his nature?
But when the narrator raised this query to a learned divine, he was told
that he must ask instead whether " 'this power [to avoid moral evil] is
proximate — that is the point.' "

This was a new word to me, and unfamiliar. Up till then I had
understood the business, but this term plunged me into obscurity,
and I think it was only invented to confuse people. So I asked him

to explain it, but he was very mysterious about it, and sent me off with no further satisfaction.

Nor did the well-intentioned inquirer find satisfaction from any of the experts he consulted. The neo-Thomist Dominicans admitted use of the term, but they declined to explain what it meant and were not at all nonplussed when told that "proximate" was being employed in a variety of senses. " 'What!' " exclaimed the narrator. " 'But Reverend Fathers, it is playing with words to say that you are in agreement because you both use the same terms, when you mean different things.' The Fathers did not answer." A prominent secular doctor overheard this exchange, and, when pressed on the same point, he replied, " 'Wait a moment, you might catch me out. Let us take it in easy stages. I distinguish: if one calls this power *proximate*, he is a Thomist, and so Catholic. If not, he is a Jansenist, and so a heretic.' 'Monsieur Arnauld does not call it,' I said, 'either proximate or not proximate.' 'Then he is a heretic,' the doctor said."

"To tell the truth," the narrator protested, "I am very much afraid that all this is pure quibbling." And surely his provincial friend would agree that "it would be something unworthy of the Sorbonne and theology to use equivocal and captious words without explaining them." So this appeal was addressed to the assembled savants:

"Now for the last time I ask you, Reverend Fathers, to tell me what I must believe to be a Catholic."

"You must," they all said in unison, "say that all the righteous have *proximate* power, leaving aside all question of meaning."

"In other words," I said as I took my leave, "one must pronounce this word with one's lips to avoid being called a heretic. Is this word scriptural?"

"No," they told me.

"Does it come from the Fathers, the councils, or the popes?"

"No."

"What about St. Thomas?"

"No."

"Then why is there any need to say it, since it has no authority behind it nor any meaning in itself?"

"You are stubborn," they said. "You must either say it or be heretical, and the same with Monsieur Arnauld. For we are in the majority, and if necessary we shall bring in enough Franciscans to ensure [electoral] victory."

The first three *Provincial Letters* entered the public domain in quick succession — January 27, February 5, February 12, 1656 — but Pascal's literary attack did not prevent, on January 31, the formal censure of Arnauld by the Sorbonne on the question of *droit*; he was thereby deprived of his degrees and expelled from the university. The reiterated complaint about the legality of the process led nowhere. Perhaps some small satisfaction was gleaned in Jansenist circles from Pascal's sardonic commentary in his third *lettre*.

> Set your mind at rest [the narrator advised his provincial friend], and do not be afraid of being heretical if you use the condemned proposition. It is only wrong in Monsieur Arnauld's *Second Letter*. Will you not take my word for it? Believe, then, the most zealous of the examiners; only this morning a friend of mine, a doctor, asked this person to define the difference in question, and wanted to know if it was no longer permissible to say what the [ancient] Fathers said, and was given this excellent answer:
>
> "This proposition," the examiner said, "would be Catholic in the mouth of anyone else; it is only in Monsieur Arnauld that the Sorbonne has condemned it." This should make you marvel at the devices of Molinism, which bring about such prodigious upheavals in the Church that what is Christian in the Fathers becomes heretical in Monsieur Arnauld; what was heretical in the semi-Pelagians becomes orthodox in the Jesuits' writings; the time-honored doctrine of St. Augustine is an intolerable novelty, and the new inventions that are daily turned out before our eyes are supposed to be the Church's ancient faith.

Yet a satirical riposte of this kind must have seemed futile and even trifling to those most directly concerned. Antoine Arnauld remained in hiding, and his sister, Mère Angelique, mourned aloud at the aggressive behavior of the enemies of the doctrine of Saint-Cyran. The anonymity of the author of the *Provincial Letters* was, to be sure, preserved, but the printers of the little tracts were from the beginning harassed by Mazarin's police — which necessitated moving the enterprise from one inconvenient venue to another. In mid-March *les solitaires* were ordered by royal edict to depart Port-Royal des Champs. "All our hermits are gone from here," lamented Mère Angélique. "Our valley has become truly a valley of tears. All the gentlemen and the fifteen pupils in the *petites écoles* are sore afflicted at having been obliged to quit this place, and they are to be pitied." On March 20 she learned that the expulsion of the nuns from both the convents of Port-Royal was imminent; this intelligence, testimony to her remarkable access to restricted information, came from a document seen on the queen mother's dressing table. Mère Angélique responded to this dire threat by passing the next three days and nights in prayer before the Blessed Sacrament.

At Mass on the morning her triduum was finished the Introit proper for that day, liturgically the Friday of the third week of Lent, was taken from Psalm 86 (85): "Give me, Lord, a sign of your goodness, so that those who hate me may see it and be confounded that you have helped me and consoled me." However much Mère Angélique took these words to heart, she could not have dreamed how strikingly they were to be affirmed that very day. It was March 24 on the secular calendar. On an altar in the choir of the chapel at Port-Royal de Paris had been placed that day, as Jacqueline Pascal recorded, "a very beautiful reliquary in which was encased in a little sun of silver-gilt a splinter of a thorn of the Holy Crown." This precious memento, allegedly taken from the crown of thorns the Roman soldiers had derisively pressed upon Jesus' brow just before the crucifixion, belonged to a priest named de la Potterie — a relative of the Arnaulds and a Jansenist sympathizer — who was well known as a collector of religious relics. Through the course of the day the sisters paid due veneration to this tangible memorial of Christ's passion. Among others who came to the choir to offer reverence to the relic were the *pensionnaires,* the young girls who were receiving at Port-Royal their education as well as their religious formation. In their number was Marguerite Périer, a child of ten who — it may be recalled — had been brought to Paris from Clermont at the end of 1653 by her mother, Gilberte Périer, in hopes of a successful treatment of an ailment in the child's eye. But various Parisian physicians had been no more able than those in Marguerite's native Auvergne to bring her any relief. Her left eye continued to fester, and its chronic swelling indicated the presence of a painful, pus-filled fistula that gave off a disgusting stench. Indeed, if anything, her condition markedly worsened during the early months of 1656. Wracked by insomnia and fever, little Margot fell into an ever more pitiable state.

She was not only Blaise Pascal's favorite niece; she was also his godchild. With her parents far away in Clermont, he and his sister, her Aunt Jacqueline, provided for her whatever therapy they could secure, and, at the same time, endured all the pangs felt by those who must helplessly watch a loved one suffering from a hideous disease. Blaise, whose own health was so wretched, had perhaps little reason to put much hope in the skill of the medical profession, but, when warned by one of the doctors that Margot's abscess might spread to her nose and throat, he wrote to his brother-in-law and urged that an operation be performed. The "operation" recommended was a fearful procedure, a cauterization that, besides the horrible pain involved, might even prove fatal. Florin Périer, so far away, could not abide the thought of a hot iron thrust against his little girl's eye. He instructed Pascal to put off any such drastic course until he could come to Paris himself and reach a decision. He arrived there on April 4, hastened to Port-Royal, and, when his daughter had been ushered into his presence, he looked with amazement into her bright and shining eye. The ulcer was gone.

This was "the miracle of the Holy Thorn." The nun responsible for the *pensionnaires,* Soeur Flavia, had of course long been aware of her young charge's unhappy and apparently incurable condition. When she had brought her girls into the choir to venerate the relic on that fateful March 24, she had, on the spur of the moment, plucked the reliquary from its place on the altar and applied it to Marguerite's eye. That evening the girl came to her and said, "Sister, my eye is healed. It doesn't hurt any more." An astonished Soeur Flavia brought the news immediately to Mère Agnès Arnauld — Mère Angélique was still at des Champs — who confided it next day to Jacqueline Pascal. Mère Agnès ordered a veil of silence to be lowered over the event, though everyone resident in the convent quickly became aware of it.

On the following Wednesday, March 29, Blaise Pascal was informed of what had happened, and at his urging the nuns invited the surgeon who had recommended cauterization to interview Marguerite. He did so, in Blaise's presence, on March 31, and confessed himself mystified at what appeared to be a complete cure, but he asked that he be allowed to reflect on the situation and to see the girl again before giving a definitive determination. In the interval Florin Périer, summoned by Jacqueline, arrived from Clermont, and to him, on April 7, the surgeon, after a second examination, formally stated his opinion that the girl had been healed by a miraculous intervention. But this attestation was not sufficient for the prudent Périer and his advisers — including no doubt his brother- and sister-in-law. At his invitation the other Parisian doctors who had previously treated Margot, seven of them altogether, assembled at Port-Royal on April 14, the Wednesday of Holy Week. After a careful scrutiny of their former patient, they signed a declaration that concluded: "Since this sort of cure of so severe a disease effected in an instant can only be termed extraordinary, to the degree that it can be understood we think that it surpasses the ordinary forces of nature and that it could not have been done without a miracle, which we believe to have been genuine."

It was a joyous Easter in 1656 for the Périers, for the Pascals, and indeed for the whole Jansenist company. They nevertheless maintained a wary reticence about the miracle at Port-Royal, as though unsure of its impact upon public opinion. It was only after the attending physicians circulated the story that it spread throughout Paris and beyond — at least so maintained Antoine LeMaître, the party spokesman on the matter. The effect at any rate was electric. The queen mother was fascinated by the accounts she heard, and dispatched the king's own doctor to see Marguerite. Cardinal Mazarin was similarly impressed, and, when Olier and the priests of Saint-Sulpice complained to the royal chancellor that crowds were being enticed to the convent by tales of bogus miracles performed there, that official blandly replied that the cure of "the little Périer" looked as though it were authentic. At the beginning of May, Mère Angélique observed that "it seems that opinions about us have softened," and she rejoiced particularly that her elder brother, Arnauld d'Andilly, had received permission to return to *les granges* of Port-Royal des Champs; perhaps the other Solitaries would soon be allowed to join him. On May 27 the Archdiocese of Paris initiated its formal inquiry, and three days later the vicar general himself interrogated Marguerite. Over succeeding months depositions were taken from twenty-five individuals, including "the father, the sister, the aunt, and the uncle of the subject."

Blaise Pascal was deposed on June 8. He recounted for the archdiocesan officials his intimate knowledge of his niece's affliction and the part he had played in verifying its cure. His was a sober chronological narrative of the facts as his scientist's eye had perceived them, and he did not hesitate to use the word "miraculous" to characterize them. Neither did the other witnesses to the event, and, on October 22, 1656, the five theologians who conducted the inquiry under the mandate of the vicar general declared authoritatively, in the name of the archbishop, that a supernatural intervention had in fact occurred. Five days later a solemn Mass of thanksgiving was sung at Port-Royal de Paris, during which Father de la Potterie's reliquary was displayed once again upon the altar. But the sight most worshipers came that day to see was the little *pensionnaire*, Marguerite Périer, now grown somewhat bewildered and perhaps jaded by all the attention focused on her.

The fifth of the *Provincial Letters* appeared a few days before the miracle of the Holy Thorn, and the sixth on April 10 — that is, just as the physicians were examining Marguerite and pondering among themselves the cause of the remarkable phenomenon presented to them. Soeur Jacqueline Pascal wrote Marguerite's anxious mother — who had remained throughout these tense weeks with her other children in Clermont — an assurance of "our brother's joy" over the marvel that had happened to his beloved niece, but, true as that observation no doubt was, not even a passing allusion to the miracle manifested itself in the sixth or in any of the *lettres* that followed until the sixteenth, written in December of 1656. Clearly Pascal believed that his polemical cause had to avoid being seen as dependent upon this wondrous incident, significant as it may have been in itself and, to him, so personally consoling.

He had indeed already shifted the focus of his campaign with the publication of the fourth *lettre* (dated February 25). No longer intent upon defending Antoine Arnauld's theory of grace before the Sorbonne — a lost cause by then — he mounted a frontal assault upon Arnauld's, and his own, fiercest enemies. "There is nothing quite like the Jesuits," he wrote mockingly to his imaginary friend in the country. "Others only copy them. Things are always better in the original." And the "original" he described through the remaining *Provincial Letters* was a dark conspiracy of corporate ambition, moral laxity, and slander, which, if allowed to prevail, would in the end subvert the very mission of the Catholic Church. Silent as he remained, in these denunciations, about the miracle of the Holy Thorn, he must nevertheless have been incensed at the ingenious manner in which the French Jesuits attempted to dismiss the import of the healing of Marguerite Périer. The Church, one of them wrote, has declared the Jansenists to be heretics, and therefore the cure at Port-Royal has been effected not in order to bolster their false teaching but rather to prick their consciences: "God, who is the Father of mercies, has desired to make one last effort to touch their hard hearts." They have denied that Jesus died for all, and yet they proclaim a miracle in their own house by the instrumentation of "a thorn smeared with the precious Blood that has been spilled for the salvation of all humankind." Not for the first time had God confounded the counsels of infidels.

The Society of Jesus, which Pascal attacked so furiously in the *Provincial Letters*, was scarcely a century old. It traced its origins back to 1534 when seven students in the University of Paris gathered in a church on Montmartre and swore vows of perpetual poverty and chastity, and pledged as well to go on pilgrimage to Jerusalem, after which, they promised God and each other, they would devote the rest of their lives to apostolic labors. Their leader was a Spaniard, Ignatius Loyola, whose personal religion embodied both the militancy and the mysticism of this golden age of Spanish Catholicism. Six years later the little band received papal approval — in return for which they offered the popes special and extraordinary allegiance — and Loyola became the Society's first General. The title in this instance was particularly appropriate: Loyola had been a soldier before his conversion experience, and the military virtues he prized — obedience to command, solidarity, perseverence — were carefully incorporated into the Constitutions he drew up to govern his new Society — or *Compagnie* as the French had it, a word with martial overtones of its own.

Circumstances prevented the pious journey to Jerusalem, but the apostolic labors were taken on nonetheless, and with astonishing success. The Society's growth was prodigious: within a few years the original seven had become a thousand, and by the end of the century fourteen thousand Jesuits were at work in every corner of Europe as well as in the ancient realms of East Asia and in the newly discovered lands in America. In France, by Pascal's time, they numbered more than three thousand, divided into five provinces; they operated more than forty *collèges* across the country, in which the sons of the ruling classes received their education — thirteen thousand of them, it was said, in Paris alone.

In many respects these élite soldiers of Christ gave the fiery aspirations of the Counter-Reformation their loftiest expression. And they brought much more than religious enthusiasm to their ministry. The intellectual vigor and discipline and communal forcefulness the Jesuits routinely displayed were not matched in any other organization of the time, ecclesiastical or secular. Included in their number were tireless missioners, spell-binding orators, astute diplomats, formidable controversialists, the leading scholars in every field, the finest schoolmasters, the most sophisticated courtiers, and — when the occasion demanded it — men courageous enough to accept death for their beliefs. Even in such an extremity the Society displayed a knack for turning defeat into triumph: when the Jesuit Edmund Campion was tortured and then executed by the English government, the incident caused a stir of protest all over Europe — a far cry from the obscurity accorded the other, largely anonymous English Catholics who suffered the same barbarities.

But for every guileless martyr like Campion the Society seemed also to produce a Robert Parsons, his comrade on the English mission. Parsons escaped Campion's bloody fate and spent the rest of his life intriguing, with scant success, against the Elizabethan and Jacobean regimes. Critics were quick to label Parsons's dubious operations as characteristic of Jesuit strategy: a kind of worldly ruthlessness, an all-too-ready inclination to let the end justify the means, a tendency to compromise one truth in behalf of an allegedly higher one, and, above all, a proclivity to identify the well-being of Catholicism with the ascendancy of the Society of Jesus. Nor were such critics by any means restricted to militant Protestants like the rulers of England, who understandably feared and despised the Jesuits as their most dangerous opponents. Almost from the beginning the members of the Society were regarded with suspicion and even hostility by many of their fellow Catholics. Some of this antipathy stemmed from simple clerical envy of the Jesuits, whose sermons were listened to more avidly than those of most priests, whose books had more impact, whose missionaries achieved more spectacular successes. It was galling to realize that kings preferred the fathers of the Society as confessors, and that ladies of high fashion regularly sought their counsel in and out of the confessional. Many bishops, jealous of their local authority, resented the canonical independence the Jesuits enjoyed — and not seldom flaunted — because of their unique links to the papacy. Members of the older religious orders thought them pushy and abrasive. The guild of theologians, at least in France, regarded them as aggressive rivals; there were no Jesuit votes cast against Antoine Arnauld in the Sorbonne, because the Sorbonne admitted no Jesuit doctors to its sacred precincts.

But at a deeper, and more elusive, level — one at which Pascal and his Jansenist friends confronted them — the Jesuits excited antagonism among not a few thoughtful Catholics simply by reason of their modernity. They were men marked as much by the values and attainments of the humanist movement as by the gospel. They lived in accord with a rule that emphasized mobility and flexibility. Within the strict and yet broad limits of that rule, they gave full scope to Renaissance individuality. *Ad majorem Dei gloriam* — for the greater glory of God — was their motto, and the world in which they proposed to fulfill it was radically different from the world that had existed before the Reformation and the proto-capitalist commercial revolution and the rise of the great nation-states. They refused to commit themselves to old customs, to be tied down to the choir and the parish, or to wear a special religious garb. Today's problems and challenges could not be solved with yesterday's methods. The ancient Fathers of the Church and the medieval schoolmen might be revered, to be sure, but it was more important to improve upon them, to accommodate them to the modern world. In all this the Jesuits seemed to disdain the venerable Christian ideal of the contemplative life and to substitute for it a dedication to frenetic activity. They gloried in the flamboyance of baroque art and indeed in all the secular achievements of their time. They judged their own accomplishments in quantitative terms: look, they said, at how many heretics we have reclaimed, at how many savages we have converted, at how many books we have published and sermons we have preached and devotions we have sponsored.

And look, responded Pascal, at how many compromises the Jesuits have made with the sinful world. "You must realize," he wrote in the fifth *lettre,*

> that it is not [the Jesuits'] object to corrupt morals; that is not their policy. But their sole aim is not to reform them either. That would be a bad policy. This is how they see it. They have a good enough

opinion of themselves to believe that it is useful and virtually essential for the good of religion that they should enjoy universal credit and govern the consciences of all. And as strict evangelical precepts are suitable for governing certain sorts of persons, they make use of them on those occasions which serve their purpose. But as these same precepts do not fit in with the ideas of most people, for these they omit them, so as to have something to please everybody.

This is why they find it necessary, having to deal with people from every walk of life, to have casuists to match such great variety.

You can readily see from this principle that if they had only lax casuists they would frustrate their chief aim, which is to embrace everyone, since the really pious want stricter guidance. But as there are not many like that, they need only a few strict directors to look after them. They keep these few for the few who want them; whereas the multitude of lax casuists is available for those who want laxism.

Casuistry is the application of general principles of morality to definite and concrete *cases* of human activity in order to determine what one ought to do or ought not to do, and also in order to decide whether and to what extent guilt should or should not be imputed to an action already performed. Casuists, then, are the experts who apply such principles to a specific instance, which, by definition, is different from all other instances. In the Catholic scheme of things every spiritual director or confessor is to some extent a casuist, because he is dealing with a particular individual to whom he is offering counsel or — in the confessional — about whose deeds he is rendering a judgment. By Pascal's time a pseudo-science of casuistry had developed in order to provide support for directors and confessors. Huge tomes were published containing illustrations of moral dilemmas and suggested solutions to them; these were for the most part imaginary cases, but not dissimilar to real predicaments in which penitents might find themselves. The authors of such manuals inescapably based themselves upon precedent and upon the accumulated opinions of moral theologians.

These latter, it hardly needs saying, did not always agree among themselves. So there evolved under the casuist umbrella a variety of ethical systems that differed according to the measure of liberty each granted to the individual when confronted by a moral precept. Some sought to limit the scope of that liberty, others to expand it. In the awkward, Latinate terminology theologians habitually employed, the school called "tutiorism" urged that strict adherence to the letter of the law was the only safe course to follow; "probabiliorism" granted that when the intent of the law was not altogether clear it was permissible to allow freedom if the arguments in favor of it were more probable than otherwise; and finally "probabilism" maintained that the individual was free to pursue a certain course of action when there were probable arguments to support it, even if counterarguments were more probable. "Probability" in this context usually had a quantitative signification: if four or five reputable casuists arrived independently at the same conclusion — that fasting during Lent, for example, was not required of a nursing mother — then that opinion could be safely followed, even though the number of reputable casuists who did not endorse it was larger.

There was nothing new about this approach to moral decision making, but given the rigorous standards championed by the Jansenists, it is hardly surprising that they approached all casuistry with deep scepticism and, further, that they equated the most liberal of these schools of thought, probabilism, with satanic immorality. The application of probabilist principles to ethical conduct amounted, in their view, to a licence to sin. At issue, once again, was the relationship between human freedom and divine grace, though in this instance once removed from the abstractions that had pitted Arnauld against the Sorbonne. And once again the chief enemy for the Jansenists was the Society of Jesus, which had made probabalism peculiarly its own and converted it into blatant laxism.

Pascal could make no claim as an expert on the science of casuistry. It is doubtful that before Arnauld and Nicole had enlightened him he had anything more than a vague acquaintance with probabalism or with any of the other moral systems routinely employed by confessors and spiritual directors. He did indeed set himself the task of reading one of the most famous Jesuit manuals — that published in 1626 by the Spaniard, Antonio Escobar — but for the other citations that appeared in the *Lettres*, beginning with number four, he had to depend upon material supplied him by his better-informed associates.

142

This is not to say that the effectiveness of Pascal's polemic was therefore compromised. Quite to the contrary. The very nature of the casuist enterprise — its accidental and anecdotal character, its predisposition to the overly subtle and to the admittedly fanciful — lent itself to the light and satirical touch that a learned amateur could readily bring into play. Unlike the professional theologian, who had to be concerned about the reaction other professionals might have to his analysis, Pascal could present the viewpoint of the ordinary Catholic, honestly perplexed by the mental reservations and the sinuous logic he discerned in the Jesuits' practical critique of moral problems. He could, and did in the *Provincial Letters,* assume the posture of an ingenuous inquirer who wanted only straightforward answers to straightforward questions about ethical propriety. In doing so he knew full well that he would find a certain amount of automatic sympathy among the audience for which he was writing. Despite the Jesuits' striking successes, despite their immense influence in church and state, despite the distinction they had attained in so many fields of endeavor — or perhaps in part *because* of all these things — they were widely regarded with distrust and dislike. Arrogance and undue ambition were attributed to them by some, wicked if undefined intrigue by others. For the Jansenists, however, the negative reaction to the Society was precise: a genuine loathing, based on ideological and moral grounds. To this feeling Blaise Pascal gave voice by denouncing to as large a public as possible the Jesuits' manipulation of probabalism.

At first he continued to use the rhetorical device of wickedly playful dialogue. His narrator described to his friend in the country how he had gone to a learned Jesuit and told him that he found the Lenten fast very trying.

> [The Jesuit asked me] whether I did not find it hard to sleep without having had supper.
> "Yes, Father," I said.
> "I am so glad," he replied, "to have found a way of giving you relief without sinning. There you are, you are not obliged to fast. I do not want you just to believe me; come along to the library."
> I went there, and taking down a book he said: "Here is your proof, and, goodness knows, it's a good one. This is Escobar."
> "Who is Escobar, Father?" I said.

143

"What! you do not know who Escobar is? The member of our Society who compiled his Moral Theology from twenty-four of our Fathers. Here it is: 'Is someone who cannot sleep unless he has had supper obliged to fast? Certainly not.' Are you satisfied?"

"What a splendid fellow, that Escobar," I said.

"Everyone likes him," answered the Father. "He asks such charming questions."

"To tell you the truth, Father," I said, "I still do not really believe it. You mean to say that it is not a sin to fail to fast when one is able to? That one is allowed to look for occasions of sinning instead of being obliged to avoid them? That would be very convenient."

"No, not always," he said; "it depends."

"Depends on what?"

"Ah ha!" replied the Father. "And if it were somewhat inconvenient to avoid these occasions, would one be obliged to do so? That is not the view of our Fathers: 'One must not refuse [sacramental] absolution to those who remain in proximate occasions of sin, if they are so placed that they cannot turn from their ways without giving rise to gossip or bringing on themselves some inconvenience thereby.'"

"What, Father! because they put these lines into their books, it has become permissible to seek occasions of sin? I thought the only rule to be followed was Scripture and the tradition of the Church, but not your casuists."

"Good Lord!" exclaimed the Father. "You remind me of those Jansenists. I can see that you do not know what the doctrine of probable opinion is. I really must tell you about it. It is the foundation and the ABC of all our moral teaching: 'An opinion is called probable when it is founded on reasons of some importance. Whence it sometimes happens that one really grave doctor can make an opinion probable. And this is the reason: A man especially devoted to study would not expound an opinion unless he were attracted to it by some good and sufficient reason.'"

"And so," I said, "a single doctor can turn conscience round and upside-down as he pleases, and always quite safely."

"It is no laughing matter," he said, "and you must not think of challenging this doctrine. When the Jansenists tried to do so, it was a waste of their time. It is too well established."

144

The perverse beauty of this system, the narrator explained to his friend, lay in its boundless flexibility. There was a Jesuit probable opinion on every side of every moral or spiritual question.

"Splendid, Father, your doctrine is most accommodating. What! to be able to answer yes or no as one chooses! Such an advantage cannot be overestimated. And now I see the benefit you derive from the contrary opinions held by your doctors on every subject. For one of them is always helpful, and the other never harmful. If you do not find what you want on the one side, you jump over to the other, and never a risk."

After having enunciated these corrupt principles — "In matters of morality one should not follow the ancient Fathers but the modern casuists" — Pascal's imaginary Jesuit went on in the succeeding *lettres* to explain away the sinfulness of, among other enormities, simony, usury, drunkenness, theft, slander, even murder ("It is lawful according to the consensus of all casuists to kill someone who intends to slap you or hit you with a stick").

With the eleventh *lettre* (dated August 18, 1656) Pascal set aside the provincial gentleman and addressed the Jesuits directly. The reason for this shift was one common enough in the arena of literary controversy. "Reverend Fathers, I have seen the letters you are circulating against those I wrote to a friend of mine about your moral teaching." Published rebuttals to his charges had inevitably come forth, not least among them the allegation that he had treated hallowed subjects frivolously. "What, Fathers, are we to accept the fantasies of your writers as articles of faith? Is no one to be able to laugh at passages from Escobar, and the fantastic and unchristian decisions of your other authors, without being accused of scoffing at religion? In ridiculing your moral teaching I am as far from ridiculing sacred things as your casuistry is from the sacred teaching of the Gospel." But in fact his adversaries had gained a rhetorical advantage, because Pascal, stung by their accusations, from this point relinquished imaginary conversation in favor of aggrieved monologue, sometimes hectoring and increasingly bitter, and, in so doing, sacrificed all of the humor and much of the charm that had made the earlier *lettres* so readable. There also crept into Pascal's still sparkling prose a measure of defensiveness and self-service absent before. "Reverend Fathers," he

145

wrote in *lettre* twelve, "you describe me as 'impious, buffoon, ig-
noramus, clown, impostor, slanderer, rogue, heretic, crypto-Calvinist,
possessed by a legion of devils.' I hope by my own defense to convict
you of more real impostures than you impute false ones to me."

In substance much of the same ground was gone over again, the
same wicked casuists quoted, and, if anything, even more bizarre examples of Jesuit perfidy alluded to. No doubt Pascal the controversialist
overstated his case, quoted his opponents out of context, and, in short,
indulged in the stratagems, not all of them honorable, that controversialists commonly employ. But the Jesuits did the same in their rejoinders to the *Lettres,* and at least in one instance they were guilty of
grave calumny: they told "a monstrous lie" in accusing the Jansenist
party of treacherously adopting Calvinist teaching on the Eucharist.
This was effrontery of the boldest kind; nothing in the writings of
Saint-Cyran or Arnauld would sustain such a charge, and the fervor of
Mère Angélique and her sisters in their devotion to the Blessed Sacrament was a byword in Paris and indeed throughout France. "We must
put an end to this insolence," wrote Pascal in his sixteenth *lettre* (December 4, 1656), "which does not spare the holiest of places."

> I appeal to all; is there anyone in the Church against whom you
> can lay so abominable a charge with so little probability? For, tell
> me, Fathers, if these nuns and their directors were 'in league with
> Geneva against the most Blessed Sacrament of the altar' (which
> is a dreadful thought), why should they take as the principal object
> of their devotion this sacrament which they are supposed to
> loathe? Why should they add to their rule the institution of the
> Blessed Sacrament? Why should they take the habit of the Blessed
> Sacrament, the name of Daughters of the Blessed Sacrament, call
> their church the church of the Blessed Sacrament? Why should
> they request and obtain from Rome confirmation of this institu-
> tion and have unceasingly, night and day, nuns in presence of the
> blessed Host to make reparation by their perpetual adoration of
> this perpetual sacrifice for the impiety of the heresy which tries
> to destroy it?

Only here, and only this once in the *Provinciales,* did Pascal allude to
the miracle of the Holy Thorn:

Cruel and craven persecutors, are the most secluded cloisters to afford no sanctuary against your slanders? While those holy virgins adore Jesus Christ in the Blessed Sacrament night and day, you do not cease night and day to publish abroad that they believe that he is neither in the Eucharist nor even on the right hand of the Father. You slander those who have no ears to hear you, nor mouths to answer. But Jesus Christ hears you and answers for them. This holy and terrible voice can be heard today, dumbfounding nature and comforting the Church. And I fear, Fathers, that those who harden their hearts and obstinately refuse to hear him when he speaks as God, will be compelled to hear him when he speaks as judge.

Sturdy as was its defense of Port-Royal, the sixteenth *lettre* also gave evidence of some tension between its author and that nerve center of French Jansenism. Despite frantic efforts, the Jesuits had not yet discovered the identity of their eloquent enemy; they assumed, not illogically, that he must have been one of the Solitaries, LeMaître perhaps or d'Andilly. "You will not fail to say," wrote Pascal, "that I belong to Port-Royal, for it is the first thing you say to anyone who attacks your excesses, as though only at Port-Royal could people be found zealous enough to defend the purity of Christian morality against you." But though he held the Arnaulds and their associates in the highest esteem, "I have never belonged to their community." Indeed, "I shall speak in such a way as to make you [Jesuits] regret that you are not dealing with a man of Port-Royal [who might] make lamentations to God so that you may be forgiven." Pascal felt no such benevolence: "I feel obliged to make you blush before the whole Church."

He repeated his disavowal even more explicitly in number seventeen (January 23, 1657). Strictly speaking, the claim was true enough; Pascal had never formally joined *les solitaires,* and he had been only an occasional guest at Port-Royal des Champs. But it was disingenuous, too. Since 1648 he had attended Mass at Port-Royal de Paris and had listened raptly to Father Singlin's Jansenist sermons; his nieces and his beloved sister, whose judgments and opinions had more weight with him than those of anyone else, were in residence there; Singlin and de Saci he had chosen for his spiritual directors; and he had taken on the defense of Antoine Arnauld and the consequent quarrel with the Jesuits because Arnauld specifically had requested him to do so and had guaranteed him his own support as a professional theologian. Perhaps Pascal did not literally "belong" to Port-Royal; but he was definitely — to invoke a term not in the seventeenth century's lexicon — a fellow traveler.

The tension at any rate persisted and indeed, as the *Provincial Letters* appeared one by one, deepened. Mère Angélique Arnauld — who remembered the often bitter negotiations related to the reception of Jacqueline Pascal into Port-Royal de Paris — never completely trusted Jacqueline's brother, who was, she suspected, too much the uninhibited intellectual and therefore too much in thrall to the world for divine grace to work in him with due effectiveness. Nor did Pascal in his rugged individualism ever fit comfortably into a partisan category. Moreover, as Mère Angélique and others in her circle gradually became convinced that the strident tone of the *Lettres* was doing as much harm as good to their cause, they also, paradoxically, thought they detected in the last two of the series — numbers seventeen and eighteen — an inclination on Pascal's part to break ranks. In fact, as later events would prove, they mistook tactics for strategy, but at the time they pondered assertions like this one with some uneasiness: "I heartily detest the five condemned propositions. Even if Port-Royal did hold them, I declare that this would not enable you [François Annat, S.J., to whom the last two *lettres* were addressed] to conclude anything against me, because, thank God, my only allegiance on earth is to the Catholic, Apostolic, Roman Church, in which I desire to live and die, in communion with the Pope as sovereign head, and outside which I am fully convinced there is not salvation."

8 Poised on the Battlements

T HE PHYSICAL and emotional demands involved in composing the eighteen *Provincial Letters* would have taxed the strength of one who enjoyed much better health than did Blaise Pascal. Nevertheless he took on with zest the grueling schedule of research and writing and revising in a subject in which he was not well versed, all of it proceeding under a veil of secrecy and with the possibility ever present of exposure and persecution. It was all the more remarkable, therefore, that he continued at the same time to pursue other studies and to go out of his way to offer personal support and solace to troubled associates. A particularly poignant example of this latter devotedness was Pascal's correspondence with Charlotte de Roannez.

In 1656 this younger sister of Pascal's intimate friend, the duc de Roannez, was twenty-three years old. Regular as she may have been in performing her religious duties, she showed no sign that she shared her brother's newfound fervor or his intention to retire from the allurements of the world; she was, on the contrary, expecting soon to contract the noble marriage suitable to a woman of her station. But in August of that year she made a nine-day retreat at Port-Royal de Paris — much of her devotion time spent in veneration of the Holy Thorn — at the end of which she felt a strong impulse to enter the convent. She dutifully consulted the spiritual director of Port-Royal, Abbé Singlin, who advised her not to act precipitously; if the vocation were genuine, he said, a period of prayerful reflection would reveal it to her. Mademoiselle de Roannez agreed to wait, and, in the company of her brother the duc and their mother, she departed Paris for the family estates in Poitu. From there she wrote to seek counsel from Pascal, whom she had known since she was a child. He replied in a series of letters — nine fragments have survived — written between September and Christmas of 1656 — between, that is, the appearance of numbers twelve and sixteen of *Les Provinciales*.

Pascal plainly hoped that Charlotte de Roannez would decide to become a nun of Port-Royal, but he was careful to keep his recommendations oblique. And he took pains not to interfere in any way with the advice of Father Singlin, with whom she was also in communication. Like all the followers of Saint-Cyran, Pascal accorded precedence in spiritual direction to the ordained ministry. But this did not mean that he or any of the unordained ladies and gentlemen of Port-Royal, like Mère Agnès Arnauld or LeMaître or d'Andilly, hesitated to offer edifying guidance if the circumstances seemed appropriate. Indeed, once they were converted, pious discourse was woven into the texture of their lives, and Gilberte Périer remembered that many anxious souls sought out her brother and requested his advice.

No doubt the general approach he assumed in dealing with Mademoiselle de Roannez was duplicated on other similar occasions. The frequent references to and quotations from the Bible, Old Testament and New; the citations from the Fathers of the Church, particularly St. Augustine; the preachment of familiar Jansenist themes — "the peace of Jesus Christ will become perfect only when the body is destroyed" — all these predictable characteristics run through this set of letters. But so does a fine sensitivity that testifies to Pascal's special relationship with this young woman for whom he cared deeply.

Apparently she had begun the correspondence by raising with him two concerns. The first was her unease at the thought of the final judgment. In reply Pascal referred her to the thirteenth chapter of Mark's Gospel, in which Jesus foretold the destruction of the temple in Jerusalem — "not a stone will be left upon a stone" — and the other afflictions that would precede his second coming and the ultimate justification of the elect. "It seems to me," he wrote somberly, "that these predictions perfectly fit our own times, when moral corruption degrades even the houses of religious committed to holiness, as well as the books of theologians. The only course is to flee from such disorder, and, as St. Mark quotes Jesus, woe at such a moment to women with child or with a babe at the breast, to those, that is to say, with worldly attachments that keep them from flight." Then, as though conscious that his application of the biblical text may have struck too close to home, he quickly added: "I wish I could read this whole chapter of the Gospel with you. Remember anyway that it concludes with an exhortation that we fast and pray in order to avoid all these calamities, that the prayer be continuous, because the peril is continuous."

Charlotte's second source of anxiety had to do with miracles and relics and with the Holy Thorn in particular, and here Pascal's answer was softer and also revelatory of his own attitude toward this difficult subject. After promising to send her a fuller account of a nun at Pontoise cured of illness "through devotion to the Holy Thorn," he confided to her "a beautiful expression of St. Augustine about such matters: 'Those who truly see miracles are those who benefit from or are improved by miracles,' for one does not see them if one does not profit from them." As for relics of the saints, "there is no doubt that the Holy Spirit abides invisibly in the remains of those who died in God's grace. For God never abandons his own, not even in the tomb, where their bodies, dead in human eyes, are alive more than ever in God's eyes, because they are without sin."

The substance of Pascal's succeeding eight letters maintained the same combination of instruction and reassurance. But their tone grew sharper in response to Charlotte de Roannez's complaints about her difficulties, especially her mother's violent opposition to her desire to join Port-Royal. "You will never detach yourself from the world without sorrow." "St. Paul has said that those who would enter into the good life will find pain and trouble in abundance. This ought to console those who realize it, because alerted to the fact that on the highway to heaven they will encounter such suffering, they should rejoice in the knowledge that they are on the right road." "The past should never disconcert us, since our only duty to it is regret for our past faults. The future touches us even less: it is totally out of our control, and we may never even arrive there. The present is the only time that is really ours, and we must use it in accord with God's will."

151

Pascal enclosed in his fourth letter, written at the end of October 1656, a copy of the document issued by the Archdiocese of Paris, verifying the miraculous cure of Marguerite Périer. This official affirmation of the Holy Thorn seemed to move him to set aside, for the moment, Mademoiselle de Roannez's worries and to compose, in almost lyrical terms, a profession of his own faith in a "miracle" of a different dimension. "One ought to profit from an occasion of this sort," he wrote, echoing the sentiments in his first letter.

If God opened himself to human beings continually, there would be no merit in believing; and if he opened himself never, there would be little faith indeed. But in fact he hides himself ordinarily and reveals himself only rarely to those anxious to do him service. This strange secret, in which God retires impenetrable to the sight of men, is a most important lesson for us to reflect upon in solitude. He remained hidden under the veil of nature with which we are enveloped until the Incarnation. And even then he remained hidden in his humanity. And finally, when he wished to fulfill the promise made to his Apostles — that he would stay with us all days, even to the consummation of the world — he chose to do so by abiding in the strangest and most obscure secret of all, in the species of the Eucharist. This is God's ultimate hiding place. Infidels, to be sure, have discovered the existence of God in the designs of nature. Christian heretics have comprehended the divinity of the man Jesus Christ. But to recognize him under the appearance of bread, this privilege has been reserved for us Catholics alone; only to us has the hidden God revealed himself so fully.

In 1657 Charlotte de Roannez took the veil at Port-Royal de Paris. The peace and certainty she sought there, however, eluded her, and the coup for the Jansenists that the entry of one of her rank represented soon vanished in a sea of troubles. Once death had deprived her of the support of Singlin and Pascal, she petitioned to be dispensed from her vows. She married a noble duc, but her domestic life proved to be no happier than her cloistered one had been. Emotionally fragile and easily bruised, she may have pondered in her last years what Blaise Pascal had once written her: "Our Lord has said that since the appearance of

John the Baptist, that is, since his own appearance in the world, and, consequently, his encounter with each of the faithful, the kingdom of God suffers violence, and the violent shall bear it away."

It could hardly have been a coincidence that Pascal dated the eighteenth of the *Provincial Letters* March 24, 1657, the anniversary of the miracle of the Holy Thorn. He did not advert in this pamphlet to the cure of his niece, but he was aware as he was writing this last *lettre* in the series that reports of other miraculous events, also ascribed to specifically Jansenist devotion, were spreading all over Paris and its environs. Crowds of the curious as well as the infirm continued to jam the approaches to Port-Royal, so much so, it was said, that every day parked carriages filled up all the nearby courtyards. In the midst of such popular enthusiasm the Jansenists' opponents were reduced to muttered objections and futile charges of fraud. Their discomfiture, however, was not destined to last for long. Confident that they stood for the truth and the right, they could wait for the notorious inconstancy of public opinion to reveal itself, as indeed it shortly did.

The immediate success of *Les Provinciales*, meanwhile, could hardly be exaggerated. They were being read and discussed in salons and presbyteries all over France. The frequent republication of individual *lettres*, their almost instantaneous translation into Latin and English, and the collection of them into bound volumes that circulated widely, all testified to their popularity. Perhaps the tantalizing anonymity of their author — preserved till 1659, despite strenuous efforts by the Jesuits to unmask him — helped to promote them. Negative reaction at any rate simply sparked more interest: when the *Parlement* of Provence ordered that copies of them be publicly burned, the publicity merely added to their sale. In September 1657, the Roman Inquisition issued a decree condemning *Les Provinciales*, whether published singly or in book form, but the Inquisition's writ had no legal standing in the Gallican Church, and Mazarin, though still officially at odds with the Jansenists, was hardly less so with the new pope, Alexander VII. And anyway the failure of the government's earlier attempts to suppress the *lettres* through harassing the printers convinced the cardinal that the time was not yet ripe to move firmly against Port-Royal.

The Jesuits for their part might protest to their hearts' content that Pascal's indictment of them was unfair; that his examples of their distortions of probabalism were drawn out of context; that their moral teaching, based upon the venerable Catholic distinction between the commandments and the evangelical counsels, was in accord with Christ's injunction to preach the gospel to all men and women of every class and condition, not just to a handful of elect souls. On this last point they were ultimately to prevail over Pascal and the narrow Jansenist ethic, but not without suffering severe and permanent damage to their corporate reputation. Thanks to Pascal's literary genius, and to Arnauld's and Nicole's knowledge of casuist literature — and thanks, too, to Margot Périer — the Jesuits could do little, for the moment, but lick their wounds and reflect ruefully upon the meaning "jesuitical" had come to have in every modern language.

The survival among his papers of the opening few paragraphs of what would have been the nineteenth of the *Provincial Letters* — undated and addressed, like its immediate predecessors, to the king's Jesuit confessor, François Annat — indicates that Pascal had not originally intended to break off his polemic at this point. Why he did so remains unclear. One reason may have been the disagreement among his allies as to the likely future effectiveness of this particular campaign; the pious Father Singlin, for instance, pointedly invoked the rash of divine interventions to urge that prayer now clearly pleased God more than did contentious broadsides. Or it may have been because Pascal simply decided he had said in this format all he wanted and needed to say. The war of words was far from over, but undue repetition would surely dull the controversialist's cutting edge. So one last time, in number eighteen, Pascal called upon the authority of the Jansenists' oracle: "The only way of reconciling these apparent contradictions, which ascribe our good deeds now to God and now to ourselves, is to recognize that, as St. Augustine says, 'our deeds are our own, because of the free will producing them, and they are also God's, because of his grace causing our free will to produce them.' And, as he says elsewhere, God makes us do what he pleases by making us desire what we might not desire." Needless to say, only the most ardent partisan could interpret these passages as "reconciling contradictions" rather than begging the original question.

The burst of energy that carried Blaise Pascal through the fourteen draining months which saw the composition of the *Provincial Letters* sustained him till the middle of 1658, when a fierce and prolonged toothache presaged further physical deterioration. This respite from the worst of his maladies, which seems to have begun about the time of his second conversion, yielded many literary fruits besides the celebrated *lettres*. Much of what has survived from this period, however, while it witnesses to the depth and breadth of Pascal's mind, also reveals his proclivity to leave work unfinished. So many bits and pieces, so many fragments, so many notes and précis for treatises that would never be written — it was as though a throng of ideas and projects jostled for his attention, as though his intellect, too fertile to remain content with the same subject for long, raced from one uncompleted inquiry to another. Yet the quality of this disjointed production attained an astonishingly high level of sophistication. In mathematics he toiled through the mystery of the cycloid and established the underpinnings for a science of integral calculus and for a theory of probability. In rhetoric he produced a piece on the art of argumentation. He wrote an abridged life of Christ and a series of profound meditations on that most tortured question of his Catholic generation, the nature of divine grace. And, taking on an enterprise destined to bring him immortal fame, Pascal now began to gather materials — recorded at odd intervals on odd scraps of paper — for an *apologie* for the Christian religion, which would be published after he died under the title *Pensées*.

But in the immediate wake of *Les Provinciales* the most pressing challenge for Pascal remained the defense of the Jansenist party in France. To this end he bent every effort, both in public and in private. The twists and turns meanwhile among the vested interests left the affair in a demimonde of uncertainty. The various synods of the French secular clergy, local and national, maintained their overall hostility toward the theories of Jansenius, but, at the same time, they routinely denounced the perversions of unbridled probabilism. The Jesuits, with Father Annat as their chief spokesman, kept up the by now accustomed drumbeat: "Fifteen times," Annat wrote after the appearance of Pascal's fifteenth *lettre*, "we have repeated what is undeniable, that the Jansenists are heretics" and crypto-Calvinists. Cardinal Mazarin, anxious to secure his credentials as a statesman worthy of a successor of Richelieu, was distracted from domestic concerns, including the Jansenist imbroglio, by the negotiations to end advantageously the long war with Spain, a triumph he achieved with the treaty of the Pyrenees in 1659. Complicating the first minister's preoccupations was the emergence of the young king — Louis XIV had now come technically into his majority — who assumed, for whatever reason, an overtly antagonistic stance toward the Jansenists, perhaps simply as a way to assert his independence from the equivocal Mazarin.

In October 1656, Alexander VII had signed a bull, titled *Ad sanctam*, explicitly repeating the earlier papal condemnation of the five propositions as they were found in *Augustinus*, thus quashing once again Antoine Arnauld's distinction between *fait* and *droit*. But this pope was no more eager than his predecessors had been to involve himself directly in the French doctrinal quarrels, and for some months *Ad sanctam* was allowed to rest in official obscurity. Then, the following spring, convinced by his advisers that the prestige of his office was at stake, Alexander pressed for the formal acceptance of the bull by the relevant authorities in France. Louis XIV agreed, as did a national Assembly of the Clergy and, after some hesitation, the doctors of the Sorbonne. Once more a formulary was prepared, this one, significantly, to be signed by nuns as well as by male religious. These negative decisions strongly intimated that the pro-Jansenist reaction to the miracle of the Holy Thorn had already begun to wane.

But besides the king and the aggregate of the French clergy and the theological faculty of the University of Paris, there was another corporate body that needed to be appeased before a condemnatory edict of the kind Pope Alexander proposed could take effect. The *Parlement* of Paris enjoyed uniquely the right to "register" and thus give validity to any Roman decree. If the *parlementaires* could be persuaded that the pope's intervention contravened the traditional liberties of the Gallican Church, then *Ad sanctam* would be a dead letter. On this ground the Jansenists chose to make their stand. Their major weapon, yet again, was the printing press. Among the spate of publications they produced, the most notable was the *Lettre d'un avocat au Parlement* (Letter to a member of the *Parlement*, June 1, 1657), written by Antoine LeMaître with Pascal's collaboration, which argued that registration of *Ad sanctam* would be tantamount to admitting a foreign jurisdiction into France. The strategy proved successful, at least to the extent that it helped to ward off for four years the harsh measures against the Jansenists taking shape in the king's mind. The *Parlement* duly "recorded" the bull, but it refused for the time being to sanction the formal subscription to its contents called for by the Assembly of the clergy.

Then, in December 1657, the Society of Jesus committed a serious blunder. It allowed one of its number — an anonymous professor of canon law — to publish an *Apologie pour les Casuistes contre les calomnies des Jansenistes* (Apology for the casuists against Jansenist calumnies), which, by attempting to justify even the most absurd uses of probabilism, managed merely to confirm Pascal's harshest charges in the *Provincial Letters*. The *Apologie* occasioned a great commotion, especially among the parish priests, who in their local synods in Paris, Rouen, and elsewhere demanded that the *Parlement* and the Sorbonne condemn the offensive book. The *curés* of Paris, not unreasonably, requested assistance in stating their case from the gentlemen of Port-Royal who had been the primary targets of the Jesuit diatribe; they were only too happy to oblige.

Blaise Pascal wrote three of the five pamphlets published in the name of the Parisian clergy. The first of them appeared on January 25, 1658. It began with a clarion call: "Our cause is the cause of Christian morality. Our adversaries are the casuists who corrupt that morality. The interest we defend is that of the consciences of the faithful who are in our charge; and the reason we speak out now with more vigor than ever against this lying system is because the impudence of the casuists grows more every day, and now [in the *Apologie*] has reached its ultimate excess." Father Escobar and his associates were once more hauled before the bar and excoriated not only for their immoral doctrine but also for their endless and mendacious intrigue.

> We are therefore under strict obligation to speak up in this controversy, and all the more so because the authors of this *Apologie* are bent upon destroying our ministry. This book is nothing but a vicious slander against the parish priests of Paris and the provinces who have opposed these disorders. *Voilà* this seditious and schismatic enterprise, behold the zenith of insolence to which the Jesuits have elevated their casuists; after having abused the moderation of the ministers of the Church in order to interject their odious opinions, now they reveal themselves ready to drive out anyone who refuses to consent to their scandalous teaching.

The Jesuits of course responded in kind, thus provoking Pascal to publish a *Second écrit des curés de Paris*, which, it was said, he composed in a single day of frenzied writing (April 2, 1658). The message was as bitter and relentless as ever.

> We see the most powerful and numerous religious order in the Church, men who direct the consciences of almost all the great people in the land — we see them leagued together in their madness to defend the most horrible maxims that have ever wounded the Church. We see them, despite all the charitable admonitions given them in public and in private, doggedly authorizing revenge, greed, sexual licence, false honor, self-love, and all the passions of corrupt nature, the profanation of the sacraments, the degradation of the ministers of the Church, and scorn for the ancient Fathers in order to substitute for them their own ignorant and deluded authors. And seeing before our eyes this flood of corruption about to submerge the Church, we make bold to cry out to our leaders, as the apostles did to Jesus in the midst of the storm on the sea, "Save us, or we shall perish."

One cannot but wonder, in retrospect, whether the literate French public, by the late spring of 1658, had begun to grow weary of this seemingly interminable quarrel, of these scathing denunciations and counter-denunciations. If not, it may have been due simply to the allure and sheer power of Pascal's prose, which no Jesuit could match (and to which no translation can do justice). Marguerite Périer at any rate claimed that her uncle believed his final contribution to this series — the *Cinquième écrit des curés de Paris,* June 11, 1658 — "was the most beautiful thing he had ever written." However that may be, Pascal ventured into new controversial waters with this little tract, touching for the first time upon the political aspect of the religious dispute.

The Calvinists, "these enemies of our faith who have separated themselves from the Roman Church" and have set up a state within a state, have justified their schism by pointing to the wickedness of the Jesuits. "These heretics have for years tried with all their might to impute to the Church the abominations of the corrupt casuists. Reflect upon the position in which the Jesuits have placed the Church": instead of letting "her holiness shine forth with such éclat that she inspires all peoples with veneration and love, they have made her the scorn and the horror of heretics. Well might the Church say to the Jesuit fathers what the Patriarch Jacob said to his cruel sons: 'You have rendered me hateful among the peoples who live around us.'"

> The Jesuits are guilty of these evils, and there are only two ways to remedy the situation: either the reform of the Society or the disgrace of the Society. Please God that they will choose the first alternative! If they do, we will be the first to make their change of heart so well known that all the world will be edified. But so long as they obstinately bring shame and scandal upon the Church, no other course remains for us except to publicize this so widely that no one will misunderstand it. In that case the Church would despair of efforts to cure them, and instead see to it that the faithful be no longer seduced and that heretics be no further estranged and that all be able to find salvation along the road marked out by the gospel.

A year later the gentlemen of Port-Royal could savor the news that the *Apologie pour les Casuistes* — its author now revealed as a Jesuit named Pirot — had not only been censured locally but had also been placed on the Roman index of prohibited books. Their satisfaction was tempered, however, when they learned that the pope, in a gesture of even-handedness, had ordered the *Provincial Letters* put on the same list.

Antoine Arnauld's famous distinction between *fait* and *droit* was central to the Jansenist controversies that dominated the religious life of France during the last half of the seventeenth century and beyond. It afforded comfort and refuge of sorts to those determined to cling to their understanding of St. Augustine's teachings while clinging at the same time and just as fiercely to their status as Roman Catholics in good standing. For Blaise Pascal the distinction grew ever more important as the papal reprimands of the Jansenist position continued to mount. He stressed it at the very beginning of *Les Provinciales*, and it remained at the heart of his polemic. It was inconceivable to him that the divinely established Church and her head should reject her greatest doctor in favor of a gaggle of contemporary Jesuits. *Droit* was one thing, but *fait* was something quite different. The pope was simply mistaken in condemning *Augustinus* as a matter of fact, because he had been misinformed. And when it came to determining questions of fact, Innocent X or Alexander VII was no more infallible than any Jean or Marie one might meet on the rue des Francs-Bourgeois. Typical of his equanimity was his reaction to the news that Pope Alexander's *Ad sanctam* of October 1656 had insisted once again that the five condemned propositions could indeed be found in *Augustinus*.

> I praise with all my heart [he wrote a disheartened Charlotte de Roannez] even the scanty zeal for union with the Pope that I discern in your letter. The body is not alive without its head, nor the head without its body. Whoever separates himself from the one or the other belongs no longer to the body and hence no longer to Jesus Christ. I know of no persons in the Church who are more attached to this unity than are those whom you call our intimates. We know that all the virtues, martyrdom, austerities, and all good works are useless outside the Church and outside communion with the head of the Church, who is the Pope. I will never separate myself from his communion, or rather I pray God to keep me in it; without it I would perish forever.

Yet another distinction, more practical than theoretical and hence less capable of succinct expression, also played a role as the contest unfolded. Public opinion, clerical and lay, remained by and large unsympathetic to the Jansenist theories about grace and freedom, to the degree, at least, that these abstruse ideas were understood. They smacked too much of Calvinist determinism and repudiated too baldly the humanism that most educated French men and women had absorbed with their mothers' milk. The repeated censures leveled by the clerical assemblies and the Sorbonne at *Augustinus* and the other publications that endorsed it tend to confirm this contention.

But at the same time the lifestyle adopted by the votaries of Port-Royal won the grudging respect even of those among the élites who had no intention of embracing such rigidities themselves. The social prominence of the members of the Jansenist party — and the sheer talent they consistently displayed — served to highlight a moral ascendancy that gained them a hearing when they raised a cry against laxity. This was especially the case when that cry was directed principally at the Jesuits, who were unpopular on other grounds. The importance of the *Provincial Letters* in this respect can hardly be overstated. The ambivalent result was that the same authoritative bodies that routinely condemned *Augustinus* condemned the *Apologie pour les Casuistes* as well. Obviously the correlation between Port-Royal's understanding of St. Augustine's teaching on grace and its uncompromising moral code was not apparent to everybody.

This was the sort of intellectual inconsistency that bothered the likes of Blaise Pascal. He knew that the dramatic success of *Les Provinciales* had itself rested upon a certain double standard. The first three *lettres* had simply poked fun at the academic dispute over grace and freedom without seriously confronting the complex problems involved, while in the last two he had attempted to address that issue, but, anxious as he had been to defend his own integrity, he had achieved only middling effectiveness. The real triumph he had scored in the controversial arena had resulted from his assault on the Jesuit casuists in *lettres* four through sixteen. Yet for him, if not for the public at large, the conclusion was obvious — namely, that laxist Jesuit confessors were precisely that because they repudiated St. Augustine's notion of efficacious grace in favor of Molina's sufficient grace. It was obvious to the author of the *Provincial Letters,* because he, a non-specialist, accepted the assurance of the Jansenist experts that the matter had been satisfactorily established in the dense pages of *Augustinus.*

Yet the agile mind of Blaise Pascal was not one to remain satisfied for long with borrowed information about so crucial a subject. Not that he rejected the instruction of Antoine Arnauld and Nicole; but as both a man of science and a man of faith he needed to explore for himself the tangled question of grace and free will, needed to work through all its implications as they affected the Christian dispensation and, not less, himself personally. So sometime after the completion of the *Provincial Letters* and the various *écrits* in behalf of the Parisian clergy — or, perhaps more likely, simultaneously with those polemics — he began to sort out the parameters of the problem and to propose a solution to it. As in so many other instances, he left this task unfinished, and it has survived as a draft in four parts, running to about a hundred pages of small print. These *Écrits sur la grace* are analytical in character and thus lack the sparkle and rhetorical flourishes that marked the controversies with the Jesuits; indeed, they appear almost conciliatory in comparison.

The opening lines of the first *écrit* are suggestive of a somewhat

161

dry scholastic disputation. "It is an established fact," Pascal wrote, "that some men are damned and some are saved. It is also an established fact that those who are saved have willed this to be so, and that God also has willed it, or else it would not have occurred. But the question remains as to which of these two wills, the will of God or that of the human being, is the mistress, the governor, the source, the principle, and the cause of the other."

Three possible answers have presented themselves. The Calvinists maintain that "God has created some men in order to save them and others in order to damn them, by an absolute act of his will and without any consideration of merit." Their distorted notion of divine justice leads the Calvinists further to conclude "that God not only permitted Adam's original sin but caused it," and that "he sent Jesus Christ into the world to redeem only those whom he predestined to save when creating them in the first place," while "abandoning and depriving of his love" everyone else. "*Voilà* the horrible opinion of these heretics, injurious to God and insupportable to humankind."

Out of revulsion toward "this abominable theory," the Molinists have adopted another "that is not simply opposed, which would have been appropriate, but is entirely contrary to it." According to their view — a reprise of the Pelagian heresy of old — God has willed conditionally to save all men. In order to effect this end, Jesus Christ was incarnated so that he could buy back every human being without exception. Grace therefore has been given to all, and God, "having foreseen from all eternity the good or bad use to which people put the aid given them, saves those who employ it well and condemns those who employ it ill." So it is that while the Calvinists eliminate ordinary human choice from the process, "the Molinists flatter it, by attributing to it ultimate responsibility of the individual's salvation or damnation." No room has been left in the Molinist scheme for the operation of God's absolute and omnipotent will, which renders it "a delusion contrary" to that of the Calvinists, but no less a delusion.

In a dialectical maneuver reminiscent of his analysis of the contrasting moral appraisals of Epictetus and Montaigne — in the *entretien* with Father de Saci — Pascal argued that in this case, too, "the disciples of St. Augustine" avoided these concomitant errors by seizing the middle ground. The fundamental distinction he drew, far from being novel, was the standard fare offered years before by Jansenius and

Saint-Cyran: "In the state of pristine innocence God could not justly condemn any human being, nor deny anyone the grace necessary for salvation. But in the state of corruption" — after Adam's sin in which all humankind was implicated — "God could with justice damn the whole race, and those born today, unless they have been snatched back from the abyss by the sacrament of baptism, are eternally condemned and deprived of the beatific vision, which must be adjudged the greatest possible unhappiness."

In the former of these states, God, "by his general and conditional will," mapped out the salvation of all men and women and granted to them "sufficient" grace to bring this happy outcome about. Note the words "conditional" and "sufficient" in this context. Adam's bad conduct was not divinely predetermined (as the Calvinists would have it), but his sinful decision to rebel against the beneficent God "has infected and corrupted the whole human race, so that it has become the object of divine wrath and retribution." Therefore, no individual man or woman can claim exemption from "universal culpability; everybody is worthy of damnation," not only because of his own sins but also because of his incorporation into the radically corrupt legacy imposed upon him by his first parents. Yet a portion of degenerate humankind "God has chosen to save by his absolute will" — a truth obstinately denied by the Molinists — "grounded wholly in his own gratuitous mercy"; for the others, they have been left in the unhappy moral predicament in which Adam's original sin, as well as their own, has placed them. The mission of Jesus Christ into the world, therefore, "has been to save that segment of humanity which God, by his absolute and omnipotent decision, and by the most efficacious means, has chosen — those, that is, whom he has predestined to merit by Christ's salvific death, in contradistinction to those whom he has left to the perdition that everybody deserves."

It was by playing off "absolute" against "conditional" and "sufficient" against "efficacious" that Pascal arrived at his conclusion, which was quite in tune with the lessons taught him by his Jansenist mentors. What sufficed in the state of primitive innocence, when God conditionally willed the salvation of all men and women, did not suffice once the human race, poisoned by sin, could be effectively rescued from its pollution only by God's absolute will to intervene through the earthly vocation of Jesus Christ. Those whom in his mercy he has chosen to save received aid or grace "efficacious" enough to persevere in virtue; but those not among the elect were given either no grace at all or only "sufficient" grace, which put them into the same perilous standing as the sinless Adam and Eve — indeed, even more perilous since now God's "absolute" choice had become the prime factor.

> Human beings therefore can be ranked into three categories. First are those who never had the faith. Second are those who are indeed blessed with the faith, but, not persevering, die in mortal sin. The third are those who embrace the faith and sustain it in charity till death.
>
> Jesus Christ obviously did not have an absolute will that the members of the first group should receive any grace through his sacrificial death, from the simple fact that they did not receive any.
>
> As to those in the second category, Christ has willed conditionally to redeem them and has afforded them some aid, which would have led them to salvation had they used it properly; but he did not choose to give them the singular grace of perseverence, without which all the rest is futile.
>
> Finally, Christ has willed absolutely the salvation of the individuals comprising the third group, and he has conducted them to it by certain and infallible means.

With this classification Pascal answered the question with which he had begun his inquiry: human choice plays a qualified part in the economy of salvation, but the divine will assumes full sovereignty, because, unless impelled by the "singular" and "efficacious" force exercised by the Creator, the creature's will remains ultimately impotent. Yet one might legitimately wonder what scope for human freedom was left in such disproportion, in such strain put upon apparently simple terms like "absolute" and "sufficient." It is difficult, in other words, to see how, given the final verdict, the *Écrits sur la grace* have awarded anything more than a nominal role in the moral sphere to free choice, and difficult therefore to see how the Jansenist view differed in substance from an extreme version of Calvinist predestination. Its harshness in any case needs no comment. Nor was this mitigated by Pascal's insistence that all Christians must believe that they belong to the elect minority, but without certainty and in fear and trembling, and that they must not presume to consign anybody, however seemingly wicked, to perdition, because such a determination was an impenetrable mystery known only to God himself. The unvarnished assertion of this grim theory possessed at least one virtue: it helped to explain the unrelenting austerities of Port-Royal, whose denizens kept ever before their eyes the gospel's warning, "Many are called, but few are chosen."

Pascal contended that the Calvinist error could be, and indeed had been, refuted by arguments from reason. The Molinists, on the other hand, had to be confronted on the ground of the traditional teaching of the Church, and to this task he devoted most of the remainder of the *Écrits sur la grace,* testing his ideas by the standards he discerned in Scripture and in the writings of selected Church Fathers and scholastic doctors. He paid special attention to the decrees and canons of the Council of Trent. Predictably his scholarship was impressive, and, if his first principles were granted, his reasoning was impeccable. At the end of the exercise he expressed satisfaction that he had in fact unravelled a perplexing dilemma. "We learn," he wrote, "from such pure doctrine how to defend both the power of nature against the Protestants and the powerlessness of nature against the Molinists; the efficacy of grace against the Protestants and the necessity of grace against the Molinists, without destroying free will with grace as the Protestants do, and without destroying grace with free will as the Molinists do."

Pascal's was a curious confidence. Of the three classes of persons he distinguished, two of them had no chance to see God face-to-face, despite the death and resurrection of Christ. And yet the fifth of the five condemned propositions — which Pascal agreed deserved condemnation — read, "To say that Christ died and shed his blood for all mankind is a Semi-Pelagian doctrine." The Council of Trent had decreed that the process of justification depended upon both the grace of God and free human choice, without, however, attempting to define the precise relationship between the two. Given the controversies that raged throughout the sixteenth and seventeenth centuries among and between the Protestant and Catholic camps, the conciliar diffidence in the face of this mystery seems to have been warranted.

165

9 "May God Never Abandon Me"

IN THE SPRING of 1658, thirty-five-year-old Blaise Pascal was at the height of his powers. The illnesses that had afflicted him since childhood remained for the time being in relative remission. The Jansenist cause he had made his own, if it had not triumphed, had secured at least a measure of toleration, thanks in large part to his own efforts. He had witnessed that cause validated by the miraculous cure of his own beloved niece: "When there are parties in dispute within the same Church," he wrote confidently, "miracles are decisive." Yet, partisan though he had become, he had maintained his independence and had followed his own genius, as the brilliant polemic he had invented for the *Provincial Letters* amply proved. And if, in his religious enthusiasm, he no longer prized to the degree he once had his long-established fame as a scientist, it never occurred to him that his capacities in this regard had in any way diminished.

Indeed, Pascal's fertile mind at this moment was brimming over with projects, one of which, however, had taken precedence. In April 1658, he delivered the first of probably several lectures to his friends at Port-Royal des Champs — or rather not so much lectures in the formal sense as learned conversations or conferences, in which he outlined for a sympathetic audience his plans to compose a definitive *apologie* for

166

the Christian religion. Even at this early and tentative stage of his enterprise Pascal made it clear that his would be no conventional defense of religious belief, going over the same old ground in the same old way. Savants who gloried in abstractions — Pascal's contemporary, René Descartes, no less than the scholastic doctors — would find scarce comfort in this *apologie*. "The metaphysical proofs for the existence of God," he said, "are so remote from human reasoning and so involved that they make little impact, and, even if they did help some people, it would only be for the moment during which they watched the demonstration, because an hour later they would be afraid they had made a mistake." He quoted St. Augustine, that shrewd observer of both the human and the divine, to the effect that whatever satisfaction such arguments afforded a person's curiosity was swiftly vitiated by the resultant pride. "Whereas," added Pascal, "those who have known God through a mediator know their own wretchedness." And here, in this latter insight, was the key starting place for a new and vibrant apologetics.

> Man's greatness and wretchedness [he told *les messieurs de Port-Royal*] are so evident that the true religion must necessarily teach us that there is in man some great principle of greatness and some great principle of wretchedness.
>
> It must also account for such amazing contradictions.
>
> To make man happy it must show him that a God exists whom we are bound to love; that our true bliss is to be in him, and our sole ill to be cut off from him. It must acknowledge that we are full of darkness, which prevents us from knowing and loving him, and so, with our duty obliging us to love God and our concupiscence leading us astray, we are full of unrighteousness. It must account to us for the way in which we thus go against God and our own good. It must teach us the cure for our helplessness and the means of obtaining this cure. Let us examine all the religions of the world on that point, and let us see whether any but the Christian religion meets it.

It should not be thought that this first public statement of the thesis of what was destined to be published innumerable times under the title *Pensées de M. Pascal sur la religion et sur quelques autres sujets qui ont été trouvées après sa mort parmi ses papiers* (The thoughts of Monsieur Pascal about religion and about other matters, which were discovered among his papers after he died) represented a new departure for its author. The idea for such a project had been germinating within for a considerable period; for how long it is impossible to say, though it would not be unreasonable to suppose that it had begun to take root in the wake of the fiery conversion of November 1654, when Pascal had suddenly discerned the reality of the God, not of the "savants," but of "Abraham and Isaac and Jacob, and of Jesus Christ." He had at any rate settled into a definite and rather prosaic methodology some time before the presentation at Port-Royal. He wrote down his thoughts and observations — his *pensées* — on full-sized sheets of paper. Some of these reflections occupied an entire page or several pages, while others were exceedingly brief — often no more than a sentence or a suggestive phrase. These short and frequently obscure scribblings were then carefully cut with a scissors from the sheet on which they had been written and preserved for later elaboration. When he spoke to the gentlemen of Port-Royal in the spring of 1658, Pascal had already begun to arrange the bits and pieces into distinct classifications. He passed a needle and thread through the corners of the written notes related in some way to each other and thus bound them into separate dossiers. By the end of the year, when his renewed illnesses prevented him from completing this design, he had put together 382 entries into twenty-seven bundles of papers, with titles like "Order," "Vanity," "Causes and Effects," "Nature Is Corrupt," "Proofs of Jesus Christ," "Christian Morality."

A genuinely persuasive apologetics had to confront a problem in epistemology: what can the human person know with any certainty about God and God's revelation? Pascal dealt with this issue bearing in mind, predictably, both the rigor and the limitations imposed by mathematics. In a short tract, written contemporaneously with the *Pensées* but, like them, unpublished until several years after his death, he had argued that nothing could be nobler in the mind than the pure reasoning of the geometrician. But in this *De l'esprit géométrique et de l'art de persuader* (The geometric spirit and the art of persuasion) he had also insisted that fundamental principles of thought — *mots primitifs*, as he called them — from which all reasoning has its inception, remained always undemonstrable. Intuitions about space, time, motion, and — specially significant for Pascal — the double infinity of largeness and littleness, in the midst of which the creature struggled in vain to find the center or the circumference, were rooted in "the heart." This conviction led him ultimately to frame the most frequently quoted, and the most frequently misunderstood, of all the aphorisms in the *Pensées:* "The heart has its reasons of which reason knows nothing." Here was an assertion, not of some emotional drive independent of and superior to rationality, but of the mysterious presence in every human being of an experiential faculty competent to furnish those first principles from which all reasoning necessarily derives. And so, Pascal concluded, "it is the heart that perceives God, and not the reason. That is what faith is: God perceived by the heart, not by the reason."

The locale Pascal first chose to explain his theories should come as no surprise. Stubbornly as he maintained that he "did not belong to Port-Royal," he had nevertheless forged close bonds with *les messieurs des granges,* with Antoine Arnauld, Nicole, LeMaître, and the others, and, by extension, with Mère Angélique Arnauld and her nuns down in the valley from the Barns and in Paris. So completely had he adopted their pessimistic view of the human condition that it could make him waspish even when dealing with those dearest to him. When, for example, Florin and Gilberte Périer proposed to arrange a rich marriage for one of their daughters, Blaise reacted harshly, asserting that "marriage was the most dangerous and the lowest of the conditions of life allowed a Christian." The same uncompromising estimation undergirded every aspect of his proposed apologetic. "It is untrue," he protested, "that we are worthy to be loved by others. It is unfair that we should think such a thing. The will is depraved. No religion except our own has taught that man is born sinful, no philosophical sect has said so, so none has told the truth." "How hollow and foul is the heart of man!" he cried. There stands no escape from perdition save the one Saint-Cyran had proclaimed years before to a cynical world: "It is clearly evident," as Pascal expressed it, "that man through grace is made like unto God and shares his divinity, and without grace he is treated like the beasts of the field."

Other, more mundane considerations also link the genesis of the *Pensées* to Port-Royal des Champs. Pascal had shown a particular interest in the functioning of LeMaître's *petites écoles,* having previously devised an ingenious method of teaching the boys to read. More recently he had prepared a similar technique for the young pupils who aspired to learn mathematics. This task had perhaps occasioned him to compose the little essay on *l'esprit géométrique*. At about the same time, Antoine Arnauld had been consulting his colleagues, including Pascal, about the manual in logic he was preparing, one which, under the title *La logique de Port-Royal,* was to exert substantial influence in that discipline over the next two centuries. Arnauld could have taken little consolation, however, in Pascal's contention, as part of his scrutiny of *l'art de persuader,* that conventional logic enjoyed only modest standing in the field of argumentation when compared to mathematics.

But these various preoccupations may well have served Pascal another purpose, an occasion for him to think through the ramifications of a distinction crucial for an understanding of his mature thought, that between the *esprit de géométrie* and the *esprit de finesse,* "between the mathematical and the intuitive mind."

> There are two kinds of mind. One goes rapidly and deeply into the conclusions from principles, and this is the accurate mind. The other can grasp a large number of principles and keep them distinct, and this is the mathematical mind. The first is a powerful and precise mind, the second shows breadth of mind. Now it is quite possible to have one without the other, for a mind can be powerful and narrow, as well as broad and weak.

However carefully thought through, however, Pascal's annoyingly inconsistent use of terminology left the door open to confusion. Did he mean "accurate mind *(esprit de justesse)*" to be equivalent to "intuitive"? It would seem so.

> In the [mathematical mind], the principles are obvious, but remote from ordinary usage, so that from want of practice we have difficulty turning our heads that way; but once we do turn our heads the principles can be fully seen; and it would take a thoroughly unsound mind to draw false conclusions from principles so patent that they can hardly be missed.
>
> But, with the intuitive mind, the principles are in ordinary usage and there for all to see. The principles [however] are so intricate and numerous that it is almost impossible not to miss some. Now the omission of one principle can lead to error, and so one needs very clear sight to see all the principles as well as

an accurate mind to avoid drawing false conclusions from known principles.

Mathematicians who are merely mathematicians therefore reason soundly as long as everything is explained to them by definitions and principles. And intuitive minds that are merely intuitive lack the patience to go right into first principles of speculative and imaginative matters which they have never seen in practice and are quite outside ordinary experience.

Pascal's conclusion, despite the imprecise use of terms, seems clear enough: one who would seek the truth must do so aware of the pitfalls that an exclusively mathematical or intuitive propensity inexorably leads to. "Judgment," he maintained, "is what goes with instinct, just as knowledge goes with the mind. Intuition falls to the lot of judgment, mathematics to that of the mind."

Some months after his presentation at Port-Royal des Champs, during the late summer of 1658, Blaise Pascal was focusing his mind once again upon a purely scientific problem. Not that he ceased gathering materials for his *apologie* and reflecting upon them; rather, this continuing activity coincided with a final foray into the mathematical thickets. The venture, coincidentally, marked the beginning of the progressive breakdown of his health that would bring about his premature death four years later. Both his elder sister and his niece recalled the circumstances vividly. "The renewal of my brother's ailments," wrote Gilberte Périer, "began with a toothache that deprived him of all sleep." In order to distract himself from tormenting insomnia he tried to concentrate on a mathematical puzzle much discussed since Galileo's time, that of the cycloid or, in the parlance of seventeenth-century France, *la roulette*. "The first thought he entertained about this was quickly followed by a second, and then by a third, and then by a host of considerations, one after another, which," said Gilberte, "uncovered for my brother, in spite of himself and even to his surprise, the true nature of this mysterious geometric figure." That may indeed have been an overstatement — one contemporary critic, while praising the "subtlety of this work" and the willingness it showed to tackle "the most difficult problems," nevertheless protested that Pascal employed "a method a little too audacious to conform properly to mathematical exactitude." However that may be,

171

certainly Pascal's investigation into the curve delineated by a point on the circumference of a circle seen as moving over a flat surface proved to be, when elaborated by later thinkers, a genuine contribution to the development of integral calculus. This accomplishment, however, meant less to Gilberte than did the fact that the inquiry at hand appeared to have relieved, at least for the moment, his *mal de dent*.

At first Pascal did not intend to publish the results of his nocturnal musings on this recondite subject. But, as Marguerite, Gilberte Périer's daughter, remembered these events, "the duc de Roannez, having called upon my uncle one morning during this time, was pleased to find his friend was feeling somewhat better," the result, it seemed, of his fruitful research into the questions posed by *la roulette*. The duc, however, was troubled by Pascal's intention to allow his opinions on this topic to remain unrecorded. Let the world understand now, said Roannez in rebuttal, that the same person who has shown himself capable of the most astute examination of these abstract riddles is also one who has given himself to Jesus Christ without conditions. "Monsieur de Roannez argued that there was a better use than a merely scientific one to make of such a discovery, that in accord with my uncle's plan to refute unbelievers it would be more than useful to show them that at the same time he knew more than anybody else about geometry and indeed about the whole subject of inferential demonstration."

Pascal not only adopted Roannez's recommendation — publication of his views about the cycloid, more than a hundred pages in French and Latin, occurred in October and again in December of 1658 — but he also issued a challenge to other researchers across Western Europe to submit their own solutions to the mathematical problems involved. A monetary reward, he announced with some fanfare, would be given to anybody who arrived at a solution more acceptable than his own. A panel of six savants would decide the issue. This rather bizarre invitation was taken up by only two other scholars — not including Christopher Wren, the architect of St. Paul's in London, who declined to participate — neither of whom satisifed the panel sufficiently to win the prize. Perhaps this negative judgment was not surprising, since Pascal had appointed the jury. At any rate the competition, such as it was, said as much about Pascal's own confidence in himself as it did about the status of contemporary mathematical studies.

And, having gone quite beyond what the duc de Roannez had urged, it testified also to Pascal's lingering ambition to enhance his reputation among the intelligentsia. No wonder the purists of Port-Royal continued to regard him with some suspicion.

Sixteen fifty-eight was a year of prodigious activity for Blaise Pascal. But the toothache that had prompted him to seek out the secrets of the cycloid proved a harbinger of unpleasant things to come. By the beginning of the following year much of the debility that had formerly afflicted him was stalking him once again. The old digestive troubles returned, as did the brutal headaches — migraine perhaps — with their attendant woes of nausea and blurred vision. And returned also were the vile medicines and clumsy therapies he had endured earlier, no more effective now than before. In February and March of 1659 alarmed friends were warning each other of Pascal's rapidly deteriorating condition, of the utter exhaustion that left him so bereft of energy he was scarcely able to hold a pen in his hand, of the languor into which he had fallen for which the physicians prescribed a diet of hearty soups and ass's milk. Such was the life he led — "if," as Gilberte Périer sadly put it, "one can call the pitiable state in which he passed his last years truly a life."

But Gilberte did not waver in her conviction that, though her brother's increasing infirmities "rendered him incapable of serving others, they were not without their usefulness for him. The great patience with which he suffered them led him to embrace the consoling thought that they were God's way of preparing him for the beatific vision." That this sentiment represented far more than merely a pietistic recollection is confirmed by Gilberte's immediate reference to Blaise's *Priere pour demander à Dieu le bon usage des maladies* (A prayer to ask God to make good use of sickness), which was composed during these dark latter years. And indeed this long prayer, this *cri de coeur,* breathes a deeply moving sincerity and poignancy.

> Lord, whose spirit is so good and so sweet in all things, and who are so merciful that not only the blessings but also the misfortunes that come upon your elect are the fruit of your mercy, grant me the grace not to question as a heathen might the state to which your justice has reduced me. You gave me health so that I might serve you, and I made a wholly profane use of it. Now you send

me sickness in order to correct me; do not allow me to use this as an excuse to irritate you by my impatience. I have used my health badly, and you have justly punished me for it; do not allow that I use badly now your punishment. And since the corruption of my nature is so profound that it spoils even your favors, see to it, oh my God, that your all-powerful grace makes your chastisements salutary for me. See to it, oh my God, that I worship in silence your adorable providence upon the conduct of my life; that your scourges console me; and that, having lived undisturbed in the bitterness of my sins, I taste the heavenly sweetness of your grace during the beneficial illnesses with which you have afflicted me.

It would seem that when Madame Périer spoke of her brother's incapability "of serving others" she had in mind principally his intellectual work, and this, with a few notable exceptions, was the case. But in other respects these years of acute suffering seemed, if anything, to heighten Pascal's sympathy for others who suffered. Not only did he contribute lavishly to charitable enterprises in Paris and in provincial centers he was familiar with, like Clermont and Blois; he also, to the extent he was able, followed the example of Vincent de Paul and visited the sick and the poor who dwelt in the hideous Parisian slums. Gilberte recounted how coming home one morning from Mass at Saint-Sulpice Blaise met an orphan girl begging on the street; he conducted her back to the presbytery and gave the priest money to see to her care and to help her secure "'an honorable position'" — all this without revealing his name. At the beginning of 1662, sick now almost unto death, he nevertheless settled a homeless family in his own house on the rue des Francs-Bourgeois.

Yet even as the shadows round Pascal deepened, his restless intelligence continued to probe into the possibility of new undertakings. About the time he turned his home into a hostel for the poor, he conceived the idea of setting up a regular carriage service that would convey passengers from one district in Paris to another for the modest fare of five coppers. Together with the ever-faithful duc de Roannez and a few other friendly shareholders, he formed a company to finance the venture, and the inaugural route, between the Porte Saint-Antoine and the Luxembourg, began operation in March 1662. Pascal meant to devote whatever profits he gained from the *voitures des cinq sols* to charitable purposes, and he ratified this intention in his last will. The system continued to expand after his death, so that it is fair to conclude that Blaise Pascal, besides his pioneer contributions to the advancement of automated computation, conic projection, hydrostatics, and integral calculus, also fostered, in a modest way, the origins of modern mass transport.

And yet, at the end of his life, proud of these accomplishments as he may have been, he consciously measured their value by a standard that must have puzzled his fellow intellectuals. In the summer of 1660, while he was staying with the Périers in Clermont, Pascal received a letter from Pierre de Fermat, the distinguished mathematician with whom he had corresponded on various technical matters over the years. Fermat lived in Toulouse, and he proposed that since Pascal for the moment was relatively nearby, the two should finally meet at some convenient place halfway between the two cities. "Monsieur," Pascal answered on August 10, "you are the most courteous man in the world, and I am certainly one who can recognize your fine qualities and admire them without limit, especially since they are joined to such singular talents." Indeed, "had my health permitted it, I would have flown to Toulouse to visit you, nor would I have allowed a man like you to have gone to the slightest trouble to see a man like me." But, he continued, "I am so weak that I cannot walk without a stick, nor sit a horse, nor even travel by coach more than three or four leagues at a time." The regret Pascal felt at missing this opportunity for a face-to-face meeting was genuine, but the reason he gave for his disappointment may have startled Fermat.

> I tell you that although I consider you the greatest geometrician in Europe, it is not this distinction that attracts me to you, but I would have sought out rather the spirit of integrity [*honnêteté*] that I am confident would have imbued your conversation. For to speak frankly about geometry, I find it the highest exercise of the mind; but at the same time I know that it is so useless that I discern little difference between one who is only a geometrician and one who is an able artisan. So I call geometry the most beautiful craft in the world, but in the end it is only a craft. I have often said that it is good to do the research, but that it cannot preoccupy our

175

energies. Thus you can see that I would not take two steps to meet you for geometry's sake, and I trust you would humor me in this regard. And anyway I am now involved in studies so far removed from mathematics that I can hardly remember what that subject is all about.

After uttering this pardonable hyperbole, Pascal concluded his reply to Fermat with a less pardonable flourish of flattery and a description of his schedule for the balance of the year. He would depart Clermont in three weeks time, he said, for Bourbon, where he would spend the month of September taking the curative waters. From there he would go by riverboat to Saumur and stay till Christmas with "the governor of Poitu, the duc de Roannez, who entertains sentiments of me of which I am unworthy." Then, after the feast, he would proceed up the Loire from Saumur to Orléans and by easy stages back to Paris. "*Voilà*, Monsieur, the pattern of my present life, of which I am obliged to give you a full account, in order to assure you of the impossibility of accepting the honor you have deigned to offer me, you, the first man of the world."

There survives no evidence of whether or not these last months of 1660 alleviated any of Blaise Pascal's illnesses or strengthened his inner resources. It would have been well had it been so, for his last great battle was at hand.

The Paris to which Pascal returned in January 1661 was anxiously awaiting the news of the death of Jules Cardinal Mazarin. That wily statesman had few friends among the elite classes, but he had earned their grudging respect as one who had proved a worthy successor of Richelieu by outmaneuvering the great nobles and the *parlementaires* during the successive crises of the Fronde, and by judiciously employing diplomacy and military force to elevate France to a position of unprecedented ascendancy in Europe. The cardinal had in effect destroyed the last traces of medieval localism, a boon for which the young king, whom he had tutored in statecraft, had reason to be grateful. But Louis XIV had also grown impatient to take the full direction of affairs into his own hands. To a degree, as the cardinal lay dying at Vincennes, he had already done so by putting to rest the burning question of who would succeed Mazarin as first minister. He would assume that responsibility himself, he proclaimed, and, once Mazarin died early in March, so he did for more than half a century. Advisers aplenty would in following years leave their mark upon the autocratic regime — most notably that consummate bureaucrat, Jean-Baptiste Colbert — but no subject would wield power as Richelieu and Mazarin had done. From the moment that this circumstance had become plain, the Jansenists had had cause to go about in fear and trembling. As recently as 1657 the teenaged Louis, no doubt under the influence of his pious mother, had expressed his distaste for Port-Royal and all its works and pomps. For an autocrat divinely chosen to guide the religious no less than the secular destiny of his people, as Louis XIV sincerely believed himself to be, any deviation from the accepted norm was an act of *lèse-majesté*.

On December 13, 1660 — while Blaise Pascal was still enjoying the hospitality of the duc de Roannez in Poitu — the king signaled the end of Mazarin's ambiguous ecclesiastical policy. On that day, with the ailing cardinal in attendance, Louis summoned to the Louvre the officers of the Assembly of the Clergy, then meeting in Paris, and told them that his conscience obliged him to bring about the extermination of Jansenism. Mazarin, supple courtier to the last, seconded his master's announcement with an hour-long denunciation of this wicked creed, which, he said, two popes and the overwhelming majority of the French bishops had condemned and which, since mildness had failed to stem its baneful influence, must now be treated with severity.

Implementation of the royal resolve followed swiftly. By February 1, 1661, the Assembly had promulgated a document that once again called for a formula of orthodoxy to be signed by all priests and religious and outlined the sanctions to be directed against those who refused. The king promptly confirmed this legislation in a letter dispatched to every diocese in France. So the dreaded prospect of formal subscription to an explicit repudiation of Jansenius — from which, it may be recalled, the *Parlement* had saved them two years earlier — once more loomed over his disciples. A sign that this time the authorities would brook no compromise came on April 23, when an officer of the court informed the abbess of Port-Royal, Mère Agnès Arnauld, that the community must accept no postulants until further notice and that the seventy *pensionnaires* resident in the two convents had to be sent back to their homes. Among the girls affected by this order were the heroine of the Holy Thorn, Marguerite Périer, and her sister, Pascal's nieces.

Soon afterward another directive closed down LeMaître's *petites écoles*, and still another called for the dismissal of Abbé Singlin as spiritual director of Port-Royal. As though such troubles were not enough, about this time the grand matriarch of the Jansenist movement, Mère Angélique Arnauld, took to her bed for good; she died early in August.

Meanwhile, the Jansenist leaders lobbied desperately to prevent any formulary from proscribing the distinction between *fait* and *droit*. The precise wording was obviously of crucial importance to them. In Paris, whose archbishop was in exile for unrelated reasons, the task of composing the document fell to the vicars general in consultation with their colleagues, the parish priests, most of whom disliked the Society of Jesus and many of whom, though not Jansenists themselves, had had cordial relations with the gentlemen of Port-Royal. Indeed, Pascal had written several anti-Jesuit broadsides in their behalf less than three years previously, and it may have been that he had a hand in preparing the statement they proposed for subscription at the end of May. This document at any rate strove for some accommodation: while it insisted upon "a complete and sincere respect" for the doctrinal censure of the five propositions, and sternly forbade "preaching, writing, or disputing anything in a sense contrary to this assent of faith," it did not explicitly require an admission that the propositions were to be found in *Augustinus*. Antoine Arnauld and Nicole, satisfied that the essential point had been maintained, recommended that their followers sign the formulary. The nuns at Port-Royal de Paris, after secret consultation with Father Singlin, did so on June 22.

The victory, however, was short-lived. The very next day the royal council, responding to widespread complaints and, more meaningfully, to the known wishes of the king, instructed the vicars to suspend circulation of their formulary, and six days after that it ordered a new and more sharply specific one to be drawn up. Early in July Louis XIV requested from the pope a definitive statement quashing the original formulary on the grounds of its vagueness, and Alexander VII, in marked contrast to the papal hesitancies of the past, complied with alacrity. By mid-August his brief had been received by the king, and by October 31, 1661, the Parisian vicars general, after some grumbling about Gallican liberties, had capitulated and issued a new formulary, which, despite the quarrelsome circumstances that had given it birth, displayed considerable restraint and discretion.

I submit myself sincerely to the Constitution of Pope Innocent X of May 31, 1653, according to its genuine meaning, as determined by the Constitution of our Holy Father Pope Alexander VII of October 16, 1656. I recognize that I am obliged in conscience to obey these Constitutions; and I condemn with my heart and my lips the doctrine of the five Propositions of Cornelius Jansenius, as found in his book titled *Augustinus,* which these two Popes and the Bishops have condemned; which doctrine is not that of St. Augustine but only of Jansenius, who has badly understood the true sense of this holy doctor.

This text was read out in the churches on November 20, with the addendum that clergy and religious had fifteen days to subscribe to it.

Blaise Pascal was neither priest nor religious, and so no signature was required of him. But though he stood in no personal danger, the new formulary presented a clear crisis of conscience for him even so. How many of those now to be coerced into publicly abandoning their principles had adopted those principles, or at least had had them reinforced, because of what Pascal had written or argued? To sign meant to disavow Jansenius, not as an obscure Dutchman who had written a thick and unreadable book, but as a prophet who had provided the intellectual grounding that determined how reason and faith could be reconciled, how human wretchedness and human nobility combined to bring about, in Christ, a curious and miraculous harmony. To sign meant to abjure St. Augustine, St. Paul, and their teaching on efficacious grace. To sign meant to surrender to the wickedness of the Jesuits.

But Pascal felt none of these ideological and polemical concerns as keenly as he did the injustice he believed the formulary imposed upon the holy women of Port-Royal. To force their signatures under the threat of shutting down the convents, confiscating their endowments, and dispersing the nuns themselves was tantamount to a demand that they repudiate a conversion process not unlike his own. These sisters claimed no theological expertise; artful argumentation and subtle distinctions were not for them. But by adhering to the values taught them by their venerated master, Saint-Cyran — and hence by Jansenius — they had achieved, in Pascal's judgment, the highest degree of spiritual excellence. They lived, now not they, but Christ lived in them. By the time the Parisian vicars put forward the second formu-

179

lary, Pascal's conviction in this regard had been confirmed by a voice from the grave.

Some months before the controversy over subscription had erupted, Pascal's sister Jacqueline had, under obedience, left Paris and gone into residence at the convent of Port-Royal des Champs, where she served as subprioress and mistress of novices. During the tense days of June 1661, she had resisted signing even the first, relatively innocuous formula, though in the end she did so. But not before she had written a strong protest to Antoine Arnauld, who had urged the sisters to conform, and another to one of the nuns still in Paris. Why should there not be raised a protest against this grotesque proceeding? she asked both of them. Why not at least a little band to assault the barricades of power? "I know the respect that is due to the authorities of the Church. I would gladly die to conserve them, just as I am prepared, with God's help, to die confessing my faith during these present travails. What are we afraid of" — the closing of Port-Royal, the loss of our goods, or of our freedom, or of our lives? "But is such a prospect not our glory, and ought it not to be our joy?" It will never be a question of "raising altar against altar," she maintained; we shall never be schismatics, for "nobody can be cut off from the Church without willing it so: the spirit of Jesus Christ is the bond that unites his members to himself and to each other. But we can rest secure within the simple limits of our sorrow and of the meekness with which we shall accept our persecution. The charity with which we shall embrace our enemies will bind us invincibly to the Church."

There is no doubt that Blaise Pascal knew these sentiments precisely. And there is very little doubt — those who knew her best attested to it in later years — that the ever precarious health of Soeur Jacqueline de Sainte-Euphémie was gravely undermined by the strain that attended this contention. She died, aged thirty-six, on October 4, 1661, and so she was spared confronting the calamity of the second formulary. As far as her inconsolable brother was concerned, she whom he loved better than anyone in all the world had died of a broken heart.

But she guided him still, as the unfolding of events soon made clear. Arnauld and Nicole, after much soul-searching, decided that it was permissible to sign the formulary of October 31. They argued that since the popes and the bishops had in effect upheld the Augustinian doctrine of efficacious grace, the reference in the formulary to Jansenius could be construed as some imagined fault in *Augustinus* rather than as material actually contained in that book. Consequently they drew up a statement intended for the use of the religious of Port-Royal when the formulary was presented to them for signature.

> Considering that in our ignorance of all these matters which are beyond our profession and our sex, all we can do is to render testimony to the purity of our faith, declaring altogether freely by our signature that, being submissive with a very profound respect for our Holy Father the Pope, and having nothing more precious to us than our faith, we sincerely and with our whole heart embrace what His Holiness and Pope Innocent X have decided about these matters, and we reject all the errors which they have judged contrary to the faith.

But to Pascal such a mode of preserving the by now sacred distinction between *fait* and *droit* smacked of the kind of mental reservation he so despised as a jesuitical evasion. Indeed, he wondered aloud whether the distinction itself, which he had so vigorously defended in the last two of the *Provincial Letters,* was worth saving. The discussions between him and his erstwhile collaborators in that venture became increasingly heated and bitter. Gilberte Périer — who had just moved her household from Clermont to Paris — reported that after one such conversation Blaise "was so overcome with sorrow that he felt physically sick and lost the ability to speak or even to understand what was being discussed." Once he had regained something of his composure he said to her: "When I see these persons I regard as those to whom God has made known the truth and who therefore ought to be its defenders ready to go away and surrender, I tell you I am so gripped by sadness that I cannot stand it, and I must surrender to it."

Yet, despite such feelings, Pascal was really not ready to surrender. He set down his thoughts on the subject in a few pages that were circulated under the title *Écrit sur la signature* (Commentary on the signature [required by the formulary]). This little tract was far from his best polemical effort — not surprisingly, perhaps, since it was written even as he entered upon his final illness, and since it was directed not against his enemies but against those mentors who had taught him whatever theology he knew. What it lacked in precision, however, it

181

compensated for by its passion. "The whole question today," he began, "is about these words, 'I condemn the five propositions in the sense of Jansenius,' or 'the doctrine of Jansenius with regard to the five propositions.' It is of capital importance to see in what manner one could subscribe to this view." Indeed it was, but the trouble with this assertion was that Pascal's quotation of the formulary was inaccurate and even tendentious. "I condemn," it read, "the doctrine of the five Propositions of Jansenius, as found in his book titled *Augustinus*, . . . which doctrine is not that of St. Augustine." Thus the statement evidently meant to say that the doctrine of efficacious grace as found in the works of St. Augustine — though different terms for it were used by different theological schools — was entirely orthodox *(droit)*, while Jansenius's understanding of it was not *(fait)*. Arnauld maintained that while this last clause was based on misinformation, such a relatively minor error could be disregarded in respectful silence as one put one's name to the formulary, so long as one also explicitly professed the predominance of the issues of faith. Not so his former pupil nor the loyal duc de Roannez and a few other notables within the party. "It must be grasped first of all," wrote Pascal, "that in truth there is no difference between condemning 'the doctrine of Jansenius with regard to the five Propositions' and condemning efficacious grace, St. Augustine, and St. Paul. It is for this reason that the enemies of efficacious grace strove so hard to have this clause included in the formula."

But, replied Arnauld and Nicole — both of them composed rebuttals to Pascal's harangue — the formulary did not in fact say what Pascal claimed it did. The censure of Jansenius, a simple mistake, did not encompass a repudiation of Augustine or of the crucial difference between efficacious and sufficient grace. Moreover, those who had erred on this point of history, popes and bishops and the doctors of the Sorbonne, were by no means all wicked Molinists, as Pascal seemed to assume. That the teaching of Augustine was allowed, indeed extolled, while Molinism was not mentioned in the formulary, provided, they said, adequate reason to declare victory and save Port-Royal from the vengeful king. Moreover, like the fervent Catholics they indubitably considered themselves to be, these embattled theologians had no stomach for an endless quarrel with the ultimate ecclesiastical authority. But Blaise Pascal had at this moment no such reservations.

The pope and the bishops have taken one side in this dispute, and they insist it is a matter of faith to agree that the five propositions are heretical "in the sense of Jansenius"; Alexander VII has in fact pronounced [in his *Ad sanctam*, October 16, 1656] that, in order to profess the true faith, it is necessary to say that the words and sense of Jansenius express the heretical meaning of the [five] propositions, and so the *fait* takes away the *droit* and becomes itself an essential portion of the profession of faith, just as one might say that the sense of Calvin about the Eucharist is heretical, which most assuredly is a point of faith.

Here was Pascal's basic allegation, that a datum of history — Jansenius's published views — had subsumed an essential doctrine of the Church — efficacious grace. To reject the first was necessarily to reject the second as well. However dubious such reasoning may have been, Pascal left no doubt as to the vehemence with which he held it. Arnauld's position, he wrote, is "so ambiguous and so timid that it appears unworthy of true defenders of the Church." As for the proposed verbal compromise: "I conclude that those who sign the formulary, pledging only their faith and not formally excluding the teaching of Jansenius, have chosen a middle way which is abominable before God, contemptible before men, and entirely useless to those who are thus personally led astray."

In this last contention, at least, Pascal proved prophetic. On November 28 and 29, 1661, the nuns of Port-Royal signed the formulary, while adding to it the profession of faith Arnauld had prepared for them. Two months later one of the Parisian vicars general came to Port-Royal and courteously informed the sisters that another codicil would be necessary, this one to the effect that they accepted also the decision that attributed the five propositions in their heretical sense to Jansenius. The pressure intensified over the succeeding months, exerted both by the king's council and by the ecclesiastical authorities, who on June 30, 1662, ordered that the formulary be agreed to by signatories "simply, and without restriction or addition." So Arnauld's tactic, to the extent that it was a tactic, had merely delayed the evil hour. By then Blaise Pascal was beyond quibbling with his friends or battling his enemies. But as he lay dying he knew he had been faithful to his principles and to the memory of the woman who, for him, had uniquely endowed those principles with nobility.

183

Late in the summer of 1661, Gilberte Périer, fearful for the health of both her siblings, persuaded her husband to set up a second household in Paris. Florin indeed required little persuading, devoted as he had always been to his in-laws and dedicated as he had always been to their various causes and enterprises. Another inducement for both of them had been the banishment in April of that year of their two young daughters, along with the other *pensionnaires,* from the convents of Port-Royal. Gilberte and her children had scarcely settled into their new lodgings in the Faubourg Saint-Marcel, on the left bank, when Jacqueline Pascal died. Then they watched helplessly as Blaise's physical condition went from bad to worse, the process hastened by the unhappy quarrel over the formulary. Relations with Arnauld and Nicole had been somewhat patched up by the spring of 1662, though the former warmth among them could not so quickly be restored. By then Pascal had turned over his house to the homeless family with whom, however, he continued to live. Gilberte regularly visited him and nursed him, but when, at the end of June, a child in the house contracted smallpox, she insisted that he move into the Périer residence. So he did, bringing his accumulated papers with him.

A large portion of these were the hundreds of sheets that comprised the remote preparation for his ambitious *apologie* in defense of the Christian religion. Three hundred eighty-two of these *pensées* — it may be recalled — Pascal had classified under various headings before the recurrence of illness had forced him to desist. At least five hundred more, together with other notations more or less related, remained uncatalogued. It is impossible to know how he might have arranged and elaborated this material had he lived long enough to do so, though scholars and editors have tried for three centuries to solve that puzzle and, in their attempts, have brought a measure of order out of the chaotic scraps of paper. Even so, a final word can never be said about Pascal's own plan for what came to be called the *Pensées,* or, indeed, whether he had had the chance to form a plan.

If Pascal's ultimate order and classification cannot be conclusively established, his objective can hardly be questioned. He aimed to effect conversion, and not only of *libertins* and atheists — few in number in his experience — but also, and more importantly, conversion of that class of upright individuals for whom religion was a respectable appendage to their existence rather than its warp and woof, those *honnêtes hommes* like his friends Méré and Mitton or like his own father or indeed like Blaise himself had once been. It follows that he wrote for a sophisticated lay audience, not for the masses, and not for priests and nuns either. He assumed that his readers knew something of the Bible, perhaps more about the classics, and most of all about the French intellectual culture as embodied especially in Montaigne. And Pascal never wavered in his methodological approach: to reach the truth in the realm of nature one must apply one's reason and experience relentlessly, never mind what conventional wisdom or authority — even the most prestigious authority, like Aristotle on the vacuum or Descartes on the soul — has to say; but within the realm of grace the truth lies only in the person of Jesus Christ, whom the authority of Scripture and of the living tradition of the Catholic Church uniquely reveals, resistant always to modern innovations like those of the Molinists. The notional distinction between faith and reason young Blaise had learned at Étienne Pascal's knees. Then the boy grew into a man who, having passed through a singular "night of fire," discovered a faith that transcended reason. Such faith had brought him into direct contact with a Reality that rendered all else trivial in comparison and that left reason hardly more than the dubious honor of demonstrating how vile was the human condition.

Much of the later, uncatalogued portions of the *Pensées* Pascal devoted to scriptural analysis. In doing so he showed himself very much a man of his century, or rather of the European epoch that had begun when the Protestant Reformers had advanced their theological claims on the strength of *sola scriptura*. Not that he was much interested in the time-worn quarrels stirred up by Luther and Calvin and their opponents; these had all been long since settled to Pascal's satisfaction in favor of the Catholic controversialists. Nor of course did he wrestle with the problems raised by a biblical criticism that developed only centuries after his death. His purpose was quite otherwise.

> Not only do we only know God through Jesus Christ, but we only know ourselves through Jesus Christ; we only know life and death through Jesus Christ. Apart from Jesus Christ we cannot know the meaning of our life or our death, of God or of ourselves.
>
> Thus, without Scripture, whose only object is Christ, we know nothing, and can see nothing but obscurity and confusion in the

185

nature of God and in nature itself. (417 in the order of the later *Pensées* proposed by Louis LaFuma)

Pascal was particularly fascinated by the Old Testament. He wondered about "the advantages, the sincerity, the particularity, the perpetuity" of the Jewish people. Intrigued by the Hebrew prophets, he wrote down long extracts and paraphrases of their predictions as well as lists of citations from Isaiah, Daniel, Jeremiah, and the others, "to show that true Jews and true Christians have only one religion" (453), or rather that one is the continuation and fulfillment of the other.

The Christian's God does not consist merely of a God who is the author of mathematical truths and the order of elements. That is the portion of the heathen and the Epicureans. He does not consist merely of a God who extends his providence over the life and property of men so as to grant a happy span of years to those who worship him. That is the portion of the Jews. But the God of Abraham, the God of Isaac, the God of Jacob, the God of the Christians is a God of love and consolation; he is a God who fills the soul and heart of those whom he possesses; he is a God who makes them inwardly aware of their wretchedness and his infinite mercy; who unites himself with them in the depths of their soul; who fills it with humility, joy, confidence, and love; who makes them incapable of having any other end but him. (449)

As was the case with the 382 classified items, many of the later *Pensées* were unintelligible jottings or, at best, hints at what might have been. "Hypothesis that the apostles were rogues" (457). "They hide in the throng and call numbers to their aid. Tumult" (504). "*Probability.* Anyone can add to it, none can take away" (653). "*Grace.* Movements of grace, hardness of heart, external circumstances" (702). And, also as before, Pascal produced aphorisms aplenty. "In all religions sincerity is essential: true heathens, true Jews, true Christians" (480). "Imagination magnifies small objects with fantastic exaggeration until they fill our soul, and with bold insolence cuts down great things to its own size, as when speaking of God" (551). "The mind naturally believes and the will naturally loves, so that when there are not true objects for them they necessarily become attached to false ones" (661). "Sneezing absorbs all the functions of the soul as much as does sexual activity, but we do not draw from it the same conclusions against the greatness of man, because sneezing is involuntary" (795).

In his musings Pascal did not spare old enemies. "Anyone condemned by Escobar is really condemned" (666). "Every time the Jesuits take the Pope unawares, the whole of Christendom becomes guilty of perjury. The Pope is very liable to be taken unawares, because he is so very busy and trusts the Jesuits so much, and the Jesuits are perfectly capable of taking people unawares for the sake of spreading calumny" (914). Nor did he hesitate to make references to famous persons, one a droll comment bearing upon both sneezing and sexuality: "Cleopatra's nose; if it had been shorter the whole face of the earth would have been different" (413). His ambivalence toward Montaigne ran through the *Pensées* like a leitmotif. "The immortality of the soul is something of such vital importance to us, affecting us so deeply, that one must have lost all feeling not to care about knowing the facts of the matter. Falseness of the philosophers who did not discuss the immortality of the soul. Falseness of their dilemma in Montaigne" (427, 409). "Montaigne's faults are great. Lewd words. His views on deliberate homicide, on death. His completely pagan views on death are inexcusable" (680). And yet the author of the *Essais* had left an indelible mark upon the spirit of the author of the *Pensées*: "It is not in Montaigne but in myself that I find everything I see there" (689). His evocation of René Descartes was blunter and without a trace of poignancy. "Write against those who probe science too deeply. Descartes" (553). "Descartes useless and uncertain" (887).

But the most famous and most challenging of all the later and uncatalogued *Pensées* was surely *le pari*, the Wager. "I should be much more afraid," observed Pascal by way of preface, "of being mistaken and then finding out that Christianity is true than of being mistaken in believing it to be true" (387). There may have been several levels at which Pascal, no stranger to the mathematical intricacies involved in gambling and in probability theory, perceived this remarkable apologetic ploy, but one stood out plainly "according to our natural lights."

> If there is a God, he is infinitely beyond our comprehension, since, being indivisible and without limits, he bears no relation to us. We are therefore incapable of knowing either what he is or whether he is.

187

Yes, but you must wager. You have two things to lose: the true and the good; and two things to stake: your reason and your will, your knowledge and your happiness; and your nature has two things to avoid: error and wretchedness. Since you must necessarily choose, your reason is no more affronted by choosing one rather than the other. Let us weigh up the gain and loss involved in calling heads that God exists. Let us assess the two cases: if you win, you win everything, if you lose you lose nothing. Do not hesitate then; wager that he does exist. Here there is an infinity of infinitely happy life to be won, one chance of winning against a finite number of chances of losing, and what you are staking is finite. That leaves no choice; wherever there is infinity, and where there are not infinite chances of losing against that of winning, there is no room for hesitation. Since you are obliged to play, you must be renouncing reason if you hoard your life rather than risk it for infinite gain, just as likely to occur as a loss amounting to nothing.

But what if one still finds an approach of this kind intellectually unsatisfying? Where in all this lies the deductive evidence? Pascal's retort was that the wager embodied a moral decision, not an intellectual demonstration or even an argument.

At least get it into your head that, if you are unable to believe, it is because of your passions, since reason impels you to believe and yet you cannot do so. Concentrate then not on convincing yourself by multiplying proofs of God's existence but by diminishing your passions. You want to find faith, and you do not know the road. You want to be cured of unbelief, and you ask for the remedy. Learn from those who were once bound like you and who now wager all they have. (418)

Here was Pascal's consistent message, expressed over and over again in the *Pensées* in many different fashions, and not always so abruptly as in the conclusion to the Wager.

The prophecies, even the miracles and proofs of our religion, are not of such a kind that they can be said to be absolutely convincing, but they are at the same time such that it cannot be said to be unreasonable to believe in them. There is thus evidence and obscurity, to enlighten some and obfuscate others. But the evidence is such as to exceed, or at least equal, the evidence to the contrary, so that it cannot be reason that decides us against following it, and can therefore only be concupiscence and wickedness of heart. Thus, there is enough evidence to condemn and not enough to convince, so that it should be apparent that those who follow it are prompted to do so by grace and not by reason, and those who evade it are prompted by concupiscence and not by reason. (835)

Blaise Pascal was destined to live only six weeks after he repaired to his sister's house at the end of June 1662. Most of that time he spent in bed, growing progressively weaker and enduring severe abdominal pain and insomnia. At first, however, since he maintained a strong pulse and developed no fever, his physicians assumed he was in no immediate danger. That Blaise did not agree with them became apparent on July 4 when he told Gilberte that he wished to make his sacramental confession. The Périer residence lay in the parish of Saint-Étienne-du-Mont, hard by and dependent upon the monastery of Sainte-Geneviève, whose domestic staff it had been founded to serve. The *curé* since 1653, Paul Beurrier, a canon-regular of Sainte-Geneviève, was widely admired as a virtuous and conscientious parish priest, with no particular intellectual or ideological pretentions. Père Beurrier duly answered Madame Périer's invitation that July day and heard her brother's confession. He did so again several times during the weeks that followed, and also paid pastoral visits to the sick man on other occasions when the sacrament was not dispensed. Pascal took much consolation from his conversations with the *curé*, who, for his part, was greatly edified by the simple patience with which Pascal endured his sufferings. "He is like a little child," the priest said to Gilberte, "he is so humble, he is submissive as an infant."

The news that Pascal had asked to be shriven had caused considerable alarm among his friends, and when he asked further that Beurrier bring him the Eucharist, his doctors strongly dissented on the grounds that the excitement involved would worsen his condition. Pascal was visibly annoyed and disappointed at this negative recommendation;

but, given the sacramental practice of the time — especially among the austere followers of Saint-Cyran — such a request from a sick person could have sounded to those around him like a death knell. "I wanted very much to receive Holy Communion," Pascal observed wryly to Gilberte, "but since I see that people have been taken aback by my confession, I am afraid that they would be even more disturbed by this, so I suppose I had better put it off."

His condition relentlessly worsened even so, and none of the medical treatments could reverse the wearing away of that frail body. He experienced moments of relief, to be sure, when he was able to talk to the mourning friends who called upon him, most movingly perhaps to Antoine Arnauld — wearing a disguise again as the persecution of Port-Royal intensified — with whom he had so recently quarreled. But now the end was only a matter of weeks. On August 3 Blaise signed his last will and testament. On August 14 he was stricken by vertigo and terrible pains in his head. Three days later he fell into violent convulsions, and that night, August 17-18, Gilberte anxiously summoned Père Beurrier. The priest adminstered viaticum and extreme unction to the dying man, who, as his sister remembered it, received these ministrations "with tears rolling down his cheeks." Then as Beurrier, in accord with custom, gave the final blessing with the ciborium containing the sacred Hosts, Pascal cried out, "May God never abandon me!" He never spoke again, and twenty-four hours later, at one o'clock in the morning of Saturday, August 19, 1662, he died, aged thirty-nine years and two months.

Epilogue

T HE FUNERAL mass for Blaise Pascal was offered at ten o'clock in the morning of Monday, August 22, 1662, in the parish church of Saint-Étienne-du-Mont. The *curé*, Père Paul Beurrier, presided, and after the service the body of the deceased was interred in a tomb located at the entrance to the Lady Chapel, directly behind the high altar.

But the ritual supplication "rest in peace" was not to be granted, at least not yet. The trouble began eighteen months later when Florin and Gilberte Périer had erected on the wall of the ambulatory of Saint-Étienne a memorial plaque honoring their brother. This epitaph, written in Latin, paid conventional and uncontroversial tribute to Pascal's virtues, stressing how he had spent his last days "meditating on the law of God — *in divinae legis meditatione.*" The moment chosen to exhibit such a eulogy, however, proved highly unpropitious. The anti-Jansenist reaction was at its height, and enemies in abundance were poised to pounce upon any gesture of resistance, however innocuous, to the prevailing opinion. The matter was quickly brought to the attention of the new archbishop of Paris, Hardouin de Beaumont de Péréfixe: the plaque, he was informed, insolently proclaimed the orthodoxy of one who had been in fact a heretic, of one indeed who had died without receiving the sacraments and without acknowledging the submission he owed to the Church. If justice were to be done, Pascal's body should be removed from the sacred precincts of Saint-Étienne, or, at the very least, the offensive memorial should be destroyed.

Péréfixe, annoyed just then by his relations with the troubled remnant of Port-Royal, was disposed to listen to overtures of this kind. He therefore summoned the *curé* of Saint-Étienne early in January 1665 and asked him about the circumstances of Pascal's death and burial. Beurrier replied that his parishioner had died a good Catholic. The archbishop, sensing the possibility of fitting this favorable report into a larger strategy, then instructed Beurrier to put his account of Pascal's last days into writing. The priest was reluctant to do so for fear of stirring up partisan animosities in his parish, but, when Péréfixe insisted, he finally agreed. The archbishop for his part saw an opportunity to steal a march on recalcitrant Jansenists, who might be shamed into conforming if they could be shown that one of the luminaries of Port-Royal had done so.

The good Father Beurrier duly wrote down his *Declaration*, which proved to be a prelude to a comedy of errors. Péréfixe directed the priest to address two questions: first, did Pascal die without receiving the sacraments? and second, did he die attached to the Jansenist party? As to the first, the priest gave an unequivocally negative response. He had known Pascal for six weeks before the latter died, he explained, had heard his confession several times, and had administered viaticum and extreme unction at the deathbed. As to the second question, Beurrier took care to distinguish what he knew under the seal of the confessional and what he had learned conversing with Pascal as one man to another. He told me, wrote the priest,

that he had formerly belonged to the party of the gentlemen of Port-Royal, but that for two years he had been estranged from them, because he had discerned that they went too far in matters related to the doctrine of grace and that they appeared to display less submission than they should to our Holy Father the Pope. Nevertheless he also said that he grieved over the widespread slackening of Christian morals, and that for two years now he had been attending to his own spiritual condition as well as to a plan he had to combat religious atheism and indifference.

Archbishop Péréfixe was delighted by this testimony, as was Pascal's old antagonist, François Annat, S.J., who eventually learned about it. It is consoling, wrote Annat in the spring of 1666, that the author of the "buffooneries" known as the *Provincial Letters* should have seen the error of his ways in time, and it is only just to give publicity to this fact. That publicity, however, had an unintended result. Pierre Nicole, in a reply to Annat published in July of that year, gently but firmly maintained that the "estrangement" of which Père Beurrier spoke had indeed occurred because of "matters related to the doctrine of grace," but not because "the gentlemen of Port-Royal" had "gone too far" in such matters. Quite to the contrary, the gentlemen of Port-Royal, by urging acceptance of the formulary of October 1661, and thus extending to pope and bishops the benefit of the doubt on the question of *fait*, had not gone far enough to satisfy Pascal. This single disagreement, he insisted, had not for an instant weakened ties of friendship, any more than Pascal's hardline position on this one issue had indicated rebellion against the Church. There was no question, added Nicole, of blaming Beurrier for this misinterpretation of Pascal's words: the *curé* was "a person of great sincerity and free from guile." He had simply taken for granted the popular prejudice that Pascal's expression "going too far" had to mean the Jansenists' unwillingness to accommodate to the authoritative teaching as stated in the formulary when, in fact, it meant just the opposite. Gilberte Périer wrote in the same vein to Beurrier himself — "I assure you, Monsieur, my brother never accused Port-Royal of any false doctrine" — while her husband, rather more formally, sent a like message to Péréfixe.

The result was one to gratify the soul of any bureaucrat. Faced by these conflicting testimonies the archbishop of Paris decided he needed to do nothing, and nothing is what he did. Besides, as he was sifting through the various alternatives, another truce between the Jansenists and their opponents was at hand. This decade of relative tranquility — "The Peace of the Church" or "The Clementine Peace," the latter term taken from the name of the pope who negotiated it, Clement IX — began in 1668, and after it collapsed into even more bitter wrangling Pascal's enhanced reputation precluded any gesture of dishonor toward his remains. So they lie now where they were originally interred, in the placidly beautiful interior of Saint-Étienne-du-Mont, only a few yards from those of Racine and from the memorial placed upon the wall of the ambulatory by the Périers. Outside the bustle of a great and pagan city pays no heed. But inside the *pensée* of one frail, brilliant, enigmatic believer seems to brood with a haunting familiarity.

> I stretch out my arms to my Savior, who, after being foretold for four thousand years, came on earth to die and suffer for me at the time and in the circumstances foretold. By his grace I peaceably await death, in the hope of being eternally united to him, and meanwhile I live joyfully, whether in the blessings which he is pleased to bestow on me or in the afflictions he sends me for my own good and taught me how to endure by his example. (737)

A Note on the Sources

MUCH of what Blaise Pascal wrote was not published in his life-time, and at least one major treatise — that on conic sections (1648) — has been lost. The authorship of the short but highly signifi-cant piece "On the Conversion of the Sinner" (1654) was formerly attributed to his sister Jacqueline. Another extremely important text, the "Conversation" with Father de Saci (1655), survives only as re-corded long afterward by the priest's secretary. Upon Pascal's death his papers passed to the custody of his surviving sister, Gilberte Périer, and ultimately to that of her son. Posthumous publication was im-mensely complicated by reason of the continuing struggles within France over the issues raised by the Jansenist party, the fortunes of which waxed and waned till Port-Royal was physically destroyed by Louis XIV at the beginning of the eighteenth century, and even after that the debates raged on. The question whether Pascal was or was not an orthodox Catholic tended to affect decisions about the publication of his religious writings and the form that such publication should take. This was particularly the case with the *Pensées*; the disordered and incomplete condition in which Pascal left his projected *apologie* of the Christian religion invited the kind of bowdlerization that in fact char-acterized the first edition (1670) and many editions thereafter. Research into Pascalian themes throughout the nineteenth century often reflected the same preoccupation, especially when French clericals and anti-clericals attempted to categorize Pascal for their own purposes. An example of this tendency can be found in the treatment of Pascal and his literary testament as late as 1932 in the article by C. Constantin in that monument of French Catholic scholarship, the *Dictionnaire de thé-ologie catholique*; this long essay (volume 11, part 2, columns 2074-2203), excellent in most respects, nevertheless seems unduly distracted by the Jansenist imbroglio.

A defining moment in Pascalian studies came at the beginning of this century with the publication of the *Oeuvres,* 14 vols., edited by Léon Brunschvieg et al. (Paris: Hachette, 1904-1914; reprint Kraus, 1965). Besides all of Pascal's extant works, this compilation contains a huge amount of supplementary material, including early biographies of Pascal, relevant correspondence, various significant Jansenist documents (e.g., Antoine Arnauld's formal propositions before the Sorbonne), even excerpts from Jacqueline Pascal's poetry. Sixty years later, taking into account further research and refinement, a similar project was undertaken by another noted scholar: Pascal's *Oeuvres complètes,* 3 vols., edited by Jean Mesnard (Paris: Desclée, 1964-1991). This collection, 3,700 pages altogether, remains, despite its title, incomplete, but it is extremely valuable nonetheless. Another collection with the same title was edited by Louis Lafuma (Paris: Seuil, 1963). In writing the present book I have used for the most part the convenient one-volume edition of the *Oeuvres complètes* (Paris: Gallimard, 1954, 1965), edited by Jacques Chevalier, a scholar who ranks as a Pascalian with Brunschvieg, Mesnard, and LaFuma. Chevalier's 1,500 pages include much supportive documentation and useful notes, concordances, and illustrations. The quotations of Pascal and his contemporaries in the text have been my own translations from the *Oeuvres,* except for the two most famous and most familiar of Pascal's works, for which I have turned to the admirable translations of A. J. Krailsheimer: *The Provincial Letters* (London: Penguin, 1967) and the *Pensées* (London: Penguin, 1966).

The *Pensées* presents particular problems to anyone who would try to reconstruct Pascal's career and thought. No consensus has ever been reached about the order in which this material was written or in what form its author might have intended it to appear. The arrangement arrived at by Louis LaFuma, *Histoire des "Pensées" de Pascal (1656-*

1952) (Paris: Editions du Luxembourg, 1954), comes closer than the others to a credible solution to the problem, and his scheme has been adopted by Dr. Krailsheimer in the Penguin translation cited above and in my text as well. Even so, the different conclusions suggested by Brunschvieg and others cannot be left out of account. For a recent and thorough discussion of the alternatives the interested reader might consult the lengthy preface to the edition of the *Pensées* by Francis Kaplan (Paris: Editions du Cerf, 1982).

The historical context in which Blaise Pascal lived has been perhaps best encapsulated in a series of relatively recent biographical studies. Nevertheless, an inquirer might well begin by perusing the translation of Georges Duby and Robert Mandrou, *A History of French Civilization* (London: Weidenfeld and Nicolson, 1965), a general account of events. Narrower in focus but very valuable is the definitive work of a leading historian of the period, Victor-L. Tapie, *La France de Louis XIII et de Richelieu* (Paris: Flammarion, 1952; English translation Macmillan, 1974, and Cambridge University Press, 1985, with a much expanded bibliography). See also P. J. Coveney, ed., *France in Crisis, 1620-1675* (Towata, NJ: Rowman and Littlefield, 1977), which contains a helpful glossary and a good bibliography, as well as an admirably lucid treatment of the Fronde. For the Paris where Pascal made his home for most of his years, see Roland Mousnier, *Paris au XVIIe siècle*, 3 vols. (Paris: Centre de documentation universitaire, 1961). For a narrative describing the European Catholic revival up to the death of Henri IV, see my book *The Counter Reformation, 1559-1610* (New York: Harper & Row, 1974), especially "The Bibliographical Essay" (pp. 367-384).

The biographies referred to above include Renée Casin, *Le cardinal de Richelieu: un prophète de l'unité* (Montsurs: Editions Resiac, 1980); Joseph Bergin, *The Rise of Richelieu* (New Haven: Yale University Press, 1991); Roland Mousnier, *L'homme rouge: la vie du cardinal Richelieu* (Paris: Lafont, 1992); A. Lloyd Moote, *Louis XIII, the Just* (Berkeley: University of California Press, 1989); Ruth Kleinman, *Anne of Austria, Queen of France* (Columbus: Ohio State University Press, 1985); Paul Guth, *Mazarin* (Paris: Flammarion, 1972); and Paule Jansen, *Le cardinal Mazarin et mouvement janséniste français, 1653-1659* (Paris: L. Vrin, 1967). Impressionistic and therefore suspect, and yet old enough now to be venerable, are Hilaire Belloc, *Richelieu, a Study* (London: Lippincott, 1929), and

Aldous Huxley, *Grey Eminence: A Study in Religion and Politics* (London: Chatto & Windus, 1941), the latter a description of the career of Richelieu's confidant, the Capuchin friar, Joseph du Tremblay.

The biographies of Pascal himself began with the memoir written by his sister, Gilberte Périer, which, despite its hagiographical overtones, remains uniquely important. Gilberte also wrote a brief account of her sister Jacqueline. Both of these pieces can be found in the various collections of Pascal's *Oeuvres* and, more conveniently, in the small book published in Paris by the Editions de la Table Rond in 1994. Gilberte's daughter, Marguerite, also left a memoir of her uncle, a kind of appendix to her mother's work.

Of modern biographies the oldest is the most extensive, Fortunat Strowski, *Pascal et son temps,* 3 vols. (Paris: Plon-Nourrit, 1922), a panoramic view that begins with Montaigne and that devotes the whole of the third volume to a study of *The Provincial Letters* and the *Pensées.* Later biographical studies assume various angles of approach, and all of them are relatively short. Worthy of attention are the books by Jacques Chevalier (1930), Ernest Mortimer (1959), Louis Chaigne (1962), Jean Steinmann (1965), J. H. Broome (1966), Jean Mesnard (1959), and Hugh Davidson (1983). Especially useful by reason of its wide scope is Robert J. Nelson, *Pascal: Adversary and Advocate* (Cambridge, MA: Harvard University Press, 1981). Albert Béguin's *Pascal* (Paris: Seuil, 1952) is not so much a biography as a thoughtful meditation. The same might be said of Romano Guardini, *Christliches Bewusstsein. Versuche über Pascal* (München: Deutscher Taschenbuchverlag, 1962; English translation, 1966), though here as elsewhere in Guardini's work there is always a somewhat troubling combination of charm and obscurity. The latest study of Pascal, Leszek Kolakowski, *God Owes Us Nothing* (Chicago: University of Chicago Press, 1995), bears the significant subtitle, "A Brief Remark on Pascal's Religion and on the Spirit of Jansenism"; it provides a splendid exposition of the Augustinian controversy. Also informative about "le milieu janséniste" is Henri Schmitz du Moulin, *Blaise Pascal: une biographie spirituelle* (Assen, Pays-bas: Van Gorcum, 1982). The work I found more helpful than any other is Henri Gouhier, *Blaise Pascal. Commentaires* (Paris: J. Vrin, 1966), which displays an erudition astonishingly wide and deep, as well as a sure grasp of the subtleties and contentions that make Pascal so compelling a figure.

Gouhier's smaller study, *Pascal et les humanistes chrétiens. L'affaire Saint-Ange* (Paris: J. Vrin, 1974), is a model of what a monograph should be.

The study of Jansenism conventionally begins with two classics, Charles Augustin Sainte-Beuve, *Port-Royal*, 3rd ed. (Paris: Hachette, 1867), 7 vols. in 6, the second (pp. 379-510) and third (pp. 7-464) of which treat of Pascal, and Henri Bremond, *Histoire littéraire du sentiment religieux en France depuis la fin des guerres de religion jusqu'à nos jours* (Paris: Bloud et Gay, 1925-1929), 8 vols., the fourth volume of which is called "L'École de Port-Royal" and pays considerable attention to Saint-Cyran, to Mère Agnès Arnauld (more important a figure, says Bremond, than Mère Angélique), and to Pascal (pp. 318-417). In conjunction with Sainte-Beuve, see Pierre Gisel, ed., *Pour ou contre Sainte-Beuve: Le "Port-Royal"* (Paris: Labor et Fides, 1993), a collection of conference papers, including Jean Mesnard, "Le Pascal de Sainte-Beuve et le Pascal d'aujourd'hui" (pp. 15-37), and Hélène Bouchilloux, "Le Pascal anticousinien d'Alexandre Vinet" (pp. 151-161), the latter reprising a scholarly quarrel of the 1840s when a critical study of Pascal was just beginning. A helpful outline of Pascal's sometimes puzzling relationship to the larger Jansenist group is William Clark, *Pascal and the Port-Royalists* (New York: Scribner's, 1902; University of Michigan facsimile, 1979).

The greatest modern student of Jansenism was the recently deceased Jean Orcibal. His *Jansénius d'Ypres (1585-1638)* (Paris: Centre national des lettres, 1989) and his *Saint-Cyran et jansénisme* (Paris: Seuil, n.d. [1961]) were particularly helpful to me, and hardly less so was his *Le cardinal de Bérulle. Evolution d'une spiritualité* (Paris: Cerf, 1965). An old book now but still useful is Nigel Abercrombie, *The Origins of Jansenism* (Oxford: Clarendon Press, 1936), elegantly written and divided approximately in half between a historical narrative and a theological analysis. Good summaries of the progress of the movement are Alexander Sedgwick, *Jansenism in Seventeenth Century France: Voices in the Wilderness* (Charlottesville: University of Virginia Press, 1977), and the first hundred pages of Françoise Hildesheimer, *Le jansénisme en France aux XVIIe et XVIIIe siècles* (Paris: Publisud, 1991). Of special interest are several of the 41 volumes of the *Chroniques de Port-Royal* published since 1950, including *Gilberte et Jacqueline Pascal* (Paris: J. Vrin, 1982) and *Un lieu de mémoire: Port-Royal de Paris* (Paris: Biblioteque Mazarine, 1991). Perhaps most compelling in this series is *La mère*

Angélique Arnauld (1591-1661). Relation, Colloque (Paris: Biblioteque Mazarine, 1992). This volume contains the homily of Jean-Marie Cardinal Lustiger, Archbishop of Paris, preached in the chapel at Port-Royal (the maternity hospital) in observance of the fourth centenary of Mère Angélique's birth (pp. 97-102); Mère Angélique's own reminiscence (written in 1655) of the beginning of the reform of Port-Royal (pp. 11-93, with abundant clarifying notes); and two important articles: Pierre Magnard, "La spiritualité de la mère Angélique" (pp. 195-209), and Perle Bugnion-Secrétan, "Mère Angélique et Pascal" (pp. 147-156). Perle Bugnion-Secrétan has also written a fine biography of the great woman: *Angélique Arnauld, 1591-1661, abbesse et réformatrice de Port-Royal d'après ses écrits* (Paris: Cerf, 1991).

One indication of the overall impact of Pascal upon Western thought is the large number of comparative studies his work has given rise to. An obviously important example is Philippe Sellier, *Pascal et Saint Augustin* (Paris: Armand Colin, 1970, and Albin Michel, 1995). A further sampling under this heading would include Michel le Guern, *Pascal et Descartes* (Paris: Nizet, n.d. [1971]), which analyses the ambivalent attitudes involved in this intellectual relationship, a theme that is also treated in Vincent Carraud, *Pascal et la philosophie* (Paris: Presses universitaires de France, 1992), especially pp. 217-345. Pascal's influence on another, more congenial group of contemporaries can be seen in Louis Marin, *La critique du discours sur la "Logique de Port-Royal" et les "Pensées" de Pascal* (Paris: Minuit, 1975), supplemented by Steven M. Nadler, *Arnauld and the Cartesian Philosophy of Ideas* (Manchester: Manchester University Press, 1989), which relates Marsenne and Pascal with Descartes and the Port-Royalists. Many of the same themes emerge in Sara Melzer, *Discourses of the Fall: A Study of Pascal's "Pensées"* (Berkeley: University of California Press, 1986), but this book does much more in its dense but compelling pages to make understandable Pascal's use of language. A somewhat similar task has been assumed by Buford Norman, *Portraits of Thought: Knowledge, Methods, and Styles in Pascal* (Columbus: Ohio State University Press, 1988), a close analysis of Pascal's shifting meanings in both his scientific and religious writings. A gallant attempt at integrating those apparently disparate works is Thomas Harrington, *Pascal philosophe. Une étude unitaire de la pensée de Pascal* (Paris: Société d'édition d'enseignement supérieur, 1982), a book marred somewhat by careless editing.

Carrying some of these associations forward are Émile Rideau, *Descartes, Pascal, Bergson* (Paris: Boivin, 1937), and Étienne Borne, *De Pascal à Teilhard de Chardin* (Clermont-Ferrand: G. de Bussac, 1962), the latter made up of papers delivered at a conference in observance of the third centenary of Pascal's death. A different kind of connection is drawn in Jean Guitton, *Pascal et Leibniz: étude sur deux types de penseurs* (Paris: Aubier, 1951). Denzil Patrick, *Pascal and Kierkegaard: A Study in the Strategy of Evangelism,* 2 vols. (London: Lutterworth Press, 1947), examines at length an intriguing compatibility. Pascal and Nietzsche would hardly seem compatible, but their connection has attracted much scholarly attention, including Enrico Castelli, *Pascal e Nietzsche* (Padova: CEDAM, 1962); J. Robert Dionne, *Pascal et Nietzsche: étude historique et comparée* (New York: B. Franklin, 1974); and Charles Natali, *Nietzsche and Pascal on Christianity* (New York: Peter Lang, 1985). The congruity of matching Pascal with Newman has often been remarked upon, but never better or more persuasively than in Mary Katherine Tillman, "The Two-Fold Logos of Newman and Pascal: L'Esprit géometrique," *Louvain Studies* 15 (1990): 233-255.

Studies on particular aspects of Pascal's life and career abound. Among those well worth attention are Louis A. MacKenzie, Jr., *Pascal's "Lettres Provinciales": The Motif and Practice of Fragmentation* (Birmingham, AL: Summa Publications, 1988), a tightly argued exposé of Pascal's literary methodology in his famous dispute with the Molinists; Pierre Guenancia, *Du vide à Dieu: essai sur la physique de Pascal* (Paris: F. Maspero, 1976); and Christian Lazzeri, *Force et justice dans la politique de Pascal* (Paris: Presses universitaires de France, 1993), which relates Pascal's critique on these subjects to those of Hobbes, Montaigne, and Nicole. Three treatments of the celebrated "wager" help to shed some light on that subtle section of the *Pensées:* Per Lønning, *Cet effrayant pari: une "Pensée" pascalienne et ses critiques* (Paris: J. Vrin, 1980), a close manuscript analysis that treats among other things the comments on the subject by Voltaire; Nicholas Rescher, *Pascal's Wager: A Study of Practical Reasoning in Philosophical Theology* (Notre Dame: University of Notre Dame Press, 1985), which examines William James's negative reaction to the wager in *The Will to Believe;* and Lucien Goldmann, "The Wager: The Christian Religion," in Harold Bloom, ed., *Blaise Pascal* (New York: Chelsea House, 1989), pp. 53-79.

201

Let the final citation belong to the historian of the last generation who did so much to bring to peoples everywhere a living picture of the past of the Catholic Church. Pierre Frieden, "Pascal et Newman. Le drame de l'homme libre," *Newman Studien* 3 (1951): 170, recounts how Henri Daniel-Rops, as a young student of seventeen, took with him everywhere in his knapsack the Hachette edition of the *Pensées*. Thirty years later, an immortal of the Académie Française, he was wont to take up again and again "the thick little book, bound in green linen, and experience once more 'the same living presence, the same emotion of marvelous proximity,' of spiritual contact." How appropriate, therefore, is the title of Henri Daniel-Rops's essay, *Pascal et notre coeur* (Strassbourg: F. X. Le Roux, 1948).

Index